5 Grams

5 Grams

Crack Cocaine, Rap Music, and the War on Drugs

Dimitri A. Bogazianos

NEW YORK UNIVERSITY PRESS
New York and London

NEW YORK UNIVERSITY PRESS
New York and London
www.nyupress.org

References to Internet websites (URLs) were accurate at the time of writing.
Neither the author nor New York University Press is responsible for URLs
that may have expired or changed since the manuscript was prepared.

Library of Congress Cataloging-in-Publication Data

Bogazianos, Dimitri A.
5 grams : crack cocaine, rap music,
and the war on drugs / Dimitri Bogazianos.
p. cm. — (Alternative criminology series)
ISBN 978–0–8147–8700–7 (cl : acid-free paper)
ISBN 978–0–8147–8701–4 (pbk : acid-free paper)
ISBN 978–0–8147–2306–7 (ebook)
ISBN 978–0–8147–2516–0 (ebook)
1. Drug control—United States. 2. Crack (Drug)—United States.
3. Sentences (Criminal procedure)—United States.
4. Narcotic laws—United States. I. Title. II. Title: Five grams.
HV5825.B62 2011
363.450973—dc23   2011028191

New York University Press books are printed on acid-free paper,
and their binding materials are chosen for strength and durability.
We strive to use environmentally responsible suppliers and materials
to the greatest extent possible in publishing our books.

Manufactured in the United States of America
c   10 9 8 7 6 5 4 3 2 1
p   10 9 8 7 6 5 4 3 2 1

For NYC

Contents

Acknowledgments

There are many mentors, colleagues, family members, and friends who have helped make this book a reality, most of whom blur the lines between the categories just listed.

I would first like to thank Lee Siegel, George Tanabe, and Fritz Seifert, early mentors who helped me focus my fire. My belief that scholarship is as much about saying interesting things about the world as it is about truth and justice owes much to Lee's passion for language, to Fritz's dedication to answering the big questions, and to the many wide-ranging conversations I have had with George.

I am also grateful to Liisa Malkki, another early mentor whose warmth and generosity exemplify what it means for a scholar to walk the talk; and to David Goldberg, who believed, from the start, that I had something to say and encouraged me to say it as richly as possible. Many thanks also to Susan Coutin, Val Jenness, Victoria Bernal, Diego Vigil, and Richard Perry, all of whom consistently provided insight and encouragement at various stages of this book.

I'd also like to thank my many friends from the University of California–Irvine, especially Paul Kaplan and Michael Braun; over the years, our friendship grew through the countless conversations we had during two of my favorite social practices: eating and drinking, usually in reverse order. I look forward to more. Many thanks also to Laura and her family, especially Aaron and Imma, two beautiful children I was lucky to help raise during the earliest stages of this book, and in whose continued growth into independent young people I will always find the deepest joy.

I am also grateful to the many people at California State University–Sacramento, especially the faculty, staff, and students in the Division of Criminal Justice who, collectively, have fostered a supportive environment of which it is a pleasure to be a part. And, in Sacramento itself, the Cuellar-Valencia family and my people in Pangaea Park have all helped create a rich sense of community, turning a new city into a new home—

Caroline, Paul and Monica, Edward, Nick, Aramis, Alexandra, Michaela, Paul and Ida, Shannon, James, Rob, Raj, Ricardo, Austin, Nick J., Mary M., Dan O., and Louise.

I am also incredibly grateful to Ilene Kalish and NYU Press for supporting first-time authors trying to say interesting things about the world, and for encouraging them to write their best. Ilene's confidence in the project, and her patience in seeing it through have been invaluable. Thanks also to the anonymous reviewers, whose willingness to engage with the book on its own terms have helped considerably, even if I have not been able to address all of their comments.

My deepest thanks, however, go to my family. My grandparents, Irma and James Jones, have modeled the highest levels of resiliency, integrity, and dignity even in the face of often overwhelming prejudice and tragedy. If I have managed to absorb even the faintest traces of my grandfather's honor and vitality, I'll be a lucky man indeed. My mother, Gail Sutherland, my father, Vasili Bogazianos, my stepfather, Peter Sutherland, and my stepmother, Carlotta Schoch, have all supported me unconditonally at every stage of my life. Individually, each has passed on traits that I strive to realize in myself—my mother's generosity, my father's humor, my stepfather's curiosity, and my stepmother's compassion.

Finally, this book is dedicated to the City and my New York family, past and present: Brandi, Sean, Chad, Jasmina, Rita and Gabe, Dot, Pinky, and Elizabeth; and, especially, my Get Open brothers—Sebastian Bardin-Greenberg, Kiambu Dickerson, Avondale Dyer, Jesse Sandler, Carlos Vasconcellos, Saundi Wilson—as well as their families, and the many other friends, musicians, and artists without whom this book simply would not have been written. Thanks also to Overtime Records, Red Five Music, Hip Hop Loves Foundation, Brüknahm, LaVibe Productions, Jazz Zoom, 58 Beats, Dina Tifferet, Lester Bowie and fam, Purchase and Avenue J, Mekka, Martial Truth, and Crazy Life Itself. Peace.

Introduction

I will not get bagged on a rock.
　　　　　—Ghostface Killah, "Run," *The Pretty Toney Album*, 2004

In all of rap's gangster mythology there is perhaps no more overused imagery than Brian De Palma's 1983 movie, *Scarface*, especially its last scene. In it, Al Pacino, in a paranoid frenzy after snorting scoops of cocaine arranged like mountains on his desk, charges onto his balcony with a military issue M-16 rifle—complete with grenade launcher—to face a small army of rival drug dealers. Before he finally falls face first into the fountain below, his body is literally perforated by bullets and sent through the railing by a shotgun blast to his back.

By the time Tony Montana, Pacino's character, died, he had become, by all accounts, a cocaine kingpin, having moved what probably amounted to tons of cocaine. Tony Montana's kingpin status and his ultraviolent death, therefore, have provided rap artists with a ready-made model of gangster heroism. And, indeed, the adoption of Scarface as an icon by self-consciously gangsta rappers is an easy connection to make. After all, how much more gangster can one get?

Even given the seeming obviousness of adopting Tony Montana as a hero, Ghostface Killah's promise—which he makes in the same song from which the above epigraph was drawn—to "die with the heart of Scarface" in order to avoid getting arrested for the equivalent of one sugar packet worth of crack cocaine seems extreme. Tony Montana, that is, died for moving tons, not grams. Perhaps, then, Ghostface's claims—along with those of countless other rap artists—are to be interpreted simply as the exaggerated boasts of an overactive imagination. Such exaggerations are all the more apparent because—as a major supplier of powder cocaine, the substance from which crack is ultimately derived—Tony Montana never sold crack. Crack dealing, in opposition to the cocaine kingpin mythology of Scarface, has always been a low-level enterprise—a retail operation dependent upon the importation of its parent substance, powder. And here lies the primary problem that this book addresses: there is actually nothing "easy" or "merely" sensationalistic about the connection many rappers make between Scarface and crack cocaine. In fact, that connection was made for them long before they ever rapped about it. More precisely, this book examines a number of interlocking contradictions at the heart of the U.S. government's punishment structure for crack that, together, comprise a highly elastic form of reasoning through which, in a strange turn, mere couriers of an inherently impure form of cocaine came to be treated *as if* they were the kingpins of global criminal organizations moving massive quantities of lethally pure drugs.

This book, thus, examines the profound *symbolic* consequences of crack's paradoxical punishment structure, although it does so from "outside" of policy. Instead, I focus on the degree to which crack cocaine emerged as a primary symbolic referent through the development of an important reflexive lyrical stance that many rap artists in the 1990s took toward their own commercialization. In doing so, they became, in essence, products that "talked back" to their producers, as well as to a music industry system that has been consistently perceived as being duplicitous and humiliating. Out of rap's confrontation with the industry that produced it, crack became *a lethal logic of work*: a grammar of social analysis in which exploited creative labor—as well as the possibilities of sustaining family and community life that such labor, it was hoped, might create—figures as central.

For me, the emotional force of these lyrical critiques came into full relief while I was performing with an independent, multiethnic New York City–based rap group that came of age during the early and mid-1990s. As part of an influential underground movement, we made music throughout the eastern United States, often recording with, opening for, or producing a number of well-known rap and jazz artists, including KRS-One, Jungle Brothers, De La Soul, Sadat X, O.C., Tha Alkaholiks, Special Ed, MF Grimm, Freestyle Fellowship, and Lester Bowie, among others. Because one of our founding members and main producers was a French-American who maintained strong connections overseas, we also recorded with a number of European artists—including Faf Larage and Shurik'N from France, and Main Concept from Germany—and performed regularly at jazz and hip hop festivals, as well as in smaller clubs and venues across the continent and in the United Kingdom.

That era in rap music saw the creation of some of the most influential albums in rap history as well as the violent deaths of some of the very artists who made such important work possible. We found out about the murder of the Notorious B.I.G., for example, before sunrise on March 9, 1997, when a choked-up road manager for Smoothe Da Hustler—whose concert we'd opened a few hours earlier—knocked on our hotel room door to tell us the news and share a drink in Big's memory. For those of us deeply involved with making music during this period—as well as, I'm sure, for those deeply involved with listening to the music made then— things did seem to change profoundly. Historical reflections on this time—whether through documentaries, television specials, or exposé-style journalism—often emphasize one of two interpretations: first, that the period was, truly, quite violent, and the deaths of those involved were, in some ways, natural outgrowths of this violence; or, second, that the rap-related violence of this time (and since) was (and still is) primarily media driven, and that the period's truest expressions occurred mainly in spontaneously generated "freestyle" gatherings in small-scale, "independent" clubs as well as on the streets throughout the city. While the first variation relies on a simplistic vision of young people from the streets somehow bringing their violence with them into the presumably nonviolent world of the music business, the second often assumes that competition and "battling" in rap are, simply, alternative, nonviolent means of expression.

Rap battles are never pure substitutions for violence, however; rather, they are dances—often literally—on and around the always precarious line between healthy competition and humiliation. A battle, in other words, is called such for a reason. Many of the most famous battle rappers who emerged from this period were quite explicitly out to ruin each other's careers. Those who emphasize the spontaneous, free creativity of the period often forget the fights, near-fights, and ever-presence of serious violence—some of which spilled over from the streets, some from conflicts begun in New York City's main jail, Riker's Island—that pervaded the climate. This climate, though, was exacerbated by the "zero-tolerance" approach of then-mayor Rudolph Giuliani's administration to "quality-of-life crimes," which—for all of the administration's talk of community— often meant little more than systematically moving disreputable-looking people out of business-friendly zones in Manhattan. It is no mere coincidence that the lyrical reflexivity which developed during this period often railed against being trapped in humiliating conditions by faceless forces of order and industry. In sum, the important creative output of this time was directly tied to the perceptions, experiences, and potential of violence and humiliation that were thoroughly woven into the fabric of daily life in the city as well as into the hopes and dreams of those young people trying to create nonhumiliating spaces of work through music.

During the many years I was involved with making music in this period, I was also involved with a young woman whose mother's addiction to serious drugs in the 1970s took a profound turn for the worse when crack cocaine emerged in the mid-1980s. The results, as anyone who has had similar experiences knows, were years of foster care for her young siblings, and long periods of her mother's total absence, which were then punctuated by chaotic visits to county jails and the mental health wards of city hospitals. As a number of researchers now suggest, the decline of crack markets—and, most importantly, the associated declines in lethal violence that began in the early-1990s—was seriously influenced by the cultural stigma that youth in communities most affected by crack cocaine attached to its users, derogatorily referring to them as "crackheads." While acknowledging that such stigma was influential in reducing real rates of violence is of the utmost importance, for those of us whose daily lives were intimately and unavoidably involved with caring for the crackheads who also happened to be family members and friends, that stigma was very real and exceedingly painful. In fact, the widespread, nonchalant use of the word in the 1990s—especially by those whose lives seemed not to have been touched, in a visceral sense, by crack—often felt like a betrayal. Through deeper reflection, however, I have come to see that this was not a betrayal; rather, it was itself an indication of the degree to which crack cocaine had clearly affected everyone, and had become a primary symbolic referent for the many young people trying to distance themselves from the desperation, humiliation, and punitive surveillance that crack represented.

My personal experiences with rap and crack, therefore, inform every page of this book. Part of my goal in it, then, is to communicate some of the power and loss that, together, constitute what I call crack's experiential fabric—the spider-webbed interconnections between policy and culture that continue to affect lives to this day. Vitally important to the whole, hence, is my contention that the intensely personal experiences engendered by the crack era were—and still are—deeply intertwined with the paradoxical reasoning undergirding the federal crack law itself, which is outlined briefly below.

Rap, Law, and the Industry

On August 3, 2010, President Barack Obama signed a law repealing one of the most controversial policies in American criminal justice history: the 100-to-1 sentencing disparity between crack cocaine and powder whereby someone convicted of "simply" *possessing five grams of crack*—the equivalent of a few sugar packets—had been required by law to serve no less than five years in prison.[1] In order to receive the same five-year mandatory sentence someone would have to be convicted of *trafficking in five hundred grams of powder.* Enacted by the United States Congress in 1988 as an update to a 1986 statute,[2] the punishment structure had created, in the United States Sentencing Commission's words, a fundamental "anomaly in the law" since no other drug in the federal system had carried a mandatory prison term for a first offense of simple possession.[3]

Hailed as a bipartisan victory, the law's repeal depended upon a number of glaring inconsistencies that advocates for rational drug policy had been highlighting for over fifteen years. For example, crack—as researchers have consistently shown—is a drug that has long been in decline. And, while rates of violent crime in the United States have also declined since the early 1990s, federal crack cases *increased* during this period, and the gap between sentences for crack and powder *grew*, which severely problematized any justification of the law's continued existence based on a link between crack and violence.[4] Likewise, while the majority of people who report using crack at least once a year are white, over 80 percent of those sentenced under federal crack laws have been black.[5]

As outlined briefly in the book's opening sections, I examine the cultural consequences of crack's paradoxical punishment, and focus on a reflexive lyrical stance that emerged in 1990s New York rap, which critiqued the music industry for being corrupt, unjust, and criminal. A consciousness of exploitation was vocalized in the very products that were themselves being exploited. Many rappers began drawing parallels between the "rap game" and the "crack game," juxtaposing their own exploits in street crime with the machinations of industry executives in the suites.

Where popular conceptions of the music industry often pit naïve artists against predatory executives, numerous rappers since the 1990s have come to present a vision of the music industry in which hustling, entrepreneurial artists from the streets *become* the industry executives in the suites. This situation creates a seemingly contradictory position for many rappers as they are both behind the scenes as executives and in front of the camera as artists, colluding in the same industry exploitation of which they are so often critical, and doing so in the very products that are being produced, marketed, and consumed on a world stage and on a global scale.

This book, then, first began as a lyrical analysis of this internal critique in which the products themselves talk back to the very system that created them, and which artists of all genres have come to perceive as intolerable. Hence, many rap artists have come to indict *the work* of the industry, in which duplicity and complexity bind hard workers to an immoral system of production. The fundamental questions, thus, that first animated this book were these: What do these products themselves say about being products, the process of becoming products, and their relationship to their producers? And what role does crime play in this uneasy, ambivalent relationship to and alliance with the exploitative practices of the entertainment industries?

Very early on, however, it became apparent that it would be impossible to understand rap's engagement with its own commercialization without also analyzing the ways in which that conflict was being accounted for in the exploding cottage industry surrounding the murders of the two most important figures in rap's merger of street and suite crime: the Notorious B.I.G. and Tupac Shakur. As the most prominent representatives of rival record labels based on opposite coasts, their feud took place in lyrics, in magazines, in awards shows, and in the streets. B.I.G. was himself a product of the 1990s New York rap milieu who later became the figurehead of Bad Boy records, the East Coast rival of Los Angeles–based Death Row Records, headed by Tupac. As the public icons of two powerful, black-owned record labels, B.I.G. and Tupac were instrumental in creating a public image of the rap industry as a business environment run like criminal cartels and street gangs. Since their murders, B.I.G. and Tupac have become near-mythical figures.

In addition to these considerations, it also became apparent during the early stages of this book that the degree to which the "real" criminal associations of rap artists have taken center stage was being institutionalized through the popularity of figures such as 50 Cent, who has been described as "B.I.G. and Tupac rolled into one."[6] After being shot nine times, the crack dealer-turned-rapper was dropped from his record label contract because, he claimed, the label executives were too scared. After making a name for himself as a hungry underground artist, 50 secured another record contract and went on to sell over eleven million copies of his debut album, *Get Rich or Die Trying.*

This book, therefore, took the shape it did because crack emerged as the "answer" to the seemingly simple question with which it began: What are the products themselves saying about being products, the process of becoming products, and their relationship to their producers? Crack, that is, figures as a broad, pervasive—even if contradictory—logic of work and labor that plays out in lyrics, documentaries, interviews, autobiographies, and, most significantly, the interaction between rap's various expressive media and the paradoxical logic of the crack laws themselves.

In order to convey crack's social complexity and symbolic power, I have borrowed a phrase from historian Raymond Williams to suggest that the American experience of crack cocaine represents the lethal core of a larger *criminological structure of feeling* that has risen to dominance in public life during the past thirty-plus years. A structure of feeling, Williams wrote, is "a particular quality of social experience and relationship"[7] that reflects "meanings and values as they are actively lived and felt,"[8] which gives the "sense of a generation or of a period."[9] I call the crack era, the period in question, the *lethal core* of this structure for one primary reason: during this time, between the mid-1980s and early 1990s, the national homicide rate rose from 8 to 10 per 100,000, and, in those neighborhoods hit hardest, to as high as *129 per 100,000*, reflecting a national death toll of nearly 25,000 people per year.[10] As the lethal core of this larger structure, crack has continued to affect perceptions of social life even as violent crime rates have steadily declined since their peak in the 1990s. In my premise, crack represents a "vital area of social experience"[11] that is rife with conflicting impulses, but still functions as an ordering gridwork "with specific internal relations, at once interlocking and in tension"[12] that often operates quite aside from what people consciously intend.

I call this structure "criminological" because it reflects the emergence of criminology, broadly conceived. As the systematic study of crime and criminal behavior, the discipline of criminology was *a theoretical intervention* into the abstract ideals of Enlightenment legal theory, problematizing, at the very least, its conception—perhaps best exemplified in the criminological canon by the writings of Cesare Beccaria—of human beings as free, rational, sovereign individuals. Criminology, however, was also *a practical intervention* into the administration of justice in nineteenth-century America, incorporating scientific and quasi-medical practices into the professionalizing forces that grew along with rapid urbanization. The actual practice of criminal justice in the United States today, therefore, is a composite of many elements: (a) early American Christian ideals of confession and repentance; (b) Enlightenment values of due process; (c) social-scientific explanations of law making, law breaking, and law enforcement; (d) the various bureaucratic practices that inevitably accompany the rise of any complex social institution; as well as (e) the popular support—sometimes tacit, at other times explicit—for the growth of state-sanctioned crime-control strategies. All of these elements only congeal into a larger criminological structure of feeling, though, in the wake of *deindustrialization*—the massive flight of manufacturing jobs from the urban core of many U.S. cities since the 1970s, and the concomitant rise of a service economy bolstered primarily by unskilled, low-wage labor.

In my conception, then, America's criminological structure of feeling reflects a collective impulse—even when, as is often the case, such impulses are driven by economic forces, and manipulated by politicians desperate for reelection in a world of increasingly unstable work patterns—to *punish away* the significant moral and material changes experienced in the latter half of the twentieth century. The results of this impulse—what sociologist David Garland has called "retaliatory legislation"—have been severe.[13] At bottom, crime and punishment in twenty-first-century America—and, increasingly, the world—have come to provide whole sets of interpretive schema through which social life is now perceived, thereby creating overlapping webs of values, meanings, and beliefs that radiate far beyond official policies and documents, and thread their way into people's daily lives and cultural creations.[14] Undergirding my premise is one simple, oft-repeated observation: the United States imprisons far more people for far more time for far more nonviolent offenses than anywhere else in the world. As a result, the third element of America's criminal exceptionalism—in addition to its high rates of lethal violence and its use of the death penalty—is this: the population behind bars has more than quintupled in the past thirty years, from less than half a million prisoners in the early 1970s to over two million presently, representing one in every one hundred U.S. adults.[15] With an additional five million on probation and parole, the more than seven million people now under criminal justice supervision represent a full one in every thirty-one U.S. adults, with some states, such as Georgia, reaching as high as one in thirteen.[16]

The multiple, overlapping experiences, then, of crime and punishment in the United States have come to suffuse the daily lives of ever-increasing numbers of Americans, saturating their senses and perceptions, and affecting the ways in which they interpret the world. These experiences now include a whole range of related elements: (a) all known and unknown offenses and victimizations;[17] (b) police stops, searches, seizures, and arrests;[18] (c) bookings, arraignments, pleas, and, more rarely, trials;[19] (d) *time*, in jails, prisons, and the various forms of supervised release that, by turns, have grown and fallen in professional favor;[20] and (e) the endless representations of crime and punishment that inundate public and private life through ever-changing media delivery systems.

A criminological structure of feeling, in other words, is a social condition in which criminal justice has become a stand-in for social justice generally. It is a condition in which the public has grown increasingly confident and vocal about its own criminological expertise, relying primarily on "commonsense" beliefs about why criminals do what they do, what law enforcement officials should do about them, and how long they should be locked up for, regardless of what other "experts"—professional criminologists, mainstream and critical—have to say about it all.[21] More importantly, the specific policies that are generated from this condition all too often reflect contradictory logics that violently overlap and stand at cross-purposes. Take gang enhancement laws, for example, which can increase sentences for felonies by anywhere from two to ten years, depending on the seriousness of the underlying charge. Such laws—which often have neighborhood-level support, but are usually associated with right-of-center, tough-on-crime advocates—are intended, in the words California's Street Terrorism Enforcement and Prevention Act, to "seek the eradication of criminal activity by street gangs."[22] Take, also, hate crime statutes, which similarly reflect an effort on the part of left-of-center advocates to send a "clear message" that hate-motivated violence simply won't be tolerated any more. Like gang enhancements, hate crime statutes also increase sentences by multiple years, depending on the seriousness of the underlying charge. The inconsistency of both efforts, however, lies in one bald fact: inmates in jails and prisons are all but required to "click up" with a *race-based gang* in order to secure even the most basic elements of survival, whether toilet paper or phone time. Prison operates according to the most reductive understandings of race, which guide almost every activity in it. Put differently, in order to show that we will no longer tolerate gangs or racism, we will, strangely, send, for extra time, "gang bangers" and "racists" to the most racist and gang-driven institution the world has ever seen: prison. Given such a radical disconnect between ends and means, one should wonder what "messages" are actually being received by gang members and racists through their enhanced sentences.

In a criminological structure of feeling, the exact same thing—time under criminal justice supervision—is believed by wide swaths of the citizenry (as well as the politicians and professionals of all political stripes who must answer to them) to perform a variety of different functions simultaneously, including, at least, the four classic goals of punishment: deterrence, incapacitation, rehabilitation, and retribution. Most often, though, justifications for such violently contradictory policies represent radically unreflexive beliefs in prison's supposed "message-sending" capabilities.

In this book, therefore, I suggest that rap music has come to serve as one of the primary means by which crack performs its work within this larger structure. I've approached rap, then, as *a complex, often contradictory, commercially bound social practice* that cannot be reduced to its political potential or violent excesses, which are often taken, simplistically, by both academic and popular critics, to be its "good" and "bad" qualities. When approached as a complex social practice, rap can be seen less as a reflection of social forces, and more as, in Williams's words, a "creative working"—"a transformation and innovation which composed a generation out of what seemed separate work and experience," bringing "in new feelings, people, relationships; rhythms newly known, discovered, articulated; defining the society rather than merely reflecting it."[23]

Rap's role in creatively working out the crack era's complicated social effects only emerges, as I've suggest above, from a specific period in rap's history, during which there developed an explicit, self-conscious, and lyrical *language of exploitation* through which many rap artists denounced routine music industry practices as being immoral and criminal.[24] "[W]e discover our epoch," Williams wrote, "not by the generalities of the period but by those points, those lives, those experiences, in which the structure of our own most significant difficulties seems to begin to take shape."[25] What began as seemingly random outbursts in rap's confrontation with its own commercialization eventually laid the groundwork for a grammar of social analysis in which empowerment and loss, creative work and servitude figure as key criminological flashpoints. In essence, the metaphor of crack in rap's confrontation with its own commercialization represents a violent logic of work in late-twentieth- and early-twenty-first-century America whose primary terms are drawn from, are shaped by, and operate within a much larger criminological structure of feeling that has risen to dominance in American public life since the 1970s.

Chapter Outline

In charting crack's lethal logic of work, which lies at the core of America's criminological structure of feeling, I draw from and weave together song lyrics, threads of legal argumentation, pieces of biography, and excerpts of interviews in an effort to register the richness, emotional force, and logical contradictions that constitute crack's experiential fabric.[26] Each chapter engages different pieces of this fabric, disentangling its multiple, overlapping, and sometimes vestigial elements in a larger effort to illustrate its social complexity as well as illuminate the inseparable pairing of policy and culture from which it grew

Chapter 1 begins by placing rap's unique expressive position squarely within the primary contradictions of crack's punishment structure as well as recent arguments condemning this structure that have come from the United States Supreme Court and the United States Sentencing Commission, among others. In short, the chapter provides a brief outline of the punitive policy contexts from which crack's experiential dynamics of feeling grew, and which also inform the rest of the book.

Chapter 2 examines the profoundly problematic rationale underlying the U.S. government's punishment structure for crack cocaine. I rely primarily on the Sentencing Commission's four reports to Congress that have consistently challenged the mandatory minimums in order to let crack's paradoxical punishment "speak for itself." This chapter analyzes the specific legal logics with which rap's conflict with its own commercialization became inextricably imbedded, and outlines how crack became the lethal core of America's criminological structure of feeling.

Chapter 3 situates the rags-to-riches, streets-to-boardroom-suites success stories that have become the most recognizable identity myths at the core of the rap industry within the broader context of rap criticism, both popular and academic, and from which two clear approaches have emerged: where one side approaches rap in order to *use* it for political ends by first rescuing the "good" parts from the commercialized aspects, the other approaches rap with the goal of *accusing* it of signaling—and, sometimes, causing—all that is "bad" in the inner city. Both attempts, however, often neglect the everyday exploitative realities within which rap's immediate productive possibilities are defined. Consequently, this chapter gives an overview of these exploitative realities in order to show how crack's social devastations became a bedrock experience for rap artists raised in the era.

In chapter 4, I problematize one of the most popular beliefs about rap's crack-infused lyrics: that they represent, par excellence, a loss of morality in the inner city. Instead, by charting the deeply moral debate at the heart of what many take as examples of the worst kinds of sensationalist superpredation, I attempt to show that, in the wake of the crack era's transformation of violence, a new moral order has arisen in which market relations have come to supplant culturally bound ones and that the young people raised in it have experienced as both power and loss. This transformation, I contend, can be seen most powerfully in the Notorious B.I.G.'s song "Things Done Changed," which creatively works out the rise of what I call "new school violence."

Chapter 5 challenges a seemingly "simple" premise underlying many popular theories that posit a clear relationship between bad parenting, crime, and rap music: no one is monitoring, punishing, or training the youth. Quite to the contrary, however, what rap, ethnographic literature on crack dealing, and research on America's declining violence rates suggest is that youth, indeed, have been engaged in very serious efforts to monitor, train, and restrain *themselves*. That these efforts have helped reduce rates of serious violence in the United States is all the more significant as youth have done so even in the midst of severe family and community disruption caused by excessive punishment and despite the near-constant public condemnation of their supposed lack of morality. This chapter, therefore, analyzes the ways in which rap's reflexive stance toward its own commercialization has consistently reflected serious efforts at restraining crack-era violence through training regimens that have been fundamentally self-imposed.

Chapter 6 analyzes the mythology surrounding the most important figure in rap's conflict with its own commercialization: Suge Knight. As the head of Death Row Records, he was at the center of the conflict with which the deaths of B.I.G. and Tupac will forever be linked. Suge stands as a powerful symbol in the rap industry because he is seen as representing two sides of the use of crack-era violence: when used in disciplined bursts it appears to provide freedom from humiliation and the violence of a life suspended by the seemingly nonviolent practices of the music industry; when an end in itself, though, violence can become a thoroughly unproductive element that signals the demise of one's productive potential. And it is precisely this balancing act between two violences that has become an essential element in the current rap industry.

The symbolism, then, of crack in rap's reflexive stance toward its own commercialization represents a moral debate whose significance lies in the widespread cultural consequences of the United States' irrational clinging to the paradoxical punishment structure of crack cocaine. In its engagement with its own commercialization, rap has come to speak to issues far bigger than itself, and, in so doing, has highlighted the degree to which crack—although a drug long in decline—has transformed into the lethal core of a much larger criminological structure of feeling that pervades American public life, and continues to radiate outward in ever-increasing carceral rings.

Crack, Rap, and
the Punitive Turn

The crack epidemic had rap representing the rules.
    —Nas, "The Last Real Nigga Alive," *God's Son*, 2002

In *Kimbrough v. United States,* one in a string of recent landmark decisions that, in effect, have made the United States Sentencing Commission's guidelines nonbinding, the Supreme Court upheld a trial court judge's decision to address the former 100-to-1 sentencing disparity between crack cocaine and powder by reducing Derrick Kimbrough's crack-related sentence by over four years.[1] Kimbrough—an Operation Desert Storm veteran with no prior felonies—had pleaded guilty to a number of drugs and weapons charges and was sentenced to fifteen years instead of the 19-to-22.5-year range that strict adherence to the sentencing guidelines would have required. Had Kimbrough been caught with an equivalent amount of powder, he would have faced eight or nine years, less than half the time he faced for crack possession. In the trial judge's view, the additional four-plus years mandated by the guidelines were "greater than necessary" to assure deterrence and public safety, and he responded by going lower than what was required. Arguing that the trial court had abused its discretion in going below the guidelines, the court of appeals increased Kimbrough's sentence to the higher number. In disagreeing with the appellate decision, therefore, the highest court in the country officially recognized what researchers, scientists, and advocates have been arguing for years: the punishment structure for crack cocaine has always been radically disproportionate to the interests of justice.

Created by Congress as an independent agency through the Sentencing Reform Act in 1984,[2] the Sentencing Commission's primary purpose was to "rationalize the federal sentencing process" by using an "empirical approach" to develop guidelines that federal courts would be required to follow.[3] The guidelines, hence, were to be followed *as law*. While *Kimbrough* is important on many levels, with future implications yet to be seen, its significance so far has been to uphold the *excision* of the guidelines' status as law.[4] The guidelines are now just that: advisory, instead of mandatory. While *Kimbrough* and the cases that led up to it have been technically concerned with the issue of due process at sentencing,[5] *Kimbrough* is significant in that both the trial judge and the Supreme Court explicitly drew on a series of the commission's own in-depth studies that have, in no uncertain terms, consistently challenged the federal government's punishment of crack cocaine.[6] In 1995, 1997, 2002, and, again, in 2007, the Sentencing Commission—the very body created by Congress to implement rational, empirically based sentencing guidelines—has detailed the irrational punishment of crack, stating, in the words of the 2007 report, that "the 100-to-1 drug quantity ratio significantly undermines the various congressional objectives set forth in the Sentencing Reform Act."[7] While President Obama's repeal of the mandatory minimum for the simple possession of crack cocaine is a significant move toward evidence-based drug policy, for over twenty years Congress clung to a sentencing structure that punished minority populations at an overwhelmingly disproportionate rate despite near-unanimous condemnation.[8]

Both the Court's decision in *Kimbrough* and the repeal of the mandatory minimum for simple possession, then, have underlined the profound irrationality at the heart of the federal government's punishment of crack cocaine. For one thing, in destatutizing the guidelines, the Court, paradoxically, allowed the commission's recommendations concerning crack to be followed in its advisory role, the way it never was followed in its mandatory role. The irrationality of crack's punishment, therefore, is at the forefront of renewed efforts at both the state and federal levels to reform a criminal justice system that has long been perceived by a broad range of critics, researchers, and politicians as being overly harsh and fundamentally counterproductive. In the words of Senator Jim Webb, whose recently proposed legislation—the National Criminal Justice Act of 2009—aims at "nothing less than a complete restructuring" of punishment in the United States, "America's criminal justice system is broken," and "[o]ur failure to address these problems cuts against the notion that we are a society founded on fundamental fairness."[9]

In fact, by many accounts, we are at a crucial bipartisan juncture in American criminal justice.[10] The year 2009, for example, saw state prison populations drop for the first time in nearly four decades, declining by 0.3 percent. But how did we get here, to a point where a mere 0.3 percent change is seen—by beleaguered proponents of rational criminal justice policy across the board—as a significant victory? This chapter gives a brief overview of how we got to this point, outlining, in the process, the contradictory policy contexts out of which crack's lethal logic of work eventually emerged, and which continue to define its experiential fabric. In addition, I discuss the "scholarly near misses" that have influenced analyses of the rap-crack intersection to this point, and suggest how we might rethink that intersection in order to move beyond reductionist accounts in which rap music and inner-city communities are taken as mere reflections of each other.

Contradiction in Crime and Punishment

Perhaps counterintuitively, given the federal government's more than twenty-year reliance on the mandatory minimum for simple possession, crack cocaine, as researchers have consistently shown, is a drug that has long been in decline. "As early as 1990," sociologist Bruce Jacobs writes in his ethnography of crack dealers in St. Louis, crack "began to show evidence of remission,"[11] and "as of mid-1998"—a few years after Jacobs began his project—"crack use, with a few rare exceptions . . . is in either nationwide decline or (late) plateau."[12] Most crack dealers, accordingly, have long been aware that they are participating in a fairly unprofitable business. In addition, many of the fears originally associated with crack— that it was, for example, instantly addictive, or, relatedly, that instantly addicted mothers would create an epidemic of crack-addicted babies— have been found by most researchers, including the commission, to be, fundamentally, baseless.[13] Likewise, although crack cocaine has been a lightning rod in the U.S. war on drugs, there has never been, in the words of the 1995 Sentencing Commission report, a "comparable crack cocaine problem outside the United States."[14]

Crack, then, is a drug supposedly in its last stages of life, whose time has come and gone, and is not even considered profitable by the very people who choose to sell it. Crack is not supposed to be important anymore; it is, it seems, just a vestige of an earlier, more paranoid era. Crack is, simply put, an anomaly. But it is precisely in this anomalous space that crack's larger social significance lies. Crack's supposed "decline"—and the wrongs believed to be magically righted through repeal of the crack law's most egregious inconsistencies—is belied by its cultural ascendance.

To be sure, arguments about the paradoxical nature of crime and punishment have been made many times before. The history of penology is perhaps most important in this regard as the field's Marxist and critical roots run deep, grounding the analysis of punishment in a profound sense of contradiction. Sociologists George Rusche and Otto Kirchheimer's classic, *Punishment and Social Structure*, is key, arguing, as it did, that, quite apart from any of its explicit goals, "the principal objective [of the modern prison] was not the reformation of the inmates but the rational exploitation of labor power."[15] Likewise, in analyzing the development of vagrancy laws in early modern England, sociologist William Chambliss argued that, rather than being "simply a reflection of 'public opinion' as is sometimes found in the literature," the laws, instead, "emerged in order to provide the powerful landowners with a ready supply of cheap labor."[16] Similarly, sociologist Richard Quinney argued that the criminal justice system primarily operates to control surplus populations made redundant "as the rate of unemployment increases."[17]

Clearly, however, Marxist analysts are not the only ones who have emphasized punishment's noninstrumental and counterintuitive effects. Sociologist David Garland, for example, has argued that punishment "should be seen not as a singular kind of event or relationship but rather as a social institution" that entails a "complexity of structure and density of meaning."[18] Similarly, in discussing what he calls the "penal imagination," sociologist Philip Smith argues that, "even where punishment looks most rationalized and bureaucratic," it nevertheless includes "unruly meanings" that "exert their insistent and surprising influence."[19] Likewise, in her analysis of the "penal spectator"—someone who "sanctions, in her approval and witnessing, the infliction of pain"[20]—sociologist Michelle Brown also emphasizes punishment's social complexity, noting that "penal meanings will always be plural and tricky to harness,"[21] regardless of how strongly we believe we can control the "messages" we think we send by punishing others. For these authors, the social significance of punishment is to be found in its complex symbolic resonance, and not its instrumental goals alone.

While critical analyses of punishment are clearly pervaded by a deep sense of paradox, even "mainstream" studies of criminal justice practice in the United States often reaffirm similar counterintuitive relationships between explicit goals and implicit functions. Take the famous Kansas City patrol experiment, which set about trying to understand the effectiveness of different policing styles on crime rates.[22] By increasing patrols in one area, keeping them the same in another, and making them purely reactive in the last, the experiment came to a fundamentally counterintuitive result: crime rates stayed the same in all of the areas, suggesting that, for all of the "common sense" about policing at the time, there was, essentially, little influence to be found between police presence and actual crime. The experiment, however, did make a strange discovery: while citizens did not report feeling any safer, they all believed that more officers were needed. In other words, the study found that the public is often in a state of always wanting more police presence regardless of the amount they actually receive. And, in a similar study conducted by some of the same authors in Newark, New Jersey, a few years later, it was found that, indeed, when police patrolled each block on foot, citizens did feel safer, even if actual rates of crime did not decline.[23] The paradox, therefore, lies in the finding that *perception*, not action, gives policing its importance. And, in an even more interesting turn, this emphasis on perception was taken up as one of the primary causative elements by criminologists George L. Kelling and James Q. Wilson in their famous "broken windows" theory of crime: "[I]f a window in a building is broken and is left unrepaired," they wrote, then the community will perceive such states of disrepair as acceptable, and "all the rest of the windows will soon be broken."[24] Dependent upon a belief that the "untended behavior" of disreputable people leads to spiraling urban decay, broken windows theory conferred a very clear importance on the connection between community fears of crime and actual crime. The spiral of decline, in their words, begins when a "piece of property is abandoned, weeds grow up, a window is smashed." As a result, "Adults stop scolding rowdy children; the children, emboldened, become more rowdy. Families move out, unattached adults move in. Teenagers," consequently, "gather in front of the corner store. The merchant asks them to move; they refuse. Fights occur. Litter accumulates. People start drinking in front of the grocery; in time, an inebriate slumps to the sidewalk and is allowed to sleep it off." And it was this theory of causation that formed the core of the William Bratton–led NYPD during Mayor Rudolph Giuliani's administration in the 1990s, which took a "zero tolerance" approach to "quality of life" crimes, turning New York City, in the eyes of many, into a "miracle" success story of contemporary policing.[25]

At bottom, from theoretical penology to mainstream crime-control policy, there is a broad consensus that the explicit goals and purposes of criminal justice may have very little effect on how the system actually operates. While the ultimate causes of and the specific policy recommendations that are generated from these paradoxical findings will always be in dispute, the criminal justice system's counterintuitive nature is everywhere affirmed. It is also in this element of paradox, however, that some of the more socially devastating aspects of U.S. crime-control policy lie.

The Punitive Turn

Called the "punitive turn" by some, U.S. crime-control policies since the 1970s have changed significantly. As a number of writers have argued over the years, the 1970s saw a strange consensus between populist "tough on crime" approaches to criminal justice policy and professional criticisms of judicial discretion that appeared to create wide sentencing disparities among different jurisdictions for similar crimes.[26] Popular concerns were, at least in part, influenced by real rises in crime, what David Garland has called a "new collective experience of crime."[27] Professional concerns, on the other hand, were often driven by what criminal justice historian Samuel Walker has called efforts at "taming the system."[28] The effects of this changing social mood—our nascent criminological structure of feeling— can best be seen in a number of films from the era in which vigilante "anti-heroes" take back city streets overrun with predatory hoodlums. Take, in this regard, the classic 1974 film *Dirty Harry*, in which Clint Eastwood, in the title role, is called "dirty" precisely because of his extralegal crime-control tactics. In one famous scene, Harry slowly grinds his shoe into the wounded leg of a writhing suspect who is whimpering about his right to a lawyer and pleading for his life. When faced with a scolding prosecutor, Harry responds with barely controlled contempt, mockingly saying how he's "all broken up about that man's rights." Take, also, 1975's *Death Wish*, in which Charles Bronson's character—who is described in no uncertain terms as a "bleeding heart liberal"—becomes a merciless vigilante after his wife and daughter are brutally assaulted. Perhaps the most interesting example of the late-seventies-era tough-on-crime mood, however, is *Escape from New York*. Released in 1981, and set in the future of 1997, the film opens with a briefly worded description: in response to a fictional *four hundred percent rise in crime*, in 1988, the federal government turned the entire island of Manhattan into a penal colony surrounded by a fifty-foot containment wall and guarded by police personnel instructed to shoot any potential escapees on sight.

In addition to this synthesis of popular and professional concerns, in 1974, an influential analysis of rehabilitation programs concluded that "the rehabilitation efforts that have been reported so far have had no appreciable effect on recidivism."[29] Often called, simply, "Martinson," this "nothing works" doctrine converged with the growing tough-on-crime trend as well as academic criticisms of sentencing disparity, giving far more scientific legitimacy to the implementation of a number of significant changes in criminal justice policy.[30] The aim of these efforts as a whole can perhaps best be summarized in a phrase: making time served better reflect time given. In many states, as well as the federal government, these efforts resulted in moves away from *indeterminate* sentencing structures as well as the serious reduction or outright abolishment of parole boards. The rationale behind these kinds of moves relied on a widespread perception that parole boards and indeterminate sentencing structures resulted in far too much leniency, giving criminals too many "breaks." Indeterminate sentences, it was believed, allowed for far too much discretion since punishments were given as ranges, such as ten years to life, rather than as a single, definite number. At some point after the minimum term had been served, prisoners would then be eligible for parole, and would have to appear before the parole board periodically to assess whether their behavior in prison, predictions of their future dangerousness, and the severity of their crimes justified early release. The effort to make time served more accurately reflect time given, then, was a move to *determinate* sentencing structures in which prisoners had to serve a specific period of time minus good time credits. After serving their sentences, prisoners were automatically freed, without having to appear before a parole board to predict their future dangerousness.

This punitive turn, however, also occurred through "truth in sentencing" laws passed in many states throughout the 1980s and 1990s, which required prisoners to serve a specific proportion of their sentences. In 1998, for example, Congress—as stipulated in a 1994 act—allocated federal grant money to those states that could prove that a majority of their offenders were serving at least 85 percent of their sentences.[31] In addition, and of specific concern to this book, during the 1980s there was an increasing reliance on the passing, at both the state and federal levels, of mandatory minimum sentences for drug and weapons charges, many of which were modeled on New York's infamous Rockefeller Drug Laws, which had been signed into law by governor Nelson Rockefeller in 1973, and reformed significantly in 2009 after decades of severe criticism.[32] Mandatory minimums *guaranteed* that a specific minimum sentence would be imposed if guilt was determined. These sentences were legislatively created punishments that did not go through the Sentencing Commission process, and were sometimes at odds with the commission's own recommendations. What was more, the mandatory minimums, in fact, trumped the commission's guidelines if there was a conflict between them.

Primarily because mandatory minimums give prosecutors an unreviewable power, some judges have come to believe that such punishment structures undermine their ability to treat like cases alike and unique cases uniquely in order to ensure fairness, proportionality, and justice.[33] By guaranteeing specific sentences if guilt is determined, the charging document filed by the district attorney *becomes* the sentence, which effectively negates the sentencing judge's ability to consider individual circumstances in order to serve the interests of justice. Legislators, on the other hand, argue that the passing of mandatory minimums reflects the democratic process at its best: elected officials passing laws that address the most serious concerns of their constituents.

The punitive turn in U.S. crime-control policy, therefore, signified a *symbolic* turn away from perceived weakness and leniency as well as a *practical* turn toward making time served better approximate time given. And, practically, this turn, in the eyes of an overwhelming number of researchers, has resulted in a fundamental paradox at the heart of U.S. criminal justice policy: in the words of prison expert Joan Petersilia, "we are both simultaneously too harsh and too lenient."[34] Petersilia's comment illustrates a now broad consensus among academics and practitioners of all political persuasions that U.S. crime policy is so rife with conflicting goals and paradoxical mandates that, rather than becoming the targeted policy it set out to be through the reigning in of overly lenient discretion, has instead become a "targeted sledgehammer"—a Zenlike word pairing that highlights its significantly counterproductive effects.

The punitive turn, while explicitly aimed at getting tough on crime, often requires, counterintuitively, that the most violent offenders be freed without any supervision after they "max out," while the least violent offenders receive both prison time and a period of postrelease supervision during which an astounding and ever-growing number of them are returned to prison for technical violations rather than the commission of new crimes. While designed to control the perceived inconsistencies of judicial discretion and to make time served more closely approximate time given, the system has, instead, wound up creating what some have referred to as America's "imprisonment binge" and its creation of a "penal state"—the quintupling of America's incarcerated population in a little over thirty years.[35]

Thus we have, for a salient example, California's recurring prison crises. In the second decade of the twenty-first century, with a total of around 160,000 inmates, each of California's thirty-three prisons is nearly at double capacity, a crisis to which governors and legislators have repeatedly responded by presenting various plans to release nonviolent inmates and build additional facilities. While such plans, in some ways, approximate the kinds of changes that advocates of prison reform have been suggesting for years, their timing and presentation in public debate indicate that, in addition to being seen as necessary steps toward alleviating an unnecessarily clogged system, they have also come to be viewed as "desperate" measures in a time of crisis. Such interpretations create backlashes against the prison reform effort since the public often sees these moves as "unleashing" criminals and drug addicts back onto the streets.[36] In addition, and in the midst of severe and recurring budget crises, Federal Masters took over California's prison health care system in 2005—controlling a significant proportion of the state's general fund in the process—after it was shown that one prisoner died every six days due to inadequate care.[37]

None of these crises, however, has been "caused" by the punishment of crack cocaine. In addition, crack has universally been seen as a drug long in decline, and the most egregious inconsistencies of its punishment structure supposedly fixed through repeal. So why, then, given crack's decline, should I spend so much time arguing that crack is vitally important to understanding our current predicament? The problem lies in the larger social effects of the 100-to-1 sentencing disparity created by the Anti–Drug Abuse Acts of 1986 and 1988. Crack was singled out, treated as one hundred times worse than the substance from which it is derived, and punished accordingly. Practically, the acts all but forced the commission to include the mandatory minimums within its own recommendations in order to avoid the even more paradoxical situation of having two conflicting sentences, both of which would be legally binding. The issue, therefore, revolves around why the United States continued to cling to an anomalous effort to punish crack offenses at a vastly disproportionate rate even in the face of overwhelming condemnation. Why, if crack has been in such a state of decline for the past fifteen years, was its irrational punishment only changed in 2010? In effect, the punishment ratio, as I detail in the next chapter, should never have been implemented, regardless of how well intentioned its creation may have been. The mandatory minimums have never made sense, and have been based, from the start, on thoroughly illogical premises that continue to provide the foundations for the new crack laws even after repeal of their most obvious contradictions. Put simply, there is no greater example of the punitive absurdity, and absurdly punitive reasoning, undergirding our thirty-plus-year experiment in mass incarceration—as well as our recent efforts to reform it—than the punishment structure for crack cocaine. Crack's punishment reflects, par excellence, what legal scholar Norval Morris dubbed the "Humpty Dumpty principle" in criminal justice: "[I]f all the king's horses and all the king's men couldn't put Humpty together again, then, by heavens, we need more horses and more men."[38] Even in the face of overwhelming condemnation and official action, crack cocaine continues to play a profoundly symbolic social role.

Scholarly Near Misses

Given the paradoxical nature of crack's punishment structure, it should be no surprise that those groups hit most heavily by the anomalous treatment of crack cocaine should also come to see themselves in similarly paradoxical ways. Take anthropologist Philippe Bourgois' argument concerning the simultaneously critical and self-destructive beliefs that crack dealers have about their roles in the underground economy: "[B]y embroiling themselves in the underground economy and proudly embracing street culture, they are seeking an alternative to their social marginalization. In the process, on a daily level, they become the actual agents administering their own destruction and their community's suffering."[39] Take, also, Bruce Jacobs's subjects, who similarly view crack dealing as "[m]ore than a source of material sustenance," and suggest that "selling crack may be one of the few meaningful arenas for the pursuit of prestige and self-worth available to a segment of the inner-city population."[40] Jacobs goes on to say that, "[a]s calamitous as market conditions may be, the choice to sell is still quite functional for some. To abandon it for something else is either to forgo a source of accomplishment available nowhere else or, worse, to stare failure in the face."[41] Crack, that is, represents a last vestige of freedom from humiliating, low-wage labor even as it intensifies neighborhood violence to such a degree that it becomes a culture of terror.

It should also be no surprise, then, that the forms of cultural expression most closely associated with those groups disproportionately affected by crack's paradoxical punishment should come to be primary ways in which many of them have dealt with the lived realities of such profound contradictions. To wit, Caesar, one of Bourgois' primary subjects, describes his own situation thus: "I was addicted to tapes for my radio. Music! That was my first addiction."[42] Similarly, Leroy, another crack dealer in the same book, describes how he deals with the irrational fear that his mere presence often seems to inspire in whites: "Sometimes it irks me. Like, you know, it clicks in my mind. Makes me want to write. I always write it down. Sometimes I write down the incident, what happened. I try to make a rhyme [rap lyrics] out of it."[43] Likewise, Angelo, an eleven-year-old friend of Bourgois' interviewees, when asked if he wanted to be a pimp or a drug dealer when he grew up, answered, "No, a rapper."[44] In other words, music—and rap music in particular—serves multiple functions for those young people caught in the middle of crack's paradoxical punishment, who are, as Bourgois' book title plainly states, fundamentally, *In Search of Respect*.

All too often, however, the relationship between rap music and street culture—in which crack figures significantly—is taken as a "mere" reflection. Even in important critical work on crack specifically and crime generally, rap is given short shrift. Bourgois, for example, barely mentions rap, even though his subjects repeatedly suggest its importance in their lives. Similarly, while rap is clearly the pervasive, ubiquitous soundtrack to sociologist Sudhir Venkatesh's ethnography of crack-dealing gangs on Chicago's South Side, it is mentioned only briefly thus: "Outside the building a car was blasting rap music"; or, "The scene was straight out of a gangsta-rap video."[45] Likewise, in arguing that the growth of the prison-industrial complex and the flight of manufacturing jobs from urban communities during deindustrialization have encouraged the "intertwining of the urban Black Belt and the carceral system," sociologist Loïc Wacquant says little about rap, stating only that these structural transformations are "further evidenced, and in turn powerfully abetted, by the *fusion of ghetto and prison culture*, as vividly expressed in the lyrics of 'gangsta rap' singers and hip hop artists."[46] In addition, in their essay on the "global triumph of capitalism at the millennium," anthropologists Jean and John Comaroff state, simply, that rap reflects a "crisis of masculinity."[47] And, in one of his articles' concluding sections, called "Hip Hop across Borders," criminologist Jock Young suggests that rap's vocalizations of "compensatory masculinity, resorts to violence and rampant individualism" are "all over accentuations of the wider culture."[48] Rap, then, seems to play important roles in many scholars' understandings of the massive changes—to the nature of work, community life, and violence—in the wake of deindustrialization. Rap itself, however, is given only minor treatment, and, more often than not, is simply referred to in its "reflecting" role.

If critical work on crime gives rap short shrift, then critical work on rap often leaves crime, and crack specifically, similarly underanalyzed. Scholars of rap often discuss crack's emergence from the aftermath of deindustrialization, then leave it alone, as if it were little more than a mere side road on rap's march to global status. In his 500-page history of the "Hip-Hop Generation," for example, journalist Jeff Chang deals with crack in only two pages, even while quoting a Los Angeles–based Crip gang member who recounted crack's massive social effects thus: "'The whole quality of life in the neighborhood just changed. . . . Folks went to jail for the rest of their life. People got murdered. It just totally devastated the neighborhood.'"[49] And, in her analysis of the often contentious debates surrounding rap music, cultural critic Tricia Rose argues that "the ground-level impact of crack, unemployment, and community destruction became a generational experience for many black youth," but similarly treats crack as just another social issue that rap music has come to reflect.[50] Likewise, in his analysis of the "culture and politics of rap," social historian Jeffrey Ogbar discusses crack only as one element among many that "all converged to foment what many would consider 'positive,' 'conscious,' 'message,' 'or 'black nationalist' rap."[51] Crack, accordingly, figures in many scholars' treatments of rap music, but does so peripherally, and little attention is paid to the specific *cultural work* that crack performs.

There exists, therefore, a significant gap in our understanding of the actual ways in which rap expresses one of the most powerful symbols of America's paradoxical crime policy. In an era in which the role of policing—and criminal justice more generally—has been reformulated around the importance of public perception, the significance of a punishment structure whose disproportionate effects on minority populations for the past twenty years have been overwhelmingly condemned by every American institution of justice likewise lies in the way it is perceived on a large scale.

Under these conditions, rather than being, simply, one social issue "reflected" in various media, crack cocaine, instead, sits at the intersection of mediated cultural forms and the logic of crime policy in early twenty-first-century America. Regarded in this light, crack acts as both *matter and metaphor*, and performs a massive amount of *practical and symbolic work*. Emerging, as it did, out of the punitive turn in U.S. crime policy during the latter half of the twentieth century, the punishment structure for crack created a legal paradox that has had lasting consequences not only for those affected most directly, but for the United States as a whole, and—given rap's undeniable global resonance—the world as well. While rap has been one of the primary means by which this legal paradox has been given voice, many rap artists—as I detail in subsequent chapters—have sought not to "magically resolve" this contradiction, but to explicitly and lyrically engage it, for better and for worse, with results that are too often interpreted, simplistically, as being either "positive" or "negative." Rap's engagement with crack cocaine, then, has included both critical and celebratory elements, all of which, however, are underlined by a profound sense of loss engendered by the growth of mass incarceration, and the necessity of lethal violence in regulating an underground economy that grew in the wake of deindustrialization.

In effect, the symbolic importance of crack cannot be understood without an honest accounting of the ways in which it has become so thoroughly interwoven into the moral and material fabric of the forms of cultural expression most closely associated with those groups affected most deeply. Correlatively, rap—especially the violence seemingly so glorified in it—cannot be understood without a thorough accounting of the irrational basis of crack's punishment structure. And, at bottom, in both crack and rap is to be found a profound struggle about the morality of work in the wake of deindustrialization. Fundamentally, both crack and rap are conceived of similarly—as ways to create spaces of nonhumiliating work in the face of severe social disruption. In the next chapter, I begin to account for the cultural resonance between rap and crack by analyzing the complicated sociolegal logics that paved the way for crack's lethal effects, and out of which its symbolic power developed.

The Invisible Hand
Holds a Gun

Law and Policy in the
Lethal Regulation of Crack

It's only crack sales making niggas act like that.
—Prodigy in Mobb Deep, "Q.U.—Hectic," *The Infamous*, 1995

In addition to repealing the mandatory minimum for the simple possession of crack cocaine, the bill signed into law by President Obama in August 2010 also reduced the sentencing disparity between crack trafficking and powder trafficking from 100-to-1 to 18-to-1. By any measure, such a reduction constitutes a significant improvement, requiring five hundred grams of powder or twenty-eight grams of crack to trigger a five-year mandatory sentence instead of the 500-to-5-gram ratio created in 1986. The final bill, however, was only one in a long line of similar bills proposed over the years.

In 2007, for example, Democratic representative Sheila Jackson introduced a bill, H.R. 265, that proposed to equalize the 100-to-1 ratio at the powder level by making possession with intent to distribute five hundred grams of either powder or crack punishable by a mandatory five-year sentence. In 2009, the same bill was again introduced by Jackson, as were similar bills by Democratic representatives Charles Rangel (H.R. 2178) and Robert Scott (H.R. 3245). Also in 2009, Republican representative Roscoe Bartlett proposed a bill, H.R. 18, that would have equalized the 100-to-1 disparity from the opposite direction: by making possession with intent to distribute five grams of either powder or crack punishable by a mandatory five-year term. What's so striking about these proposals is the casinolike way in which the various drug quantities are arrived at, with government officials coming up with numbers seemingly out of thin air. Some aimed to create a 1-to-1 ratio by increasing crack amounts to powder levels, while others intended to create the same ratio by decreasing powder levels to crack amounts. Given such extremes, the final 18-to-1 ratio would appear to be a compromise. And, while any reduction in the crack-powder disparity should be seen as a victory for advocates of rational drug policy, the new ratio, even though a clear improvement, seems especially random since it is based—like the 100-to-1 disparity it has replaced—on no scientific evidence. Why 18-to-1? Why twenty-eight grams? Why not thirty-seven, or fourteen, or six? As a consequence, the thoroughly illogical premises on which the 100-to-1 ratio had been based will remain. Eighteen-to-one is no more logical than 100-to-1, and that very illogicality has had profound consequences for real people in real communities whose lives have been unalterably affected by it.

Unfortunately, the casinolike quality of these congressional debates makes light of the lethality that has so indelibly marked the crack era. Such haphazard reductions—the seemingly random fluctuations of drug quantities—will never, by themselves, be able to address the significant symbolic power that has grown from the social disruption incurred as a result of our illogical policies. Where chapter 1 provided an overview of the punitive contexts out of which crack's experiential fabric was born, this chapter traces the ruthless illogicality at the heart of the U.S. government's punishment structure for crack cocaine. I rely primarily on the Sentencing Commission's four reports to Congress that have consistently challenged the mandatory minimums in order to let crack's paradoxical punishment "speak for itself."[1] It is from the lethal wake of this illogicality that crack's symbolic role in rap's confrontation with its own commercialization develops.

Speed of Passing

The paradoxical punishment of crack cocaine begins with the speed of the law's passing in 1986, which deviated from the normal committee process, suggesting the degree to which crack's punishment was out of the ordinary from the start. As Senator Chiles, for example, remarked, "[I]t is historical for the Congress to be able to move this quickly."[2] Similarly, commenting on criticisms made at the time, Senator Rockefeller described the bill's process as "moving too fast and frenetically."[3] Other senators were quite clearly critical, arguing that "none of us has had an adequate opportunity to study this enormous package. It did not emerge from the crucible of the committee process."[4] In addition, Representative Lott warned that "[i]n our haste to patch together a drug bill—any drug bill—before we adjourn, we have run the risk of ending up with a patch-work quilt . . . that may not fit together into a comprehensible whole."[5] But it was Senator Hawkins who, while defending the urgency of its passing, presaged the far-reaching symbolic impact of the law with which this book is now concerned: "Drugs pose a clear and present danger to America's national security. If for no other reason we should be addressing this on an emergency basis. . . . This is a bill which has far-reaching impact on the future as we know it as Americans and as we mature into the next century."[6] In effect, the quotations above suggest that crack—like opium, marijuana, and powder cocaine before it—was, from the start, a deeply symbolic matter, and, therefore, the law against it represented, for some, an attempt to head off potentially far-reaching future impacts that justified a "fast and frenetic" process to push it through. For others, its passing reflected a historical sense of emergency whose effects were potentially problematic. But perhaps most controversial, the speed of the bill's passing "left behind a limited legislative record,"[7] and "[r]elatively little debate surrounded the proposals to attach mandatory minimum penalties"[8] to crack possession. In addition, while the congressional subcommittee consulted with law enforcement officials, it did not hold public hearings. Most significant here, however, is the fact that the 100-to-1 sentencing disparity between powder and crack ultimately reached was, in the words of the 1995 report, "deliberate, not inadvertent."[9] In sum, even though it had bypassed the normal route, the disparity that emerged was, in every sense, deliberately and intentionally created.

Fears of Crack's Simplicity

The speed of the act's passing was also tied to much larger, overlapping fears concerning crack—most of which have since been debunked by many writers—that had been exacerbated by numerous media sources. The 1995 report, for example, states that, "[i]n the months leading up the

1986 elections, more than 1,000 stories appeared on crack in the national press, including five cover stories each in *Time* and *Newsweek*. . . . *Time* called crack the 'Issue of the Year' . . . *Newsweek* called crack the biggest news story since Vietnam and Watergate."[10] These media-generated fears came to a head with the cocaine-related death of college basketball star, Len Bias, who died two days after being selected as the second pick in the 1986 NBA draft. While the toxicologists at the time argued that the cocaine found at the scene of his death was not crack, Eric Sterling, who "played a significant staff role in the development of many provisions of the Drug Abuse Act of 1986, testified before the United States Sentencing Commission in 1993 that the 'crack cocaine overdose death of NCAA basketball star Len Bias' was instrumental in the development of the federal crack cocaine laws."[11] Len Bias's death, in other words, pointed to something more, solidifying a paradoxical equation between crack's simplicity of production and its potential danger.

Making Crack

As many writers have suggested, crack's pharmacological simplicity represents the importation of the middle-class high of powder cocaine to the streets via a simplified form.[12] Crack has been described as the "fast food version of powder cocaine," and one of the "most successful . . . drug innovations,"[13] whose origins lie in the earlier innovation of freebase, a smokeable form of powder. The process of turning powder to base, in fact, is an attempt to return the cocaine to its prepowder state—to "free" the drug's pure "base" from its impure, crystalline form.[14] When powder is made, coca leaves are first mashed up with either gasoline or ether, producing a coca paste. This paste is then dried with hydrochloric acid, and the resulting white powder is now sniffable. When powder is mixed in water with baking soda or ammonia, the hydrochloric acid that had been added to the original paste in order to dry it is removed. When what is left is dissolved in ether and heated, the liquid evaporates, and the result is smokable, producing "vapors of relatively pure cocaine."[15]

Because powder cost around one hundred dollars a gram in the late 1970s when freebasing became popular, it was not a drug of choice in inner-city neighborhoods. Crack emerged in the mid-1980s and was, like freebase, a smokeable form of cocaine. In order to make it, one mixes powder in water with baking soda, which is then heated and, when dry, forms into "hard smokeable pellets."[16] While crack is inherently not as pure as freebase since it does not go through the final purification step, the cooking process simultaneously creates "crack rocks" that can be easily packaged and sold in smokeable form.

Where freebase was made by middle-class users, crack was made primarily by lower-class dealers. And, while the processes of making the two drugs are almost identical, the final purification of powder into freebase is seen as a complex but dangerous process, while the making of crack is, almost without exception, seen as crude and simple. It is "technically simple and relatively quick and requires few tools or laboratory supplies,"[17] being "easily produced in a pot on a kitchen stove."[18] The crudeness of crack's production is matched by the immediacy of its effects during consumption. Smokeable cocaine enters the bloodstream more quickly than sniffable powder, "providing a powerful rush."[19] Hard and brittle, crack is de-refined powder that gets right to the blood.

While almost identical, the two sibling forms of smokeable cocaine were perceived by Congress as having distinctly different potentials of danger. In truth, freebase is inherently more dangerous than crack. According to the commission, "[M]any resisted the freebasing process because of its complexity and potential danger. Ether, a highly volatile and flammable solvent, will ignite or explode if the freebase cocaine is smoked before the ether has evaporated entirely."[20] Interestingly, then, the fact that crack was an inherently less dangerous form of base came to be, paradoxically, an indication that it was more dangerous. The danger of crack, that is, lay in its potential to spread beyond the confines of upper-middle-class consumption because it was, by nature, less dangerous and, therefore, could be more easily adopted by users who feared the freebasing process. Thus, crack's simplicity of production—despite the admittedly safe nature of the substance itself—was one of the rationales underlying claims that it was far worse than any previously known form of cocaine.

Fears of Crack's Impure Purity

Fears surrounding crack's simplicity were also intimately tied to fears of its purity, which was a logical fallacy from the start. Actually, the very process of making crack militates against its purity. As the commission states, "the baking soda used in converting the powder cocaine remains as an adulterant in the crack cocaine after conversion, reducing the purity."[21] Since crack is made—and only exists as "crack"—after such impurities are added, crack is an inherently impure form of cocaine. In treating it otherwise, especially knowing how it was made, Congress created another layer of paradox: crack, although known to be impure, was treated as if it were pure—a deliberately treated impure purity. This anomalous treatment of crack as an impure purity can best be seen in relation to the way methamphetamine is treated by the law. While any "impurities created in the manufacturing process of crack cocaine count toward the weight of the drug for purposes of both triggering the mandatory minimum and determining the guideline sentencing range," for meth, by contrast, "the threshold quantities are triggered solely by the weight of pure methamphetamine."[22] Because the impurities added in the process of making crack are counted in the punishment scheme, the added impurities are, in effect, treated as if their addition had actually increased the purity, and, by extension, crack's dangerousness. Strangely, then, when applied to crack, the weight-driven scheme underlying its punishment suggested that the more impure the crack, the more harshly it should be punished. As a result, crack came to be punished more severely for being what it cannot be: pure. Thus it is that the punishment of crack was based, from the start, on a practical and logical impossibility.

Simple Possession: From Couriers to Kingpins

The greatest significance of America's paradoxical punishment of crack cocaine, however, lies in the punishment structure for "simple possession" that was created in the 1988 update of the 1986 act. According to the commission, the 1988 act "made crack cocaine the only drug with a mandatory minimum penalty for a first offense of simple possession. The Act made possession of more than five grams of a mixture or substance containing cocaine base punishable by at least five years in prison."[23] The creation of a mandatory minimum prison sentence for simple possession, consequently, "established an anomaly" in the law: being caught with five grams of crack became an incentive for people "to bargain with the prosecutor for a plea to trafficking offenses to avoid the possession mandatory minimum penalty that would otherwise apply."[24] For this reason, the much more serious charge of trafficking in other substances came to carry a lesser sentence than the "simple" possession of crack. Essentially, the simple possession of an impure, less dangerous form of cocaine came to be punished one hundred times more harshly than the purer substance from which it was made.

Crack's strange place in law—however anomalous—was clearly the result of a specific kind of reasoning. And this reasoning was at the heart of both the crack laws and what would soon become known as the "Kingpin Strategy"—the official federal law enforcement strategy created by the Office of National Drug Control Policy in 1993, which was itself established by the 1988 act. The strategy, ultimately, was "designed to ensure that federal enforcement efforts are focused on major trafficking organizations."[25] Enforcement agencies, therefore, were to focus their primary efforts on "'the identification and targeting of drug Kingpins and their supporting infrastructure.'"[26] The simple possession of five grams of crack cocaine—the amount, again, of a few sugar packets—was to be taken as *a legal presumption* of serious trafficking. According to the commission, the mandatory minimum for simple possession was taken "as a means of aiding the enforcement community's efforts against crack cocaine traffickers by *setting up a presumption that possession of five grams of crack cocaine meant the possessor was a trafficker.* It was thought that possession of as little as five grams of crack cocaine was an indicator of distribution rather than personal use."[27] In the words of Senator Chiles, "Those who possess 5 or more grams of cocaine freebase [crack] will be *treated as serious offenders. . . .* Such treatment is absolutely essential because of the especially lethal characteristic of this form of cocaine."[28]

And it is here—in the legal presumption of seriousness based on a five-gram quantity—that crack's anomalous place in U.S. crime policy becomes one of the most powerful symbolic demonizations in late-twentieth-century America. This formulation, in which "drug quantity *would serve as a proxy* to identify those traffickers of greatest concern,"[29] in essence, created a specific culpability-by-the gram calculus by which those caught with a few sugar packets of crack would be treated *as if* they were serious traffickers just slightly below the kingpins—the Scarfacelike heads—of global criminal enterprises.

> For the kingpins—the masterminds who are really running these operations—and they can be identified by the amount of drugs with which they are involved—we require a jail term upon conviction. . . . Our proposal would also provide mandatory minimum penalties for the middle-level dealers as well. Those criminals would also have to

serve time in jail. The minimum sentences would be slightly less than those for the kingpins, but they nevertheless would have to go to jail—a minimum of 5 years for the first offense.[30]

Another, even more problematic contradiction at the heart of the law, however, was that crack, while treated as more lethal than any drug before it, has always been a low-level enterprise.

Crack's Inherent Retail Status

The Kingpin Strategy, which, ironically, came to treat simple possession as if it were complex distribution, targeted an enterprise that occurs primarily at the retail level. In the words of the commission, "Conversion of powder cocaine to crack occurs at both wholesale and retail levels,"[31] but "rarely, if ever, is [crack] imported into the United States. Instead, powder cocaine is imported, with some of it later converted into crack cocaine."[32] Not only is crack inherently impure, but it is only created at the lower levels of distribution, adding yet another level of contradiction to its punishment rationale. The more significant problem, though, lies in the fact that, "[t]heoretically, each level closer to retail sales involves *less culpable individuals trafficking in lesser quantities of drugs.*"[33] It should follow, then, that if crack is a low-level operation, its dealers should also be less culpable, and, by nature, cannot be kingpins. But this reasoning was never used by Congress. And so, the express purpose of the crack laws—to target the Scarfacelike masterminds of criminal enterprises that traffic in massive quantities of inherently lethal drugs—was fundamentally and thoroughly illogical from the start. It was a Kingpin Strategy that, at every step of the way, deliberately treated impure product as if it were that which it could not be. The punishment ratio, at bottom, was a rationally created irrationality.

In addition to their retail status, which militates against the use of a Kingpin Strategy against them, crack distribution networks have never been organized according to hierarchical models. By definition, a Kingpin Strategy assumes that there are, in fact, kingpins to be found. And, allied with this implicit feature of such a strategy is the assumption that kings must sit at the top of their organizations, a premise that, in turn, assumes a vertical, hierarchical structure. Since 1995, however, the commission—relying on the overwhelming consensus of the research community—has never found evidence that crack distribution systems were ever organized in such a way. According to the commission, as well as the research on which it relied, early crack distribution networks—which created a "market open to any person with access to cocaine and a desire to distribute"[34]—did undergo a period of "consolidation," suggesting some kind of hierarchical reorganization. Even so, "'Despite a systematic effort to locate vertically-organized crack distribution groups in which one or more persons dominates, no such groups have been located, and no distributors report knowing of such groups. Instead, freelance crack selling dominates most drug street scenes.'"[35] The Kingpin Strategy—intended as it was to ferret out and dismantle large-scale criminal enterprises—has never had evidence to justify its use against crack dealing. Crack has always been a low-level enterprise "dominated by a 'cottage industry' of small-group and freelance distributors."[36] Even more important, however, crack's low-level status stimulated the creation of a "large supply of retail dealers" who, in the testimony of law enforcement personnel quoted by the commission, are "'almost immediately replaced,'" providing a "'seemingly unending well of crack dealers.'"[37]

While the rationale underlying the punishment of crack cocaine was—and will continue to be, even though the 100-to-1 ratio has been reduced to 18-to-1—thoroughly illogical and irrational, it is the violence that came to be associated with its low-level distribution system that has been most devastating to the communities that it affected directly. And it is precisely this violence that animates—through its sheer disrupting force—the kingpin mythology that provides the backbone for rap's crack-infused lyrics. In short, the magnitude of the social experiences on which the rap-crack connection relies betrays an emotional core that cannot be explained away as easy sensationalism or mere reflection.

Crack's Violence

One of the most commonly invoked assumptions about the United States, both nationally and internationally, is that we have far more crime than any other industrialized nation. When one looks more closely at crime-specific rates cross-nationally, however, the belief that America is, overall, the most crime-ridden developed country seems clearly overstated.[38] In truth, when crime rates are disaggregated, the United States has lower rates of property crime—including serious property crime such as motor vehicle theft—than many other countries. This finding also tends to hold when we look at less serious violence, such as assault. There is, though, one fundamental difference that remains: while our rates of violence are similar to those of many countries, the United States stands alone among industrialized nations when it comes to lethal violence. Indeed, this finding has led some to argue that "crime is not the problem"; rather, it is lethality.[39]

If we look at America's homicide rate over time, we can see something interesting. Basically, between the late 1960s and the early 1990s, the homicide rate doubles, from around 5 per 100,000 to around 10 per 100,000. And, within this thirty-year period, there are two major spikes. The first rises in the late 1960s and falls by the early 1980s; the second lasts from the late 1980s to the early 1990s. The homicide rate, along with the violent crime rate generally, has fallen steadily since, and is now at early 1960s levels. While the causal mechanisms underlying the first spike are difficult to parse out, many writers have argued that it reflects a confluence of social forces. Policy analyst Alfred Blumstein, for example, has argued that, coupled with "the movement of the baby-boom generation into and then out of the high-crime ages of the late teens and early twenties," the "marked growth in violence between 1965 and the early 1970s may have been, at least in part, a result of the decline in perceived legitimacy of American social and governmental authority."[40] Even more important for this discussion, however, is the second spike, which, according to a wide range of scholars and researchers, should, in Blumstein's words, "almost certainly be laid at the crack epidemic."[41] We can say for sure, therefore, that the crack era coincided with a serious rise in lethal violence; but it is far more difficult to separate out the causes of this violence. Regardless of the original rationale for the punishment structure of crack cocaine, though, fears about crack's potential violence—as well as rising rates of real violence—came to be seen, not surprisingly, as requiring new kinds of law enforcement responses.

Modeled on the New York Police Department's Operation Pressure Point in 1984, which was a new kind of police response to drug dealers on the Lower East Side of Manhattan, a number of sweeping police tactics were soon introduced throughout the country with several key features: large numbers of searches and arrests; the questioning of anyone even perceived to be a buyer or seller; intensified foot patrols in housing projects and subways; and increased surveillance across the board. The resulting high arrest rates "received much praise, including honorable mention from [drug] Czar [William] Bennett."[42] The perceived success of this operation influenced the creation of similar operations across the country: the Tactical Narcotics Team in New York; Operation Invincible in Memphis; Operation Clean Sweep in Chicago; Operation Hammer in Los Angeles; and the Red Dog Squad in Atlanta. According to one group of researchers, "In 1988, about one-fourth of the NYPD was reassigned to newly launched Tactical Narcotics Team."[43] Significantly, the names of the task forces themselves suggested their mode of operation—tactical, invincible, and geared toward sweeping the streets clean by hammering out drug crime. And it is precisely this volatile mix of an exceedingly harsh punishment structure and more intensive forms of policing that makes the lines of causation in the United States' second homicide spike difficult to dissect cleanly.

Writing in the late 1960s, just prior to America's imprisonment boom, legal scholar Herbert Packer famously argued that, "[r]egardless of what we think we are trying to do, when we make it illegal to traffic in commodities for which there is an inelastic demand, the effect is to secure a kind of monopoly profit to the entrepreneur who is willing to break the law."[44] This "crime tariff," as Packer called it, lies at the core of what criminologist Jerome Skolnick—whose research figures prominently in the USSC's reports—has dubbed the "the Darwinian Trafficker Dilemma": an illegal business environment in which increasingly harsh police tactics and punitive policies effectively imprisoned many of the older, more established dealers who were then, as mentioned in the discussion above, "immediately replaced" by younger, less experienced freelancers.[45] As many researchers now contend, the effects of imprisoning so many older adults can have serious effects on what criminologist Robert Sampson has called "collective efficacy": a community's ability to maintain law and order—to police itself—through neighborhood-level networks of informal social control, which include families, peer groups, and faith-based institutions, among others.[46] Similarly, criminologist Todd Clear has argued that this process—what he calls "concentrated incarceration"—is a form of "coercive mobility" whereby whole neighborhoods are destabilized "by increasing levels of disorganization, first when a person is removed to go to prison, then later when that person reenters the community."[47] Likewise, sociologist Elijah Anderson has argued that the loss of "old heads" in inner-city communities—neighborhood mentors who intervene in the lives of troubled youth, providing informal moral guidance—has resulted in a deeper transformation in which moral authority now resides with young people for whom drug dealing has become a "way of life."[48] Consequently, what both the commission and the research on which it relies suggest is that the mix of harsh punishment and new enforcement strategies—which, ironically, were intended to protect community cohesion[49]—lead to the systematic destabilization of informal, neighborhood-level controls through coercive mobility.

Crack Markets

Clearly, the discussion above suggests that the violence of the crack era cannot simply be laid at the feet of crack itself. Even more important in problematizing the reasoning behind the punishment of crack cocaine, however, is the broad consensus among researchers that the lethal violence of the crack era was caused neither by the pharmacology of the drug nor by the actions of addicts; rather, the lethality of the era was a product of the systemic features of crack markets themselves. For example, in one of the most important studies of homicide patterns in 1988, during one of the biggest rises in homicide in the United States, it was found that 39 percent of all murders and 74 percent of all drug-related murders were associated neither with the psychopharmacological effects of the drug nor with the economic compulsion of its addicts, but with the market-based arrangements and relationships engendered by trafficking. The authors concluded that *"the vast bulk of crack related homicides occurred between dealers or dealers and users."*[50] In trying to account for the systemic nature of crack-related violence, therefore, much of the research on which the commission's reports rely attributes it to one primary element: the underground market in crack cocaine that was significantly influenced by coercive mobility. Thus it is that systemic violence is believed by many to be dependent upon the stability of the market. The crime tariff imposed on the structure of the crack market created an unstable, Darwinian environment, which led to a far more complicated role for neighborhood violence: while clear lines of causation may be difficult to decipher, the role of systemic violence in America's homicide patterns clearly indicates that the harsh punishment of crack, coupled with more intense police responses, aided in the creation of a social context in which lethal violence came to be a necessary form of business regulation. In quoting Skolnick, the commission underlines this point precisely: "'[I]n an underground economy, you can't sue. So you use violence to enforce your breaches of contract or perceived breaches of contract."[51] In addition, not only did violence become necessary but, as the commission contends, the use of violence as a form of regulation in the volatile, Darwinian environment of the crack trade made its actual practice worse than the violence used in other drug markets. Violence during this time became especially "'ruthless' and 'pitilessly' savage"[52] and "was more likely to characterize the unstable crack markets than more established drug markets and distribution systems."[53]

Perhaps most important is the commission's consistent citing of a broad consensus among researchers that "'crack selling was concentrated in neighborhoods where social controls had been weakened by intensified social and economic dislocations in the decade preceding the emergence of crack.'"[54] In citing the "increasing social and economic disorganization of the nation's inner cities beginning in the 1980s"[55] as a primary element in crack's emergence as well as its later instability, the commission explicitly tied crack-related violence to what economists Barry Bluestone and Bennett Harrison famously called the "de-industrialization of America": the massive flight of manufacturing jobs from the urban core of many U.S. cities throughout the 1970s and 1980s.[56] Sociologist William Julius Wilson's research on the effects of this transformation in Chicago, for example, have been instrumental in drawing attention to deindustrialization's powerfully dislocating consequences and the degree to which such effects have since permeated every aspect of social life. "The social deterioration of ghetto neighborhoods," Wilson wrote, was the "central concern expressed in the testimony" of the thousands of inner-city residents he surveyed and interviewed for multiple research projects conducted over a number of years, unequivocally supporting a fundamental finding: "Neighborhoods plagued by high levels of joblessness are more likely to experience low levels of social organization."[57] In addition to Wilson's work, research on the effects of deindustrialization in the inner city and beyond has focused on the ways in which community members are often caught between working in the unskilled, low-wage sector in which they often face humiliation, or in the underground economy in which they face the possibilities of extreme violence and incarceration. This predicament, as many researchers argue, does not revolve simply around ways of providing a living but, even more significant, represents attempts to do so in ways that maintain a sense of personal autonomy and self-worth even in the face of severe structural and community dislocation.[58]

Essentially, then, the commission's reports underline what many researchers have argued many times before and since: that crack dealing is "[l]ike any other capitalist enterprise" and is "motivated by profits and the control of a particular market or markets."[59] In anthropologist Philippe Bourgois' words, the "underground economy is the ultimate 'equal opportunity employer' for inner-city youth,"[60] and, contrary to previous literature, which characterizes them as "badly socialized" and not sharing in "mainstream values," most people in the underground economy are *"frantically pursuing the American Dream."*[61] In this way, the crack era inaugurated a specifically lethal conundrum—having to rely for one's livelihood and self-worth on a practice that simultaneously terrorizes one's own community in ways not previously experienced. It is, however, in this effort on the part of inner-city community members to create spaces of nonhumiliating work that the necessity of pitiless, ruthless violence in regulating crack markets—made unstable through excessive punishment and enforcement—comes to create some of its most devastating effects.

Relying on numerous studies, the commission has concluded that one of the most far-reaching effects of lethality becoming a necessary regulatory mechanism is that "nondrug violence" becomes "'intensified' by the cocaine marketplace (and specifically the crack marketplace) because systemic violence creates a setting in which violent behavior generally is deemed acceptable."[62] What the consensus concerning the intensification of non-drug-related violence suggests is that the Darwinian Trafficker Dilemma raised the stakes of the crack trade to such a degree that, in its wake, existing patterns of neighborhood violence were aggravated so immensely that extreme violence became, in essence, the norm.

This pattern of intensification can be seen, for example, in sociologist William Sanders's analysis of the drive-by shooting as a tactic in gang warfare.[63] He argues that drive-bys are "far superior" strategies, which—contrary to common perceptions that posit revenge as their only motivation—are rational tactics intended to protect one's own territory by preemptively destabilizing one's enemy. Drive-bys are mobile, hit-and-run "forays" that, by their very nature, introduce unpredictable danger into the most mundane of situations, instilling in communities and individuals the fear that deadly violence "can happen anywhere, anytime."[64] Unpredictable lethality is a destabilizing deterrent precisely because it violates domestic space, throwing expectations of safe zones into chaos, becoming devastatingly unnerving for the victims. Most important, however, is Sanders's suggestion that, while the drug business was not a major motivation for drive-bys in the early 1980s, "by 1988, many of the gang-related drive-by shootings . . . did appear connected to the sale and distribution of crack cocaine."[65] While crack did not create these kinds of destabilizing, invasive tactics, the necessity of violence as a regulatory mechanism is believed by many to have increased their prevalence, helping to create a much more ubiquitous sense that extreme violence in the service of regulating market instability was normal. As a result of this market instability, the lethal violence that became its necessary regulatory force had disastrous collateral effects on whole communities by escalating other, non-drug-related forms of violence, thereby normalizing lethality as the "final arbiter" of disputes more generally.

Similarly sweeping changes to violence during the crack era are also thoroughly documented in anthropologist Lisa Maher's ethnography of women drug users in Bushwick, Brooklyn, during the early 1990s.[66] For Maher's subjects, crack itself—with its jagged, shardlike appearance and its energetic high—became symbolically important, standing as a rugged symbol for a rugged time. While heroin was perceived as smoother in both appearance and feeling, crack was viewed as a more appropriate drug for a new, more brutal reality.[67] And, importantly, this reality was characterized by a number of interrelated qualitative changes that radically altered one of the primary ways in which Maher's interviewees were able to make a living: street-level sex work.

Complicating Philippe Bourgois' claim that the crack trade was an "equal opportunity employer," Maher argues, instead, that crack-era changes were deeply gendered, and negatively affected women's opportunities in the underground economy.[68] Because of widespread beliefs that women were unable to display the kinds of extreme violence that the unstable crack trade required, women's options in the emerging crack marketplace were severely curtailed, reproducing the same kinds of narrow opportunity structures they faced in the mainstream. And, as a consequence of these narrowing opportunity structures, other niches of female underground labor were also devalued. Just as the crack trade flooded street-level drug markets with novice dealers, so too were street-level sex markets flooded with novice sex workers, which devalued specific sex acts through increased competition and a strange process of cross-commodification. As an example, going rates for oral sex were correlated with the price for drugs. Since crack was cheap, often around five dollars per vial, and women users provided oral sex in order to buy it, blowjobs were also priced down to five dollars. Women sex workers who primarily used heroin, however, were able to charge ten dollars, which matched the going price for a bag of heroin.[69]

In addition, male customers—influenced, as were many, by the media-perpetuated myth that crack use was tantamount to "chemically-induced sexual slavery"[70]—assumed that all street-level sex workers were enslaved "crackheads" willing to do anything to get more.[71] Street-level prostitutes were now expected to do any number of acts that had previously been considered "deviant" by sex workers themselves, who perceived such non-normative sexual requests as a total compromise of principle. Just like Bourgois' male drug-dealing counterparts, Maher's female subjects continued to maintain an overriding sense of self-respect and dignity even in the face of coercive humiliation.[72]

As a related consequence of devaluation, the potential for violence also increased. The physiological effects of cocaine on male sexual performance, for example, compounded this potential since crack-using dates would often get frustrated with their inability to perform and then act out violently.[73] In addition, these devaluating forces also began to reduce the role of male pimps in street-level sex work since there was far less money to be made from such arrangements. While seemingly a benefit for female sex workers, this change also removed a basic deterrent presence on the streets: the threat of violent male retaliation toward violent male customers. Many women, therefore, developed informal "pseudo-pimping" relationships with men who, in turn, demanded money, drugs, and sex, but provided little in the way of actual protection. More often than not, such relationships made things worse.[74]

With increased competition among workers, less money for more work, greater expectations by dates for non-normative sex acts, increased possibilities of violence, and fewer people to watch one's back, sex work—like drive-by shootings—became dependent on the erratic, unpredictable crack trade. While sex work has always been risky and stigmatized, the crack era exacerbated its worst elements. Crack reorganized both drug and sex markets, reproducing gendered structures of opportunity, but infused them with far more violence and instability. And these collateral effects—this normalization of market-based drug violence—are exactly what have made crack such a powerful element in America's criminological structure of feeling. At bottom, crack cocaine signifies a primary break with what came before, and a new reality that is perceived—by drug dealers, sex workers, and whole neighborhoods—as fundamentally altering the organization of social life.

The Sentencing Commission, relying on numerous research reports, has also suggested that these changes in violence can best be understood as a conflict between two different kinds of street gang formations that take shape in the crack era: "cultural" and "entrepreneurial." "Cultural gangs," according to the commission, "are established primarily for social purposes," such as protecting ethnic and neighborhood affiliations, "with drug distribution a subsidiary purpose of the gang. . . . Entrepreneurial gangs, on the other hand, are established to further the financial objectives of the organization and not the gangs."[75] In charting the character of some of these changes in the late 1980s, for example, sociologist Felix Padilla argued that Latino gang culture in Chicago was beginning to change from culturally based to entrepreneurial and instrumental as neighborhood gangs "functioned as the training ground for teaching vital drug-dealing business skills."[76] Similarly, in looking at Los Angeles gangs in the late 1980s, Skolnick—while noting that violence has always been central to cultural gangs acting in accordance with older codes of violent conduct—argued that entrepreneurial gangs "employ violence to control or expand their drug business and markets. Thus, depending upon the stability of the market, the entrepreneurial gang may be more or less violent than the cultural gang."[77]

While academic research has played a key role in elucidating some of the causal relationships behind this transformation from culturally based violence to market-based violence, there has also grown a quite large subgenre of autobiographies written by former gang members in which such changes are described in narrative form.[78] Perhaps the most famous of these former gang members is Monster Kody, who was a street soldier in the Eight Tray Gangsters, a Los Angeles–based Crip gang, during the 1980s. His autobiography vividly illustrates these kinds of transformations. After recounting, in detail, his participation in numerous lethal episodes, Monster, near the end of the book, describes the changes he found hard to contend with after being released from Folsom Prison in 1988, at the height of the crack era, after serving four years. In his words, "This new, highly explosive atmosphere was a bit frightening. . . . [It was] a more advanced, horrifying form of the reality I had known. It was shocking."[79] It was, however, a friend's explanation of these changes that is most significant: "It's the dope, man, it has torn the 'hood up. . . . [N]othin' is stable. . . . Everything is fragile, more so than ever before, cause it's all about profit."[80] And, in the following quotation, Monster's friend further underscores the degree to which the search for profit in a ruthlessly unstable marketplace is understood to play a primary role in increased levels of lethal violence.

> Check this out, there are some homies who got a grip from slangin',
> but they don't come around 'cause they think the homies who ain't
> got nothin' gonna jack 'em. And the homies who ain't got nothin' feel
> like those who do got a grip have left them behind. So there's a lot of
> backbiting, snitchin', and animosity around here now.[81]

In effect, through the intensification of violence via market-based relations, interpersonal trust at the community level itself was corroded.
Old ways of violence, although brutal to outsiders, are thought to maintain neighborhood solidarity, codes of honor, and familial relationships.
Instrumental violence, on the other hand, is corrosive. Underscoring
these trust-corroding effects, the commission quotes another former
gang member: "'Now you might see a neighborhood that is Blood and
Crip together. But that's because they got something going on with drugs.
They got some kind of peace because of drugs.'"[82] In a strange turn, then,
the abstract forces of the marketplace that led to the corrosion of community trust simultaneously helped create fragile alliances of peace among
former enemies, providing them with a new set of concerns all centered
on one primary activity: making money. Thus it is that crack's intensification of bloodshed laid the foundation for a "new school violence," which is
the subject of chapter 4.

Unmistakably, what the commission reports, the research on which it
relies, the ethnographic work on crack dealers and sex workers, as well as
the autobiographies of gang members all suggest is that changes in neighborhood violence were due neither to the inherent dangerousness of the
drug nor to the people dealing and using it but, rather, to the inherently
impure, nonkingpin nature of crack, whose already fragmented distribution networks became further destabilized through excessively harsh
punishment structures and task-force-style policing. Crack transformed,
through intensification, older gangs into *networks*, no longer governed by
culturally based codes, but by the abstract, impersonal, structural conditions of pricing and supply and demand. Likewise, sex work—which
was one of the only viable options for female users who had been barred
from the drug trade—also became violently unstable and more socially
isolating. The crack era, that is, deprofessionalized *all* underground
work—practices that, while clearly illegal before, had been at least dependent upon and structured around well-understood rules. In the Darwinian environment of the crack era, young men who didn't know the drug
game, and young women who didn't know the rules of the sex trade were

the period's primary victims as well as its primary offenders, both experiencing and helping to create the social ruptures of the time. Violence came to ebb and flow according to market conditions that had nothing whatever to do with neighborhood status, respect, or protection. Older patterns of neighborhood-based affiliations were supplanted by the necessity of using violence to regulate unpredictable markets that traded in impure purities, and were staffed by an unending supply of low-level dealers who, despite their low-level status, were treated as if they were kingpins of global criminal organizations. In such a paradoxical situation, the one "cause" of the violence can never be fully parsed out. Significantly, however, the paradoxical core at the heart of crack's punishment rationale made it so elastic that any finding came to justify its continued existence. "New" findings about the low-level, retail-based, horizontal nature of the crack trade—which contradicted the original Kingpin Strategy underlying the mandatory minimums—came, strangely, to be proof that crack dealers alone were the primary engines driving the violence.

Crack's Networked Violence

By the mid- to late 1990s, the kingpin rationale that originally justified the 100-to-1 disparity no longer seemed part of the equation. Take, for example, the following quotation from the testimony of Steven Wiley, chief of the FBI's Violent Crimes and Major Offenders Section, given before the Senate Committee on the Judiciary in 1997 about the importance of crack in street gangs' supposed centrality to the skyrocketing drug trade:

> Almost overnight a major industry was born, with major outlets in every neighborhood, tens of thousands of potential new customers and thousands of sales jobs available. In slightly over a decade, street gangs have become highly involved in drug trafficking at all levels. Intelligence developed through investigation has revealed extensive interaction among individuals belonging to gangs across the Nation. *This interaction . . . is more a loose network of contacts and associations that come together as needed to support individual business ventures.*[83]

These small, entrepreneurial groups soon came to be viewed as having "advantages over larger, gang-directed groups because their limited size presents a more difficult target for law enforcement, making group leaders less likely to be discovered."[84] Effectively failing to provide any evidence for the punishment ratio's original justification, law enforcement's quite logical response to crack's horizontally structured distribution system has since been to target the only people who have ever been involved—the "unending supply" of low-end dealers who are "almost immediately replaced." Paraphrasing the testimony of a defense lawyer, for instance, the commission has stated that—in their elastic adaptations to crack's low-level system of distribution—"undercover agents and informants hold out for higher quantities in a single sale, come back repeatedly for additional sales, and insist that powder cocaine be cooked into crack cocaine before accepting it."[85] While originally justified as providing law enforcement with more ability to ferret out kingpins, the punishment structure, instead, has allowed for "'more bang for the buck' in crack cocaine cases than any other kind of drug case because a very small quantity increase results in a very large sentence increase, and because the simple process of cooking powder cocaine into crack cocaine results in a drastic sentence increase."[86]

It is perhaps not surprising, though, that the low-level, horizontally structured crack trade came to take on such importance in the 1990s. After all, the 1990s saw the rise of the "network" as a primary way in which political, economic, and social relationships were being reconceived.[87] Networks, in sum, were viewed as key in reshaping the relationship between markets and national sovereignty since the modern interstate system was believed to have lost importance through the rise of an interdependent nexus of markets. In this kind of framework, the geographical and jurisdictional boundaries of the nation-state model were sometimes seen as hindrances to capital flow as increasingly diversified corporate giants came to require more leg room. This weakening of the nation-state system through the undermining of sovereignty, however, still needed to rely on some kind of governmental stability since political upheavals scare away investors. While fierce countermovements to the aggressive search for stable investment opportunities cry out for identity and national sovereignty in the face of potentially homogenizing globalism, both need each other; "market democracy," that is, gives such movements something to hate.[88]

But this kind of debate about the role of networks in global reorganization found expression in all kinds of works of fiction as well. Published in 1995, Neil Stephenson's novel *Snow Crash*, for example, created a fictional world where former countries were called "franchises," suburban communities were termed "city-states," and criminal justice organizations were completely privatized.[89] His vision was a refeudalized system held together by virtual worlds in which even seemingly trivial activities like delivering pizza were to be analyzed, hypothesized about, monitored, and surveilled, raising the stakes to life and death. In Stephenson's take on the relationship between market-based networks and national sovereignty, even pizza delivery came to have the scientific method applied to it, becoming "pizza management science" in the process. It was a fictional account of a factional world held together only by commerce, where pizza delivery, courier services, and taxicabs ferried people and goods across networks, and political resistance was more of an individual affair, happening in the margins and spaces in between.

Networks also played key roles in reconceiving the relationship between national security and criminal justice functions since they seemed to become increasingly similar as cross-border crime (e.g., drug sales, money laundering, human trafficking) became more of a foreign policy issue, helping to standardize hitherto nationally distinct rules for jurisdiction, evidence collection, and prosecution. In a world of increasingly unstable flows, cross-national policing—as opposed to modern warfare—seemed better suited to managing risky populations. And, because modern armies are only designed to fight other modern armies, new models were believed to be needed. Smaller, more adaptable, horizontally structured paramilitary organizations were thought better equipped to deal with criminal organizations that were increasingly perceived as mobile, lethal networks.[90]

While the importance of network thinking in the relationship between sovereignty and markets has been underlined by many, such importance, as cultural critic Thomas Frank has suggested, perhaps took its most triumphalist tone in the self-congratulatory proclamations of the business world in the 1990s.[91] Deliberately at the forefront of the "new" economy, for example, was *Fast Company*, which, in the words of its 1995 manifesto, aimed to be "the handbook of the business revolution."[92] After proclaiming the advent of a new age in business, the manifesto then described the forces leading the way: "With unsettling speed, two forces are converging: a new generation of business leaders is rewriting the rules of business, and a new breed of fast companies is challenging the corporate status quo." The document went on to say that "[n]o part of business is immune," and that, most tellingly, the *"nature of work is changing."* This business revolution, in their words, was going to be as "far-reaching as the Industrial Revolution." The manifesto continued, claiming that an economy driven by technology and innovation makes old borders obsolete. Smart people working in smart companies have the ability to create their own futures—and also hold the responsibility for the consequences. The possibilities are unlimited—and unlimited possibilities carry equal measures of hope and fear. . . . We will chronicle the changes under way in how companies create and compete, highlight the new practices shaping how work gets done, showcase teams who are inventing the future and reinventing business. . . . A new community needs its own legitimate heroes and heroines, its models and mentors.

Significantly, however, crack dealing never underwent these kinds of transformations so highly touted in the 1990s precisely because it had always been, from the start, a networked "cottage industry." In many ways, then, crack's "actual" existence presaged much of the virtual discussions about the "new economy" since crack never transformed *from* vertically structured organizations with kings at their heads. As horizontally structured, smaller-scale organizations, crack-dealing crews represented the underground version of the much-vaunted "fast company," but they were denied the very inventiveness so often attributed to the legal business organizations that, unknowingly, mimicked the crack economy. Approached as if they were tentacled superorganizations with Mafialike capabilities, crack crews, in reality, were the very embodiment of the "new" economy's heroes, albeit in their underground, lethal manifestations.

The Invisible Hand Holds a Gun

In a Kingpin Strategy of drug enforcement, the focus is obviously on the king. But in a network strategy, the focus centers on the network itself, which, as opposed to a king, is neither "alive" nor can it be "seen." In the paradoxical punishment of crack cocaine, this focusing away from kingpins and toward horizontal networks of inherently low-level dealers created a specific kind of symbolic criminalization. In creating an anomalous culpability-by-the-gram calculus, the punishment structure for crack saw the emergence of a strange form of responsibility without intentionality, a kind of strict liability—crime without mens rea. The low-level dealers targeted by law enforcement were punished as kingpins, but never—like the business heroes of *Fast Company*—given any of the inventiveness often ascribed to the kingpins of other enterprises, criminal or legal. Instead, they were ascribed a kind of *primitive sophistication* that, although revolutionary in its supposedly dangerous simplicity, required no ingenuity on the part of dealers themselves.

Crack's role in the transformation of violence came to represent a new ruthlessness, at once crude and sophisticated, a kind of *revolutionary simplicity*. And it was crack's very simplicity that appeared to portend a series of complex social devastations. As the horizontal structure of the crack trade was revealed, it came to be taken as a crude form of sophistication that both presaged the rise of network society in the 1990s and demonized the criminal form it took. Crack dealers never were kingpins, but in taking them as such, the punishment structure symbolically downplayed their intentionality while upgrading their culpability. As the 1990s saw business leaders at the helm of a new revolution, crack dealers became the crude, ruthless heads of an inherently simple drug product that, in a strange turn of self-generation, *moved itself*. In its infinitely elastic, paradoxical punishment structure, crack became the sophisticated actor in the equation, the dealer its simple pawn. Crack became a form of cocaine that, in some kind of Darwinian survival effort, attached itself to a ready, steady, "unending supply" of low-level dealers that it shed as necessary. As with cutting off limbs to stop the spread of gangrene, or excising portions of flesh to get rid of a cancer, the punishment structure for crack treated them like kingpins in word only, and, in actuality, viewed them as appendages requiring amputation. In the paradoxical treatment of crack cocaine, then, *the drug itself became the kingpin*, and the dealers existed only as the media through which a newer, more intelligent manifestation of cocaine moved itself. In essence, crack, not its dealers, was ascribed a new kind of twenty-first-century networked-based criminal intelligence.

Unlike *Fast Company*'s reverence for "smart people working in smart companies" who "have the ability to create their own futures," crack dealers—through the paradoxical rationale underlying crack's punishment structure—came to be seen as mere pawns used by an inanimate-yet-intelligent drug to ensure its own survival. Crack's underground version of the "changes under way in how companies create and compete" showed that such changes occurred long before the mid-1990s, and that they were lethal and systemic, and not created through the innovations of business leaders.

Conclusion

In the 1990s, the business world celebrated itself, positing its own innovations as the prime mover of a new revolution. Simultaneously, however, rap artists—many of whom had grown up in the worst of the crack era—began memorializing the lethality that underlined those changes. Where the business world talked about networks without violence, rappers knew that violence was the real regulatory mechanism underlying these very same deregulated networks. A "crack kingpin," in other words, is a contradiction in terms. To be sure, there have been dealers who were more violent and made more money than others, but a crack kingpin is a logical impossibility. The connections made by rappers between Scarface and crack introduced at the beginning of this book, therefore, are neither accidents nor mere efforts to sell records through sensationalist crime drama. Instead, they represent a legally enforced logical disconnect: Pacino's Scarface was killed on the balcony of a sprawling mansion, while Ghostface Killah "hops fences" and "jumps benches" in a desperate effort to avoid getting "bagged on a rock," and face a punishment structure that treats him like Scarface, but knows he is inherently low-level. Rap's crack-infused lyrics, hence, are not to be understood simply as an issue of what rappers should or should not be saying. Rap's Scarfacelike boasting also shows that, in a new, deregulated, networked, deindustrialized world, the only way to get hold of the market is to meet its instability with bodily violence—that, more often than not, *the invisible hand holds a gun*.

In the next chapter, I suggest that—while mainstream innovators like *Fast Company* aimed to create a "handbook of the business revolution" in which "legitimate heroes and heroines" were showcased—rap's reflexive stance toward its own commercialization came to provide its own handbook of the underground business revolution. Crack came to symbolize, paradoxically, hopes of creating spaces of nonhumiliating work in an era of excessive punishment, while simultaneously expressing moral outrage at the duplicity of a sociolegal environment that had knowingly underwritten the normalization of lethal violence. As B.I.G. rapped, in a song aptly titled "The Ten Crack Commandments," "I been in this game for years, it made me a animal / There's rules to this shit, I made me a manual."[93]

Rap Puts Crack to Work

Royalty checks equal to crack in the street.
      —Sean Price in Boot Camp Clik, "And So," *Chosen Few*, 2002

I want to begin this chapter with a description of two images. The first is a poster for rap star 50 Cent's semiautobiographical movie *Get Rich or Die Trying*, which shows him from the back, with arms spread out in a Christlike pose, one hand holding a semiautomatic pistol, and the other a microphone. The other is a Reebok sneaker ad, which features Jay-Z, whose life similarly reflects 50's rise from crack dealer to rap star to corporate executive. The ad is split into two panels. In the left panel, he is shown sitting in a chair wearing a pinstriped suit with a view of the New York City skyline in the background. The right panel shows only his right arm, which has a number of rubber bands around it, and which foregrounds the wall of a high-rise housing project. The caption on top of the ad reads, "I got my MBA in Marcy Projects."[1]

These kinds of rags-to-riches, streets-to-boardroom-suites success stories have become some of the most recognizable identity myths at the core of the rap industry. The significance of this mythology, however, lies not in the mere *fact* that street and suite are fused, but in the characterization of both crack and rap as *specific kinds of work*. Equating rap work with crack work, though, is no simple exercise in exaggerated sensationalism. Instead, this equation signifies a moral indictment at whose heart lies duplicity: the duplicity of a white-collar world that intentionally preys on vulnerable artists; and the duplicitous nature of a punitive infrastructure in which mere couriers of an inherently impure product are held solely accountable for the community destabilizations that only the forces of deindustrialization and coercive mobility could ever have produced. In rap's confrontation with its own commercialization, both forms of legal duplicity compound and confound each other, merging in an emotional core of social betrayal. In this chapter, I situate the everyday exploitative realities within which rap's immediate productive possibilities were—and still are—defined, and out of which crack emerged as a metaphor for this collective experience of humiliation.

Putting in Work

To be sure, the notion that crime is a form of work is nothing new. In fact, the entire trajectory of American sociological criminology since the middle of the twentieth century has suggested precisely this point. Whether conceived as an innovative, rational response to a system of cultural values that overemphasizes the accumulation of wealth, as sociologist Robert Merton famously proposed,[2] or—as the sociologists Clifford Shaw and Henry McKay argued[3]—as a way of life so entrenched that it becomes, simply, one more lifestyle choice among many, the working life of crime has long figured in criminological analysis. And, as I discussed in chapter 1, ethnographic portrayals of crack dealing have consistently shown that dealers themselves view crack as an alternative to the humiliations of low-wage labor.[4] Given such a history, it should be no surprise that rap artists also call crack "work." This can be heard, for example, in Boot Camp Clik's warning to "stash the work in your sock" to avoid getting "knocked" by the police.[5] Or in Jay-Z's boast about having whole blocks "pumping my work."[6] But the importance here lies in the kind of work that crack represents, which, more often than not, rests on the concept of "grinding." Take Jay-Z's description of how he transitioned from Marcy Projects—a large public housing development in the Bedford-Stuyvesant neighborhood of Brooklyn—to the record industry. In his words, he entered the rap game with hundreds of thousands of dollars: "Nine to be exact from grinding G-packs."[7] References to grinding have become so ubiquitous that the Clipse—a Virginia-based duo whose entire oeuvre revolves primarily around intricately constructed metaphors that all relate back to cocaine base—became famous through their debut single, "Grindin." Incorporating cocaine into biblical allusions, Pusha T raps, "My grind's about family, never been about fame / Some days I wasn't Able, there was always Cain."[8] Or take Raekwon the Chef—an original member of the highly influential New York City–based group, Wu-Tang Clan—who includes a picture of himself in the liner notes of his famous first album, *Only Built for Cuban Linx*, which shows him cooking up crack on the stove, clearly suggesting how he got the name Chef.[9] Likewise, the songs of Ghostface Killah—another original member of Wu-Tang—are peppered with references to dealing both crack and powder. To wit, his 2006 release is called *Fishscale*, a slang term for high-quality cocaine.[10] There is also Fat Joe, who, in his 2004 hit, "Lean Back," describes how he got his other name, Joey Crack: as a youth, Joe recounts, he "was too much to cope with / That's why motherfuckers nicknamed me cooked coke shit."[11] Perhaps, though, the perfection of rap's connection to crack can best be seen in the chorus of a Juelz Santana song called, simply, "I am Crack": "Touch the coke, touch the pot, add the soda what you got: Me."[12]

And so, regardless of the pervasive rivalries between rap groups from different regions in the United States, from the East to the West to the South, cooked cocaine features as a primary symbol that provides a key reference through which work, as a broad category, is organized. And, most important, despite rap's penchant for drug-kingpin mythology and jewel-encrusted swagger, the ways in which the work of crack is actually depicted lyrically, instead, reflect a very different conception. As noted above, crack work, across the board, is described as hard, street-level grinding, characterized by cramped kitchens and pots and pans, whose mundane routineness is often punctuated by bursts of lethal violence. Undoubtedly, the figure of the "hustler" in rap is everywhere apparent, and crack dealing is clearly involved with hustling.[13] But it is in the concept of grinding that the specific work of crack is to be found. Hustling suggests the relative ease of profit, of "getting over," of "flipping" money to make more. The hustle is smooth and fast. Grinding, on the other hand, signifies a particular kind of hustling, and it is one that does not retain the same sense of ease. Grinding suggests difficulty—cooking, churning, twisting, pressing. While the hustle represents the swagger of success after it has been realized, the grind suggests all of the many dues paid before that success became reality—the ruthless competition, the social disruption, and the intensified violence that crack-era hustlers had to negotiate. As discussed in the previous chapter, crack stands—for dealers and users alike—as a rugged symbol for a rugged time, having radically restructured the nature of hustling itself. Grinding, in short, reflects a specific crack-era hustle that is inseparable from the period's most devastating effects, and its use is meant to recall those very same experiences.

At the same time, rap's references to crack do not occur alone. Instead, such references occur alongside connections to criminal activity of many kinds. Take, for instance, the advertising blurb for a DVD series called "Straight from the Projects: Rappers That Live the Lyrics," which boasts that "3 people were shot while our cameras were rolling . . . . 7 people . . . were shot and killed before the film was completed. This the realest ghetto shit ever filmed!"[14] And, in a tragic irony, C-Murder, one of the rappers featured in the DVD, has since been sentenced to life in prison for the very crime his name represents.[15] In addition, his police mug shot is prominently displayed on the March 2004 cover of hip hop magazine *The Source*, along with the mug shots of nine other rap artists. The issue, "Hip-Hop behind Bars: Are Rappers the New Target of America's Criminal Justice System?" describes the legal troubles of no fewer than thirty rappers, many of whom are multi–platinum-selling artists who have been incarcerated, or who were—at the time of the issue's publication—awaiting sentencing for charges including aggravated assault, gun possession, sexual assault, drug trafficking, robbery, and murder.[16] Similarly, in fall 2004, Court TV—in association with Russell Simmons, the manager of pioneering rap group Run DMC and cofounder of legendary label Def Jam—aired a special, "Hip Hop Justice," that promised to "'investigate and reveal [the] underexposed history between law enforcement and hip hop's biggest stars.'"[17]

Certainly, these emphases on rap's criminal associations are part of a larger fascination with "reality" in entertainment generally—from "Gangland" episodes on the History Channel to the gossip-fueled backstabbing of "Big Brother." But it is the degree to which the "reality" of rap has become so thoroughly intertwined with that of crime that is most pertinent; indeed, the stakes faced by many rap artists are often far more "real" than those faced by contestants on reality shows who get "voted off."[18] In turn, these life-and-death stakes are precisely what make rap's conflict with the music industry so painful, infusing the rap game–crack game equation with an emotional core that cannot be so easily explained away as mere sensationalism.

While the still-unsolved murders of the Notorious B.I.G. and Tupac Shakur have had the most impact on the public presentation and reception of rap's criminal affiliations, the 2002 murder of old-school rap pioneer Jam Master Jay—who was the DJ for Run DMC—has also prompted significant concern within the popular press.[19] There are now, we are told, "rap cops" who specialize in knowing about the rap "underworld" where drugs, guns, and music-industry disputes are thought to produce a volatile, often deadly mix.[20] One of these rap cops has even published a book called *Notorious C.O.P.*, which is, clearly, a direct reference to the Notorious B.I.G.[21]

While these violent aspects of rap's criminal connections have become more visible in recent years, it was not long ago that the way in which rap music itself was made, while not officially criminal, was seen as being akin to theft. Because of its reliance on sampling, in which digital copies of short pieces of existing music are "looped" to form continuous beats, rap has played an integral role in shaping the contours of copyright law. For example, in a 1991 case that was to become a landmark for the law and practice surrounding digital sampling, a New York district judge began his opinion with the famous command, "Thou shalt not steal," and ended by recommending that rapper Biz Markie be brought up on criminal charges for sampling pieces of someone else's song.[22]

Given the extent of these overlapping criminal connections, it should be no surprise that many rap critics have felt compelled to address such concerns above all else, focusing primarily on rap's most "obvious" transgressions, especially its explicit, even celebratory violence, homophobia, and misogyny. And, within the context of rap criticism, both popular and academic, two clear approaches in dealing with rap's explicitness have emerged: where one side approaches rap in order to use it for political ends by first rescuing the "good" parts from its commercialized and degraded aspects, the other approaches rap with the goal of accusing it of signaling—and, sometimes, causing—all that is bad in the inner city. Both approaches, however, wind up, ironically, reproducing many of the same problematic logical connections that undergird the crack laws. Just as crack was seen as a form of crude sophistication, a revolutionary simplicity, so, too, has rap been viewed as a similarly "simple" impure purity. For many critics, rap is a social practice whose primary importance is thought to reside in its as-yet-underrealized potential for social critique. Rap, therefore, must be purged of its impurities, and redeployed for political ends—to "free" rap's pure "base" from its impure, overly explicit form. For others, rap's transgressions are mere reflections of either mainstream America's long love affair with sensationalized violence, or the worst elements of inner-city youth culture. For most of these critics, though, such debates often depend on a larger issue, what is often called the "authenticity debate."

Authenticity

As early as 1990, historian Mike Davis, although not concerned with rap scholarship as such, was already critiquing a tendency within the academy to interpret rap's explicit, vocal tirades as "counterhegemonic" resistance to oppressive social forces. Writing about the complicated social history of Los Angeles, Davis argued that gangsta rap suggested a far more cozy "synergy between gangster culture and Hollywood" than many critics admitted.[23] Likewise in the 1990s, cultural theorist Paul Gilroy addressed similar issues, challenging the eagerness with which many writers had embraced rap's overt defiance, arguing that they had too readily taken it as a sign of the "uniqueness, purity and power" of black vernacular culture.[24] Gilroy also questioned rap's emphasis on narrowly conceived versions of street culture and the "'hood" as "the essence[s] of where blackness can be found."[25] He asked "which 'hood are we talking about?" and highlighted the fact that both rap and the scholars who write about it present a specifically "Americo-centric" vision of the world.[26] In his view, such writers often presented an "absolutist" conception of ethnicity in which the "community is felt to be on the wrong road, and it is the intellectual's job to give them a new direction, firstly by recovering and then by donating the racial awareness that the masses seem to lack."[27]

As the above critiques suggest, during the 1990s, academic work on rap was often concerned with analyzing what then appeared to be a fairly marginal(ized) yet vital African American subculture born from inner-city life. While a number of early histories traced the roots of hip hop throughout the African diaspora,[28] rap scholarship became very much concerned with the issues of racial and ethnic marginality and rap's possibilities for political resistance.[29] Rap was often conceived of primarily as an "authentic" development of African American cultural expression that had potential for black political voice, but was also under threat from various forces of commodification that appeared to be enlisting its stylistic innovations for such mundane things as selling cereal. Cultural critic Tricia Rose's argument that "[r]ap's capacity as a form of testimony, as an articulation of a young black urban critical voice of social protest, has profound potential as a basis for a language of liberation"[30] exemplifies this mid-1990s vision. At bottom, what both Davis and Gilroy saw as the aggressive claiming of rap often reflected attempts to parse out its political potential from its seemingly more sensational and commercialized aspects.

Since then, however, scholarship on rap has proliferated, and there have been a number of challenges to that mid-1990s vision. Gilroy's critiques of rap's Americo-centrism have since been reiterated by a number of newer scholars who are, instead, concerned with the global dimensions of rap music and hip hop culture. While not denying the fact that rap's roots are in African American cultural expression, scholarship in the 2000s has often focused on hip hop as a vehicle for youth in a multitude of different ethnic and national contexts to fashion alternative identities for themselves, thereby challenging the notion that rap is primarily a black American voice of social protest.[31] Rap scholarship must now contend with a number of significant factors that have made the promise of its political potential seem problematic at best. Because of the primary observation that, regardless of what rap may represent or what its political potential may be, it is undeniably one of the most popular, commercially successful forms of cultural expression today, earlier concerns with rap's liberatory power have been complicated by issues of global identity formation in the wake of hypercommercialization. Even given such complications, however, much criticism still revolves around efforts to purify and deploy rap music as if it were merely an instrument in larger political struggles.

While Gilroy's argument about the problematic notion of authenticity has provided an important lens through which rap has been reenvisioned, many of the same issues he wrote against in the 1990s remain. In fact, the authenticity debate is still very much at the center of how fans, journalists, and academics approach rap's violent and sexual explicitness. And, in turn, at the heart of this debate lies a key distinction: the difference between "rap" and "hip hop." The distinction's importance can perhaps best be encapsulated in a now-famous line by pioneer rap artist KRS-One: "Rap is something you do, hip hop is something you live."[32] In this conceptual schema, rap is believed to be only one, heavily commercialized, commodified, and appropriated element within a larger hip hop culture. Where hip hop is viewed as a broad cultural efflorescence, rap is often seen as that which the entertainment industry has been able to profit from most efficiently. Thus, for many, the term "rap music" is automatically pejorative, while "hip hop" suggests something grander, more pure, organic, and authentic. Along these lines, what often remains at the heart of this distinction is the desire to use rap in order to harness its political potential after first rescuing it from the forces of commodification.

To be sure, the distinction between rap and hip hop is not without historical basis. In the early days of its emergence out of predominantly black and Latino neighborhoods in the Bronx, Brooklyn, Queens, and Manhattan during the 1970s, rap had not yet come into its own and, instead, was simply the lyrical accompaniment to the musical stylings of local disc jockeys who first employed rappers to "hype" up the crowds during local block parties. Throughout the 1970s, pioneer deejays such as Kool Herc, Grandmaster Flash, and Grand Wizard Theodore developed the techniques of using two record turntables simultaneously, cutting back and forth between records in order to lengthen the pared-down drum and bass breaks in classic rock, funk, and soul songs. These "break beats" became the elements over which rappers would "talk" during parties—boasting about the deejay, calling out the names of neighborhoods and friends, and telling stories in rhyme form. Break beats also provided the sounds to which "b-boys"—literally, break boys—would "battle" each other using the acrobatic movements that were to become the foundations of break dancing. Along with graffiti writers, who used walls, benches, and subway cars as canvases for their spray paint art, rappers, deejays, and break dancers formed what were, and still are, considered to be the four elements of hip hop culture.[33]

During the early 1980s, when hip hop was becoming more popular and record labels got interested in trying to package the phenomenon, rappers became the most recognized and commercially important element in hip hop, and eclipsed the popularity of the others. Clearly, as early-1980s films such as *Breaking* suggest, there were attempts to mass market both graffiti and break dancing. Rap, however, was seen as a far easier element to package since it could be condensed into a song, recorded, and sold in smaller "units." Much like crack, which arrived soon after, rap was often viewed as a "fast food" version of popular music since it could—like cocaine cooking on a kitchen stove—be made with far less equipment, personnel, and, most important, investment capital. The subsequent popularity of rap music—over and above deejaying, breaking, and graffiti writing—was made possible, therefore, by the successful transformation of New York City block party culture into the saleable form of the rap song. As a result, much of the current popularity of rappers can be traced back to this original pressure of marketability.[34]

Even given this history, it is often believed by many writers—past and present—that rap's commercial ties automatically make it suspect. In other words, there is assumed to have been a period in which hip hop culture was uncommercialized, and to which rap can and should return. This belief, though, is problematic on multiple levels. Rappers, in fact, were hired by deejays precisely to make themselves more commercially successful. From its beginnings, then, rap has always been in the service of selling hip hop. Undoubtedly, the intensity of that commercial aspect has grown exponentially since then, perhaps making it seem as if there had been some period—albeit very brief—in which hip hop culture just "was." Once this assumption of initial purity is made, however, the resulting critiques of rap are exactly what Paul Gilroy wrote against in the 1990s— efforts to parse out the "good" aspects from the "bad," the original purity from the commercial, as well as the offensive from the political. Public discussions of rap, therefore, often assume that its violent explicitness reflects either authentic ghetto truth reporting, commercial pressures to be shocking, or, simply, wider cultural problems. Rap, that is, remains, for many people, something to be reclaimed from the pressures of commerce and used to reinvigorate the political potential of hip hop culture that is believed to have been diluted. Resultantly, the existence of crime and violence in rap is often taken as if it were already proof of commodification— as if the presence of violence could only either be the truth of inner-city life, or an aspect generated by the record industry.

Many critics now begin by proclaiming the "death" of civil-rights-era political involvement. According to media critic Todd Boyd, for example, the civil rights era "is past and people need to accept that and act accordingly."[35] Hip hop is then presented as the vehicle through which a new generation—the "hip hop generation"—can harness its as-yet-underrealized political power. In the words of activist George Martinez, "I believe that Hip Hop is the engine and cultural vehicle for the next phase of the civil and human rights movements. But we have to make a distinction between the rap industry and Hip Hop culture. . . . Because Hip Hop comes from the streets, our politics must come from the same place."[36]

Even to this day much of the public debate about rap continues to be dominated by the uses of "Hip Hop Culture," in capital letters—what it is, what it should be, and how it should best be put to use. Rap's relationship to the music industry is often treated as secondary and parasitic, and the "streets" are very often prioritized as an initial organic rawness that was later coopted and commercialized. There are now attempts to reclaim hip hop back from Gilroy's argument that rap music is only one element in a much larger "Black Atlantic"—an alternative public sphere created through the intercontinental expressive creativity of the African diaspora—that, from its start, has always implied far more cultural and ethnic hybridity than is often allowed by American critics. Take, for instance, sociolegal scholar Imani Perry's statement that "[h]ip hop music is black American music. Even with its hybridity."[37] Or, take sociologist Kristine Wright, who, in a 2004 issue of the journal *Socialism and Democracy* devoted entirely to hip hop, states her belief even more clearly: "I cannot join the club of *hip hop started as a voice of oppressed black and brown youth but now it's worldwide* . . . because for these oppressed black and brown youth, little has changed and hip hop is still *their* voice."[38] Much of the debate, then, continues to focus on pinpointing where hip hop's "true essence" lies and what direction it should take in the future: "At its essence," Wright states, "hip hop is making a way from no way, and in the case of mainstream hip hop, it has been a legal hustle for many youth from ghettos who would not have had many other opportunities."[39]

Perhaps some of the strongest critiques of rap's explicitness, however, have come from feminist writers who have been participants in hip hop culture but are now trying to reconcile rap's critical potential with an apparent increase in its sexually degrading depictions of women—to rescue, again, rap music from its slide into ugly, commercialized transgression. In her analysis of what it "mean[s] to be a woman in the Hip-Hop generation,"[40] for example, cultural scholar Gwendolyn Pough's primary aim is "ultimately to recognize the political potential within it [hip hop]."[41] Similarly, in her 2008 book, Tricia Rose hopes to "arm young black men and women, and everyone else, with powerful critical tools so that they can expose and challenge the state of commercial hip hop."[42] For Rose, "Hip hop is in a terrible crisis."[43] In sum, throughout the authenticity debate, rap, more often than not, is viewed as a social instrument that can and should be cleansed, rather than as a complex, commercially bound social practice that will continue to take its own forms regardless of how hard critics—academic or popular—work to purify it. While the 1990s saw critics trying to decode the seemingly nonpolitical in order to understand rap's importance for resistance, in the early twenty-first century, many are now trying to decode the obviously commercial in order to understand rap's role in the dilution of a potentially resistant "Hip Hop Culture."

Given these efforts to reclaim rap from crass commercialism and global appropriations—to put rap to use in reclaiming hip hop culture—it is perhaps not surprising that they have found their nemesis in efforts to accuse rap of illustrating the profound depths to which the nation's youth have fallen and the degree to which they are preyed upon by the morally corrupt messages of glorified violence.[44] Journalist Juan Williams, for example, has claimed that rap is part of a "twisted popular culture that focuses on the 'bling-bling' of fast money associated with famous basketball players, rap artists, drug dealers and the idea that women are at their best when flaunting their sexuality and having babies."[45] Tied to what he calls a "culture of failure that is poisoning young people," "hate-filled rap music" signals "the desperate need to pull a generational fire alarm"[46] that, in his view, was sounded by comedian Bill Cosby in his highly controversial speech during the fiftieth anniversary of the *Brown v. Board of Education* decision.[47] While Juan Williams has complained that "violent, oversexed gangstas"[48] brag about "how many times they've been shot,"[49] the issue of rap-related violence, it seems, lies less in rappers bragging about being shot than in the fact that so many rappers have been shot in the first place. Perhaps more to the point, though, is this: getting shot has become part of *the work of rap*. In other words, lethal violence has become a central element in a multi-billion-dollar global entertainment industry. Take, in this regard, the comment of underground rap artist MF Grimm, who was confined to a wheelchair in 1994 after being shot multiple times. After describing what it felt like to have a bullet enter his neck, ricochet in his head, and exit his mouth, he says, "At the time this happened, I was getting [record] label offers. When I got shot, the labels all wanted to separate from me. Now it's part of your deal."[50]

Thus, where one side of the debate approaches rap in order to use it by rescuing the "good" parts from its corrupted elements, the other approaches rap in order to accuse it of "poisoning" our youth. While many critics initially approach rap—in Raymond Williams's phrase—as a "creative working," such approaches are, more often than not, narrowly directed by only a few overriding goals: defining the "essence" of hip hop, describing how that essence has been diluted, and suggesting how it can be cleansed and redeployed for political ends.

Ironically, in focusing almost solely on rap's instrumental uses and abuses, both sides rely on the exact same assumption that often dominates debates about the relationship between media explicitness and actual behavior: in cultural scholar T. Denean Sharpley-Whiting's words, "the stereotype of sexual availability in hip hop provides a bridge to all other verbal and physically exploitative acts."[51] This "commonsense" belief that media violence directly influences real violence, in fact, lies at the heart of this book's central premise: in America's criminological structure of feeling, almost all issues of social justice are recast as issues of criminal justice, which must rely, for legitimacy, on causal claims. As I showed in the last chapter, however, the danger of such efforts lies in reading too much causation into too little evidence. Just as crack was viewed as an impure purity requiring a disproportionate effort to combat, so, too, is rap—when narrowly conceived as a "bridge" between lyric and violence— treated as an impure instrument whose sole importance lies in being purified and redeployed. And, also like the crack laws, such purification efforts depend upon a few interlocking contradictions.

First, while explicit content in rap—and, indeed, all media—appears to have increased exponentially since its mainstream success in the 1980s, actual rates of violent victimization have decreased precipitously for the past fifteen years. For men and women of all ethnicities, victimization rates in every single category are now at levels not seen since the early 1960s.[52] By arguing, as Sharpley-Whiting does, that rap's explicit content "gives men and boys every reason to continue gender violence,"[53] or that, in Juan Williams's words, rap reflects a "culture of failure that is poisoning young people," both sides fall into the same logical trap that has plagued anyone who has ever argued—as many continue to do—that media content has direct consequences for real behavior: media violence does not match real violence. This is no small point, for declines in violent victimization have been significant, and have occurred even while the percentage of all crimes reported to the police has steadily increased since the early 1990s.[54] Simply put, overly culturalist explanations of real-world violence will overpredict the phenomena they are trying to explain. Since the vast majority of people who consume violent content—whether rap or otherwise—do not become violent offenders, then, logically, violent content is neither a "bridge to all other verbal and physically exploitative acts" nor does it mirror a "culture of failure that is poisoning young people." Statistically speaking, the correlation—between real violence and media violence—has moved in the opposite direction. The point is not that media violence is wholly unproblematic, but that overly culturalist explanations are reductive, and mask a far more complex reality, which requires equally nuanced analyses to disentangle.

The contradiction discussed above is also intertwined with a similar paradox long noted in criminological research: while the majority of people who have experienced serious childhood trauma do not become hard-core offenders, the overwhelming majority of hard-core offenders have experienced some of the worst forms of such violence. Put another way, most serious victimizers have themselves been the most seriously victimized.[55] Unfortunately, this knowledge has been frustrating for researchers because they still have been unable to predict, with any modicum of precision, which victimized children will go on to victimize others. This finding is replicated time and again and cannot be dismissed—as those who believe "personal responsibility" is the only element that matters in explaining criminal behavior would do—as an "abuse excuse."[56] In truth, real-world offenders rarely offer such excuses for their own actions. As criminologists Robert Sampson and John Laub found in their reanalysis of and followup to one of the most extensive longitudinal data sets ever compiled in the history of criminology, "men who desisted from crime, but even those who persisted, accepted responsibility for their actions and freely admitted getting into trouble. They did not, for the most part, offer excuses."[57] In short, real-world violence begets more real-world violence, but does so in complex ways that cannot be predicted or mapped directly.

These frustrating findings about the blurry lines between offenders and victims are also replicated in numerous qualitative studies. For example, in her analysis of young women's experiences of gender violence in urban St. Louis, sociologist Jody Miller reveals the following stark realities of her young male interviewees, many of whom were engaged in serious criminal activity, including drug dealing, retaliatory violence, and gang rape: 75 percent had seen someone robbed, 70 percent had seen someone shot, 53 percent had seen someone stabbed, and 48 percent—two points shy of half—had seen someone killed.[58] In addition, 15 percent had been shot themselves, 58 percent had been threatened with a weapon, and 65 percent had been robbed.[59] Depressingly, this blurry picture of the offender-victim relationship reflects, for both young men and young women, "a continuum of violence that began at home":[60]

> [A]bout 50 percent of the youths [in this study] . . . had witnessed domestic violence. A sizable portion also reported having been physically abused: 31 percent of girls and 28 percent of boys reported physical abuse, and 14 percent of girls reported having been sexually abused by a family member. In all, 66 percent of girls and 63 percent of boys reported some exposure to family violence—as witnesses, victims, or both.[61]

Philippe Bourgois' ethnography of crack dealers in Spanish Harlem during the mid-1980s also shows the complicated offender-victim continuum in far more personal detail. Consider Caesar, described by his best friend Primo as being "the meanest" participant in the neighborhood's brutal gang rape rituals, whose potential for extreme, unpredictable violence was legendary, earning him a place as the foremost crackhouse security guard. "The only person who disrespected the . . . premises while Caesar was on duty," recalls Bourgois, "was a jealous young man high on angel dust. He was subsequently carried away . . . with a fractured skull" after Caesar hit him repeatedly with a baseball bat.[62] Born to a sixteen-year-old, unwed, heroin-addicted mother who, at the time of Bourgois' research, was serving a 25-year sentence for murder, Caesar's early years illustrate, par excellence, the overlapping forms of serious violence that characterize the backgrounds of many similarly situated youths. Raised by his grandmother, Caesar, according to his childhood friend Eddie,[63] was routinely abused "in front of everybody in the streets—like with bats and sticks for being one minute late."[64] He was also beaten with wires, and was once cut after his grandmother threw a knife at his chest. After numerous behavioral problems, Caesar was eventually sent to a reform school, where he describes seeing "'the counselors holding down the kids naked outside; and the counselor beat him down; stripped him up; and threw him outside in the snow and shit. . . . I was about twelve or thirteen.'"[65] Caesar's increasingly violent outbursts eventually led him to "an experimental Special Education facility at a hospital for the criminally insane . . . where psychiatrists were pioneering psychotropic treatments with tranquilizers."[66] At some point during all of this, Caesar's sister was murdered, stabbed seventeen times and left in a project stairwell.

While not quite as extreme as Caesar's, Primo's upbringing also shows similarly harrowing patterns of violence and childhood trauma. In graphically describing his own participation in neighborhood gang rapes, for example, Primo recounts how, in his teens, he had been socialized into the ritual by Ray, his boss, whose "ruthlessness and . . . cruelty were an integral part of his effectiveness at running his network of crackhouses smoothly."[67] Ray was older than Primo and was known by the whole neighborhood for being especially brutal. "'I know that nigga' since I was little,'" Primo remembers. "'He was weird man. Used to think he would rape me or something. . . . I'm only fifteen, boy. And he used to talk crazy shit like, "One of these days I'm gonna get that ass." And I used to wonder if that was true. I never used to dare to be alone with him.'"[68] Primo's fears were not unfounded. Ray, along with his "best childhood friend, Luis, once raped an old male transient in the empty parking lot" next to the crackhouse.[69] In an effort to communicate to Bourgois just how much this and other acts solidified Ray's fearsome street reputation, Caesar—a wildly violent presence himself—says this: "'Ray's a fuckin' pig; Ray's a wild motherfucker. He's got juice. . . . On the street that means respect.'"[70] Ray and Luis, in fact, were the ones who regularly scheduled the gang rapes, and recruited other adolescent boys from the neighborhood, many of whom—like Primo—had grown up fearing their older counterparts, and were highly motivated to not look weak in their eyes. As Primo admits, "'Back in those days I was younger. My dick wouldn't stand up. It was like nasty to me; I wasn't down with it. I can't handle that.'"[71]

The violent complexities outlined above by no means excuse their obvious horror, but one must acknowledge—in order to adequately account for rap's reworkings of crack's intensified brutality—the intersecting webs of violence that begin in the most intimate of neighborhood settings and into which many young boys and girls are regularly recruited through fear and coercion. As children of the crack era, many rap artists have surely grown up in such environments, being both victims and perpetrators to varying degrees, even if they lyrically embellish their own street credentials. A few, perhaps, may have been like Ray or Caesar. Some, like Primo. Many more, no doubt, have experienced numerous variations of these realities. In short, rap's seemingly obvious transgressions cannot be so easily excerpted from their embeddedness in violent continua and reduced to mere content choices, corruptions of a formerly pure political engagement, or simplistic media-causes-violence connections that are tenuous in the extreme. As long as it is assumed that rap's creative reworkings of crack-era intensifications should only be in the service of an essentializing hip hop identity politics, then rap's more complicated elective affinities with specific sociolegal logics and real-world violence will continually be reduced to mere instruments. If approached, however, as a complex, commercially bound social practice whose political commentaries, violent tirades, and commercial aspirations coexist, as they do, even within the same album, song, or line, then investigations of rap's social complexities can move beyond this "imprisoning framework," and begin charting, in detail, how these specific logics thread their way throughout rap's various expressive media.[72] In the next sections, I outline one such logic—the development of rap's confrontation with its own commercialization—in order to show how crack first developed into an explicit language of exploitation through the mid-1990s New York City rap underground.

The NYC Rap Underground

Since rap's beginnings, New York City has always been its spiritual home. During the late 1980s, though, a number of regional rap scenes emerged across the United States and challenged New York's dominance as the primary center of rap music production, often and repeatedly producing more commercially successful and socially controversial music.[73] The effects of being the spiritual home of rap, while simultaneously being a commercial failure, in many ways, put much of New York rap on the defensive. And, out of this defensiveness, there developed a strong sense of being "underground" by default.[74] By the 1990s, New York rap had adopted an explicitly underground ethic, which revolved around open-mic nights at well-known clubs such as the Nuyorican; freestyle lyrical battles at the movable Lyricist Lounge parties; on-air performances on the Stretch and Bobbito radio show; the circulation of "white label" records (low-budget or under-the-radar records put out with little fanfare or identifying information) by a small handful of independent record labels and artists; and quasi-legal mixtapes by local deejays that featured unreleased and exclusive material from sought-after artists. In New York rap's pervasive sense of being automatically underground, then, making rap came to be seen as hard work. New York rap in the 1990s was stressed and angry, which became a significant part of its public presentation. For all of its talk of killing and violence, Los Angeles–based gangsta rap, instead, was specifically designed to sound easy and smooth. By contrast, New York rap made every attempt to sound the way the actual work of rap was perceived as being. As a consequence, this ubiquitous sense of being underground-by-default gave rise to a complicated lyrical reflexivity in which the music industry came to be viewed as not only overly complex, but intentionally duplicitous.

Much like other cultural forms, underground rap in 1990s New York encompassed a set of conflicting beliefs all anchored by a central tension between artistic respect and commercial success. And those who were a part of the underground held to a number of overlapping positions. For some, the underground was taken very seriously and signified clear differences from what were considered mainstream values and practices. For them, the rap underground was similar to the do-it-yourself ethics of punk, hardcore, and grunge—e.g., a commitment to independent, artist-run record labels and live performances.[75] For others, the underground was not so overtly political, but was conceived as something dark, sinister, urban, below law and order, even postapocalyptic.[76] This "grimier" aspect of the underground neither embraced nor dismissed overt political engagement; rather, it actively encouraged a raw, dirty—street—vision of music making and rhyme writing. The underground was thought of as a proving ground where the possibilities of being beaten—both lyrically and physically—were real; people took their words and music seriously, and often believed they were carrying on the "true" tradition of rap's street origins. Ghostface Killah's warning, for instance, on Raekwon's 1995 album, *Only Built for Cuban Linx*, exemplifies this: "I don't want niggas sounding like me on no album. . . . For real, 'cause I'ma approach a nigga."[77] There were still others who were part of the underground only because they could not be part of the mainstream. For them, the underground was not necessarily a choice, but a stopping point from which, it was hoped, they would move on to mainstream success. This is illustrated, for example, in Redman's frustration with mainstream artists on his 1994 song, "Basically": "Why is it every time that a multiplatinum artist always uses the underground to make a comeback? Is it fair to the hardcore niggas that rap?—that don't give a fuck about the radio?"[78] Most significant, however, was that all of New York rap was underground simply because so few New York City acts were as successful as their West Coast rivals. The issue of respect at the heart of New York rap in the 1990s, therefore, was articulated as an explicit prioritizing of lyrical mastery over money. This is perhaps best expressed in a now-famous line from O.C.'s 1994 underground classic, "Time's Up": "I'd rather be broke and have a whole lot of respect."[79]

The underground, thus, encompassed a number of different, often conflicting, impulses, desires, drives, and visions. Despite such conflict, lyrical skill, ingenuity, originality, and delivery were highly prized qualities. Lyricism was the overriding prerequisite for respect, and lyrical content was heavily scrutinized, judged, and compared. Out of this milieu, which had developed a pervasive sense of being underground-by-default, there also emerged an explicit, overt chronicling of rap's rapid commercialization within lyrical content; it was a consciousness of exploitation that was vocalized in the very products that were themselves being exploited. This explicitness is perhaps best captured by Nas, whose 1994 album is widely considered to be one of the most important and influential rap records of the period: "Somehow the rap game reminds me of the crack game."[80]

As I outlined briefly in the book's introduction, much of the lyrical content that emerged from this scene focused explicitly on the music industry, critiquing it for being corrupt, unjust, and criminal. Like Nas, many rappers began drawing parallels between the "rap game" and the "crack game," juxtaposing their own exploits in street crime with the machinations of industry executives in the suites. New York rap in the 1990s, and the underground aesthetic that defined it, was predicated, in large part, on a certain reflexive stance—on being a commodity that "talked back," as much to itself and its own traditions as to its exploitation by industry executives. This reflexive stance was neither hidden nor ironic; it was, in every way, an explicitly moral struggle.

But what was it specifically about "the industry" that drew such heated response? Why such anger? After all, it was the industry that, in many ways, had helped rap grow beyond the confines of New York City. As I chart below, this anger grew from the history of the music business itself, which is now perceived by a broad range of artists as being intentionally duplicitous. In rap's conflict with its own commercialization, formerly esoteric legal arrangements—that, until then, had been understood only by very few—were openly and lyrically castigated.

The Industry

Much of rap's anger at the music industry revolved around a number of interrelated issues, all of which can be encapsulated in two key imperatives: "Own your masters," and "never give up your publishing."[81] These imperatives represent two primary, and complicated, streams of revenue in the industry, both of which are dependent upon a two-pronged system of ownership: the compositions underlying all songs and the master recordings of them.[82] First, music publishing is often seen as the esoteric key to making money in the industry, and, since music publishing started as the printing of sheet music, it developed—like book publishing—after Gutenberg invented the printing press in the 1400s. Because of its grounding in the distribution of print, music publishing is also undergirded by copyright law, the global intellectual property infrastructure underlying the ownership of books.[83]

Put simply, copyright is the right to make and distribute copies of artistic works fixed in any medium. Although countries have different philosophical notions behind their respective copyright traditions, currently— because of international treaties and trade agreements—most countries are far more alike than they are different in their practical treatment of copyright policy. In the French tradition, for instance, artistic works are considered extensions of the creator's personality. These "moral rights"— *droit morale*—are believed to inhere in each and every creation. In the American tradition, the moral rights of creators end where the rights of the copyright owners begin.

All copyright regimes, however, make two important distinctions. First, there are authors and there are owners, and the two do not have to be the same person. It is the ownership of authorings that forms the material base of copyright law.[84] Just as the ownership of tangible assets allows owners to reap profits from exchanging such possessions, so, too, with the ownership of intangible assets. Second, owners only own the "expressions" of ideas, not the ideas themselves. Once an idea is "fixed" in a medium of expression (e.g., paper, canvas, magnetic tape, and, now, digital code), then that specific fixation becomes copyrightable. In other words, without a way to prevent others from making copies of a work I own, I cannot control its distribution and subsequent consumption.[85] And, in fact, this seemingly clear separation between those who own and those who author is often a key flashpoint in rap's conflict with its own commercialization.

While popular opinion often reflects a belief that the interests of creators lie at its heart, early copyright law actually developed first as government-granted monopolies given to printing companies—publishers—in order to prevent others from making copies of printed work. In return, governments were able to generate additional revenue, and, since all works had to be registered in the publisher's records, they were also able to exercise a certain amount of control over the content of what was printed, thereby censoring, and often criminalizing, material believed to be dangerous politically and morally. In order to enforce these arrangements, some publishing companies were allowed to have their own police forces, and many people were jailed for blasphemous, seditious, and obscene libel.[86] While the British Statute of Anne in 1710 officially gave these rights to "authors"—the creators of the published works—rather than to publishers, authors often signed these rights away in order to enjoy the wider distribution that publishers could provide. And, as we shall see, it is precisely this element of signing away—and the unintended consequences of doing so—that lies at the heart of rap's anger at the music industry.[87]

Early music publishers, then, were in the business of printing and circulating sheet music, and, until the late nineteenth century, dealt only in the music of "serious" composers such as Beethoven and Mozart. But, with the increasing popular success of figures such as Johann Strauss in Vienna, Gilbert and Sullivan in England, and Puccini in Italy, sheet music regularly began to sell over a million copies per composition or song.

During this time in the United States, Tin Pan Alley—an area in Manhattan named for the sounds of aspiring songwriters plinking out hopeful hits on pianos—became home to large music publishing houses.[88] Tin Pan Alley, in many ways, marks the beginnings of the music industry as it is both understood and practiced today since most of its activities were focused on one primary goal: creating and publicizing the next hit song. Songs were written, promoted by being played live in print music stores, bought, sold, and given free to famous vaudeville performers in the hopes of further popularity. This one primary goal was made possible by the system of copyright that gave the owners of compositions the sole right to profit from them. And, more often than not, it was the larger publishers who benefited most, as they could afford to buy the rights to songs enjoying local success in the hopes of even wider popularity. It was not until the 1920s, however, that the music business—a system in which money from copyrighted songs was generated from the sale of sheet music—became the record business, after Thomas Edison's first sound recording in the 1870s stimulated the growth of mass-produced sounds. The development of "talkie" motion pictures also expanded the production, distribution, and consumption of music since it was an integral part of the new form. These technological changes allowed for the second kind of ownership: the "master recordings" of songs. While sheet music allowed for the distribution of "underlying compositions," "master recordings" allowed for the distribution of those compositions as they were recorded by specific "artists." Thus, the modern music industry was born.

While technological changes were, quite literally, instrumental in expanding the music industry as we now know it, the underlying system of collecting money from the circulation of owned songs remained, although not completely unchanged, the bedrock of the business. Consequently, music publishing—and, in turn, the heart of the music business itself—is not technology dependent: copyright owners make money regardless of how their songs get to an audience. In the modern music industry, therefore, there are a number of different streams of revenue, depending upon the various entities' proximity to both the copyrights and the master recordings of copyrighted songs. There are, then, two key roles played by talent: those who write and those who perform, either live or on record. In addition, there are two key roles played by management: those who publicize songs, and those who allow for recordings to be made. The modern music industry, thus, revolves around a few key players (as well as the lawyers, managers, and publicists who operate among them): songwriters, performing artists, publishers, and record companies.[89]

Songwriters write the songs; publishers promote those songs to performers in exchange for a large piece of the songwriters' copyrights; performers pay the copyright owners in exchange for the right to perform the songs; record labels advance money to performers, now called "recording artists," and market and promote the recordings of those copyrighted songs. And from these relationships, two main streams of revenue are created. The sale of "units"—music fixed in physical forms such as compact discs—generates what are called "mechanical royalties."[90] All mechanical royalties are first collected by record labels who then pay both the publishing company and the recording artist. Unless negotiated differently, publishers are paid a "statutory rate," derived from the Consumer Price Index and announced by Congress, for each song used. Publishers then pay the songwriters, whose share is set in an agreement with the publisher. Depending upon their contracts, recording artists are usually paid around 15 percent of the SLRP—the suggested list retail price of each unit (pronounced "slurp"). From this total, a number of deductions are made, including, among other things, the amount of the artist's original advance. The artists keep whatever is left. Because record label deductions are so notoriously difficult to understand, many artists are unaware of just how much their royalties will be impacted by them. Many artists, in fact, see few if any mechanical royalties; many more actually wind up owing their record companies for what are called "unrecouped expenses."

Performance royalties, on the other hand, are paid only to copyright holders and not to artists. Performing rights organizations such as ASCAP, the American Society of Composers, Artists, and Performers, require public venues to pay blanket license fees for the use of their song catalogues. They also track the airplay of their registered songs. After deducting their own operating expenses, performing rights organizations then pay publishers and songwriters. The arrangements among these players, however, are handled individually, and are enshrined in the recording contract, the "holy grail" for many young, hungry artists, and the site of some of the worst forms of exploitation. Perhaps the most difficult element of these contractual arrangements is that there are no "boiler plate" deals in the music industry guaranteeing any of them. While the music business, like most businesses, is complex, it is the nature of the recording contract that makes the industry seem so different from others.

The crux of this difference lies in the length of the recording contract, which is, most often, based on numbers of albums, not years. Hence, a "six-album deal with a million dollar advance" may sound nice, but, in reality, the stakes are quite high.[91] Take the million-dollar advance. Record companies will "advance" artists a sum of money to cover the recording costs of the record, which, among other things, includes studio time, producer salaries, as well as any guest performers. The advance is simply a loan that the artist must pay back before seeing any of the royalties generated by the album's sales. Now, take the six-album deal. In the words of one industry self-help guru, "Of all the inequities in the recording contract, the very worst, in my opinion, is the label's total lack of commitment as to how long your actual engagement will last. . . . Most contracts these days span a nebulous length of time that . . . keeps going until the label says they're no longer interested."[92] In truth, a six-album deal may mean the artist's entire career. First, most albums take months simply to record. Second, the artist must then deliver the finished album to the record company. If, however, the label does not find the album to be commercially viable, it may send the artist back to the studio to record more songs. In addition, even if the label executives like the album, they then must decide when to release it in order not to interfere with any current projects. Many times, the release date—even for finished, commercially viable albums—may be pushed back indefinitely, until the product is no longer considered a worthwhile commodity and is "shelved." While many businesses are complex, the record business is one of the few in which its employees can be bound to their employers for unspecified periods of time with little recourse other than to buy back their contracts, which can be prohibitively expensive.

Many contracts also stipulate that the master recordings of the album's songs will remain in the label's possession even after an artist leaves its employ. Possession of the masters, therefore, allows the label to continue selling copies made from it in as many forms as possible. For most artists, then, giving up their rights to the masters signifies a relinquishing of future profit, a loss of control over their work, as well as the emotional pain of losing access to something they have spent years creating. In effect, artists may be "shelved" while simultaneously being denied access to the very creations that lie unused on the shelf. If shelved, artists can neither work nor leave, but remain in a state of suspended *contraction*.

This suspension is experienced as deeply painful precisely because it suspends the working lives of artists, keeping what they have produced under lock while preventing them from producing anything else. For this reason, unfair contracts in the music industry hold the possibility of suspending the working lives of artists indefinitely through one ill-formed decision.

Because of these perceived inequities, since the late 1990s, lobbying groups such as the Recording Artists Coalition have helped promote a public vision of the music industry in which naïve artists are used and exploited by record label executives. For example, spearheaded primarily by rock and pop stars such as Don Henley, Courtney Love, and the Dixie Chicks, what came to be called the "artists' rights movement" and the "new music activism" by musicians, journalists, and industry folk during the early 2000s made waves in the business, garnering support from a number of powerful groups such as the American Federation of Labor–Congress of Industrial Organizations (AFL-CIO) and the American Federation of Television and Radio Artists (AFTRA), as well as from government officials and lawmakers.[93] There have been government-sponsored hearings on record-label accounting practices and contract lengths, and artists have become vocal about such issues in the popular media. These activist artists have repeatedly referred to the music industry as a "plantation system" akin to "indentured servitude" and slavery. As musician Steve Albini has written in a famous piece called "The Problem with Music":

> Whenever I talk to a band who are about to sign with a major label, I always end up thinking of them in a particular context. I imagine a trench, about four feet wide and five feet deep, maybe sixty yards long, filled with runny, decaying shit. . . . I also imagine a faceless industry lackey at the other end holding a fountain pen and a contract waiting to be signed.[94]

Faceless industry lackeys holding contracts perhaps best captures the negative image that many now hold of the music industry. Singer-songwriter Tom Waits, for example, has claimed that "the record companies are like cartels, like countries for God's sake. . . . It's a nightmare to be trapped in one. I'm on a good label now that's not part of the plantation system. But all the old records I did for Island [Records] have been swallowed up and spit out in whatever form they choose."[95] Waits goes on to say that "[t]hese corporations don't have feelings, and they don't see themselves as the stewards of the work. . . . Most people are so anxious to record, they'll sign anything. It's like going across the river on the back of an alligator."[96] Echoing a similar sentiment about the facelessness, deceitfulness, and general ruthlessness of the corporate basis of the music industry, Don Henley has claimed that "newer artists don't want to rock the boat" since many are "still starry-eyed idealists and haven't been around long enough to be mistreated," and that "other artists simply don't understand the issues or are too self-absorbed." He goes on to claim that "even the midlevel people who love music have to march in lockstep with corporate policy."[97] For many artists, established and aspiring, the *work of music*, then, revolves around two key flashpoints: *complexity* and *duplicity*. The duplicity lies in bringing naïve artists into a situation of complexity in which they often have little knowledge, and then tying them to one ill-formed decision, possibly suspending their productive potential indefinitely.

In fact, this notion of duplicity lies at the heart of legal scholar Susan Shapiro's famous reformulation of Edwin Sutherland's classic definition of white-collar crime: in Shapiro's words, "The violation and manipulation of the norms of trust—of disclosure, disinterestedness, and role competence—represent the modus operandi of white-collar crime."[98] Sutherland made criminological history in the 1940s with his original definition—"a crime committed by a person of respectability and high social status in the course of his occupation."[99] In reorienting the definition away from the status-based criterion at its core, Shapiro aimed to "liberate" the potentially powerful concept from the "imprisoning framework" that a status-based criterion, in her argument, had imposed.[100] For Shapiro, a status-based definition reflects a moralistic focus on "who" should be blamed for white-collar crime at the expense of explaining "how" such crimes actually operate. All white-collar crime, in her formulation, shares one primary element: duplicity. In Shapiro's words, white collar "'robbers' become *confidence* men, women, and organizations and induce victims to part with their money or property with lies, misrepresentations and deceptions rather than with brute force."[101] These white-collar robbers, whom Shapiro calls "agents," have a monopoly on information that their victims, whom she calls "principals," cannot verify because they lack the required knowledge and expertise. Relationships between white-collar agents and their principals, in other words, are *asymmetrical*.

This asymmetricality was also famously outlined by legal theorist Marc Galanter while analyzing the effects of people and organizations on legal rules.[102] Galanter classified legal actors into two ideal types: "repeat players," who are mainly organizations that specialize in certain kinds of litigation over time, and "one-shotters," "who have only occasional recourse to the courts."[103] Ultimately, according to Galanter, the repeat players—because of greater resources and organization—are really the "haves" of the system, and its "unreformed character" is able to uphold the ideals of fairness and equality while, at the same time, "accommodating inequality." For Galanter, the only way one-shotters can hope to redistribute the balance of legal power is to organize and consolidate among themselves.

At bottom, the pain articulated by so many artists reflects the outbursts of random one-shotters experiencing humiliation at the hands of an asymmetrical business structure created and maintained by repeat players who regularly induce artists "to part with their money or property with lies, misrepresentations and deceptions rather than with brute force." The pain felt by artists, therefore, is so often articulated in emotional language precisely because their musical creations are both commercial "products" and repositories of emotional meaning, often representing years of hard physical work as well as intangible creative labor. Recall Tom Waits, for example, who stated that it was a "nightmare to be trapped" in the plantationlike system of the music industry. Such emotionality suggests far more than a simple loss of "property," and, instead, signifies *a number of overlapping betrayals* that coalesce to suspend the working life of artists and prevent access to the products of their own labor.

In rap's reflexive stance toward its own commercialization, then, these emotional outbursts have taken on collective properties with specific guiding logics. In equating the rap game with the crack game, rap artists have developed a language of exploitation that unites promises of violent retaliation—which I explore in more detail in chapters 5 and 6—with a moral revulsion at the breaking of implied trust by the repeat players of the music industry. In this way, the metaphor of crack in rap's confrontation with its own commercialization has become a grammar of social analysis that fundamentally concerns the possibility of fashioning—by force if necessary—productive lives in the midst of social instability. Many of rap's retaliatory promises, as we shall see, revolve around efforts to bring the regulatory methods of one business—crack dealing—to bear on the asymmetrical nature of another in order to rebalance the distribution of power, and negate the music industry's humiliating effects. Crack, hence, represents a method of *violent redress*, as well as a system of *busi-*

ness regulation that eschews the legalistic methods of the Recording Artists Coalition, and, instead, shoots from and at the gut.

In rap's conflict with its own commercialization, crack serves as a bridge connecting a white-collar industry predicated on a violence of suspension, and a street industry whose work is regulated by the ever-present threat of lethality. Much of rap's violent content, therefore, represents neither the simple creations of "violent oversexed gangstas," the political yearnings of a resistant subculture, nor the mere reflections of social conditions. Instead, in equating the rap game with the crack game, rap artists have indicted *the seeming inseparability of work and violence*—the humiliating, faceless violence of an industry whose ruthless complexity has a centuries-long history, and the ruthlessness of the street in which violence itself has become a means of production. And it is to the emotional impact of that inseparability that I turn in the next chapter, analyzing the specific ways in which rap artists have accounted for the lethality of the crack era.

4

Things Done Changed

The Rise of New School Violence

I can see there's no place to run.
—Masta Ace, "A Walk Thru the Valley," *Slaughtahouse*, 1992

In recent years, a number of local governments across the United States have tried to outlaw what many have taken to be signs of moral decay in the nation's young: baggy pants. The theory is that the style began in prisons—where, as a suicide-prevention measure, inmates are often not allowed to have belts—and then spread to the mainstream through the oversized clothing styles made famous by numerous rap stars. While some of the penalties in these new laws include fines, others include jail time. The reasoning behind these attempts—some of which have passed, while others have failed—is often quite clear: "'Hopefully,'" as one Louisiana representative proffers, "'if we can pull up their pants, we can lift their minds while we're at it.'"[1] This assumed relationship between youth, intelligence, and moral decline can also be seen in the following quotation from a Florida city commissioner: "If you ask six of these kids, "What are your grades?" four will tell you they're making C's, D's, and F's.'"[2] Or, as one New York state senator's campaign slogan reads, "Raise your pants, raise your image!"[3] While aimed at saving such sagging youth from the perils implied by the state of their trousers, these goals mask a deeper fear: in the words of one former New York police captain, "'I policed all over the city. . . . The first indicator of whether a young person was in trouble was the way they dressed.'"[4] Such efforts, however problematic they may sound to some, are based on a very old kind of reasoning about the connections between morality and the young. In the previous chapters, I suggested that the seemingly simple rap game–crack game equation belies a tremendous amount of social complexity and emotional pain, reflecting a moral outrage that develops from a multifaceted sense of social betrayal. All too often, however, these moral transformations are interpreted—as the above examples suggest—as all-or-nothing affairs in which youth, especially, face a zero-sum game: morality is either present or absent, lost or given. In this chapter, I problematize the notion that rap's crack-infused lyrics represent moral *loss*. Instead, by charting the profoundly moral debate at the heart of what many would take as examples of the worst kinds of sensationalist superpredation, I show how rap creatively reworks one of the crack era's most devastating transformations: the rise of a new moral order in which market relations supplanted culturally bound ones. This moral transformation has been experienced as both power and loss by the young people raised in it and reflects their *adaptations* to the social disruptions of coercive mobility and disproportionate punishment.

Youth in Trouble

Indeed, the perils faced by the young—and the perils they then portend for us—have long been a central concern of modern industrial society. Some of the more prominent examples are often found in popular culture. Charles Dickens's visions of Victorian London in which orphans and runaways vie for scraps in the streets are perhaps the most famous. But more recent illustrations abound. In television, for instance, the 2006 season of HBO's *The Wire*—critically acclaimed for its evenhanded, in-depth chronicling of the drug war in Baltimore, Maryland—follows three young friends whose adolescent lives split into painful tracks of violence, addiction, and family collapse. The season shows the helplessness even the most motivated mentors often experience when facing the overwhelmingly disruptive forces at work in such environments. In cinema, Francois Truffaut's *400 Blows* remains a classic portrait of troubled youth, and its last scene—in which the young protagonist escapes an abusive juvenile justice system only to come up against the vast expanse of an ocean—is a bleak representation of the "no way out" predicament that youth so often seem to face. Similarly haunting, and no less impressive, Mira Nair's *Salaam Bombay* follows the difficulties faced by youth on the streets of Bombay and in the Indian juvenile justice system. And, even more recent,

Central Station, Tsotsi, and *City of God* have all offered American audiences rare glimpses, however mediated, into the international visions of youth in trouble.

But in the United States, perhaps the most prominent example of fears surrounding the worlds that youth must create for themselves is William Golding's 1954 novel, *Lord of the Flies,* which, although British, has been standard reading in many American high schools. In it, a group of young boys, stranded on an island with no adults, wind up creating a small society of ever-increasing, murderous brutality. To be sure, the examples above are not all cut from the same cloth. Some, clearly, are bleaker than others. Some are explicitly about crime, while others are not. But underlying them all is fundamental concern: that the worlds created by the young—as well as the worlds they are often forced to inhabit—are at odds with adult morality, suggesting that adults will no longer have a place once morality is lost and refashioned. Not only *can* youth create worlds for themselves, but, most disturbing for many, the young might very well create worlds—and, with them, new moral orders—that will be far more ruthless than those created by adults, and might turn out to be, to borrow a phrase from chapter 2, "pitilessly savage." The implicit logic of the fears surrounding the moral orders created by the young, however, holds that "we" have the right moral code, and that it is always in danger of being lost.

As legal historian Lawrence Friedman has shown, the development of the juvenile justice system in the United States during the 1800s was, in many ways, based on fears of the younger generation's potential to lose or destroy the moral codes of its parents.[5] Early juvenile justice was based on the explicitly paternalistic common-law tradition of *parens patriae,* in which the state was to take over as parent if the welfare of the child was in danger.[6] This fear of moral loss, as Friedman recounts, can be seen in the fact that, in the early years of the system, most youth were brought to the courts by their parents, not by the police. In other words, some parents "*used* the courts, as a club over rebellious children. It was a weapon in a culture clash—a clash of generations, especially between old world parents, at sea in America, confused about values."[7] While intended, in many respects, to provide a safe haven away from the harsher punishments of the adult system, early juvenile justice came to rely on a strange practice: it placed those youth actually found guilty of a criminal offense with those youth who were not charged with a crime, but were simply poor. In Friedman's words, it lumped "bad and bad-off children together."[8] The system, then, was animated by causal beliefs concerning the ever-present *potential* for crime that youth in poverty represented. And, perhaps not coincidentally, the growth of juvenile justice also coincided with early criminological theories that, as criminologist Nicole Rafter has shown, were united in a "concern with the criminal's poor intelligence."[9] This concern, she argued, "formed the bridge between criminal anthropology"—which famously claimed that criminals were evolutionary "throwbacks"—"and its successor, defective delinquency theory, which identified criminality with 'feeble-mindedness.'"[10] Crime, hence, lay coiled in waiting, and its ever-present potential could be read in the outward signs of skulls, body shapes, IQ scores, and, most important for this discussion, the actions and styles of the young.

This practice of putting the guilty with the potentially guilty—which stemmed from the fear of moral loss as well as the urge to protect youth from that potential—led to the creation of a system that was explicitly designed to shield youth from the pains of adult punishment, but, paradoxically, came to expose them to far greater punishment. Often called "net widening," this unintended consequence of creating more punishment through efforts to create less eventually spurred many to afford more due process rights to those caught up in the juvenile justice process. Essentially, the history of juvenile justice showed that "saving" the children really meant punishing them for crimes they had not yet committed but one day might. It reflected a pervasive fear that a loss of control over the young's moral development would mean a total loss of morality itself, a situation that is indefinitely, always on the horizon. It is a widespread fear that the next generation will be missing an essential component of full humanity and personhood. The potential, that is, seems dire, and requires immediate and serious measures such as punishment to prevent.

This ever-present, almost-here moral loss that has characterized the treatment of youth—and that requires the equally strong force of punishment to counteract it—also characterizes the treatment of crack, which, as I showed in chapter 2, was originally perceived as just such a harbinger of moral and social decay. And this is precisely what the paradox of *impure purity* suggested—a drug so simple that its danger lay in the fact of its apparent nondanger. Crack, although less dangerous than freebase, and inherently less pure than powder, was threatening primarily through potential and possibility. It is no coincidence, then, that criminologist John DiIulio's famous article, "The Coming of the Super-Predators," appeared in 1995, just after the peak of crack-era violence, and stands—and will stand perhaps forever—as the most apocalyptic account of potentially dangerous, morally lost youth to date.[11]

DiIulio had become concerned about a new breed of ruthless youth on the horizon—"ever-growing numbers of hardened, remorseless juveniles who were showing up in the system"—and pronounced that "Americans are sitting atop a demographic crime bomb." He was concerned about "elementary school youngsters who pack guns instead of lunches," "kids who have no respect for human life and no sense of the future." Describing his own research in juvenile facilities, he claimed to encounter an ever-present "buzz of impulsive violence" and was frightened by young people with "vacant stares and smiles" and "remorseless eyes." DiIulio, thus, perfected the connection between youth and moral decline, calling his insights "the theory of moral poverty": "Moral poverty is the poverty of being without loving, capable, responsible adults who teach you right from wrong."[12] For DiIulio, "Moral poverty begets juvenile super-predators" who "live by the meanest code of the meanest streets," which "reinforces rather than restrains their violent, hair-trigger mentality."

Given that rates of juvenile violence—like all violence rates—have been steadily declining since the 1990s, this kind of rhetoric might seem at least outdated if not outrageous. This emphasis on moral poverty in the making of superpredators, however, is very much alive and well. The "baggy pants" laws with which this chapter began are simply its newest, seemingly trivialized manifestation. Indeed, this kind of reasoning was evident in comedian Bill Cosby's speech during the fiftieth anniversary of the *Brown v. Board of Education* decision, in which he railed against the "lower economic and lower middle economic people" who were not, in his words holding up "their end" of the deal.[13] He exclaimed that "people with their hat on backwards, pants down around the crack" must "be a sign of something," and that, fundamentally, it signaled that people had forgotten how to parent, with profoundly negative results. "Looking at the incarcerated," Cosby claimed, "these are not political criminals. These are people going around stealing Coca Cola. People getting shot in the back of the head over a piece of pound cake!"

And it was Cosby's supposed pulling of "a generational fire alarm" that has inspired journalist Juan Williams to place highest blame on "bad parenting, drug dealers, hate-filled rap music and failing schools."[14] Williams has argued that "alarming dropout rates, shocking numbers of children born to single mothers and a frightening acceptance of criminal behavior . . . has too many black people filling up the jails."[15] For both Cosby and Williams, rap signifies little more than a "self-destructive message being beamed into young, vulnerable black brains."[16]

Thus, from Victorian London to the *favelas* of Brazil, from academic criminology to frustrated journalists and entertainers, fears about the ever-present potential for moral decay mark public debate at every turn. And, for many, it is precisely rap's focus on crack that represents moral loss par excellence. This moral transformation, I contend, can be seen most powerfully in the Notorious B.I.G.'s song, "Things Done Changed," which suggests that morality is never an all-or-nothing affair, even in the most murderous circumstances, and that the young people who adapted to the social disruptions of the crack era left their own accounts of how violently painful those adaptations have been.[17]

Things Done Changed

The still unsolved murders of the Notorious B.I.G. and Tupac Shakur remain two of the most important events in rap's history. Their murders provide fundamental events around which current artists orient their own careers, and remain crucial to the ways in which the rap industry is conceived of by both fans and insiders. In fact, the entire industry can be considered a postmurder environment. Biggie and Tupac are exemplary figures as they represent the possibility of success; they are also cautionary figures as they illustrate the severe stakes that are always at play in the rap industry. Their conflict, according to journalist Kevin Powell, marks the point at which the rap industry as a whole "took this violent turn that hadn't been seen before."[18] While Tupac's murder was deeply traumatic for many, it was not necessarily a surprise. Tupac's near misses with death had already become the stuff of legend by the time he was killed. After being shot five times, acquitted for shooting two off-duty police officers, and sentenced to prison for sexual abuse, Tupac achieved a level of street credibility that far outstripped many rappers' lyrical embellishments. For many, his own violent death seemed only a matter of time. As the epitaph above a famous mural after his death read, "live by the gun, die by the gun."

But Biggie's murder, almost a year after Tupac's, and under similar circumstances that are still unresolved, seemed to solidify this "new violent turn" in hip hop. Biggie's album titles also suggested an eerie prescience concerning his own fate. After all, his 1994 debut album was called *Ready to Die*. And it is "Things Done Changed," the first song on *Ready to Die*, that anchors this chapter, focusing, as it does, on one fundamental issue:

the emergence of a new kind of crack-era, homicidal ruthlessness in the inner city that, in many ways, seems to underline DiIulio's description of juvenile superpredators. The song illustrates the association between crack and youth violence and is a key in describing the transformation— discussed in chapter 2—of culturally bound violence into a new, entrepreneurial, and far more unstable form.

The five-minute narrative introduction starts with the sounds of Biggie's mother giving birth, and follows his life as he goes through various stages of street-induced stress. The introduction ends with a guard saying "you niggers always come back" over the sounds of clanging prison bars. Biggie responds contemptuously, retorting that he'll never be seen in prison again since he's "got plans, big plans."

Biggie begins the song with a question, asking his listeners to recall a time in the not-so-distant past in which neighborhood camaraderie, old hair styles, and, most significant, children's games dominated the scene. People back then wore "waves" and "corn braids," while kids pitched "pennies" and played "skelly." As he puts it, everybody was "all friendly." This old school friendliness is further emphasized by his depiction of community cohesion in the next line, which recounts "lounging" young men, who—while still being members of local "crews"—spent much of their time just hanging out on the "avenues." To be sure, Biggie suggests an exaggerated degree of camaraderie, but his descriptions of relaxed friends and childhood games serve to underscore a sense of innocence that, importantly, sets up what follows. In "1993," Biggie states bluntly, these same crews are now "getting smoked." The next lines go on to delineate how the 1990s mark a profound transformation in the nature of violence itself. Emphasizing the speed, brutality, and seeming impatience of violence in this new age, Biggie warns that talking "slick" will get your throat "slit" since true street hustlers don't play that "shit." The juxtaposition is clear: in this new era, things happen faster and are more brutal. There is no mediation or argumentation, only violence. People no longer "lounge" on the avenues, and the children are no longer pitching pennies on the sidewalk. In the crack era, violence happens fast and is intended to be final. His reference to childhood games has an unmistakable point: people don't play anymore. The antes have clearly been upped, and things are different.

Interestingly, the next lines of "Things Done Changed" seem to reflect DiIulio's superpredators exactly, illustrating a certain glee in this new-found lethality. In this new lethal age, instead of lounging on the avenues,

Biggie and his friends would rather hold guns for fun, smoke weed in building "hallways," and play craps "all day." They also wait for old school crews to start "fighting" so they can preempt their outdated attempts by "lighting" them up with gunfire. And, importantly, the first verse ends in a clear warning: "step away" with those old school "ways"; things done changed.

Biggie, thus, suggests that new ways of being violent in the crack era fundamentally depend on a change from fistfighting to gunplay. Only "stupid motherfuckers" rely on hand-to-hand combat or, even worse, "kung fu." To illustrate, Big recounts a fight in which one of the men tried to "scrap" and wound up with holes in his "back," suggesting the man's fearfulness in running away as well as the ruthlessness of his opponent who shot him regardless. Biggie's references to fistfighting and martial arts recall older traditions of violence that no longer apply, as well as fighting styles that involve discipline and training rather than wild gunning. The old ways, that is, are too complex; in this new age, things need to be kept simple and deadly. The more hectic and real things get, the more simple and lethal people need to be.[19] Simplicity and lethality go hand in hand, and, in a battle between simplicity and complexity, the more lethal wins.

"Things Done Changed," then, clearly resembles a certain superpredator vision of neighborhood life in the wake of the crack era. It also suggests the violent glee of a new generation's rise to power. Take, for example, the last line of the second verse in which Biggie asks the listener to consider "our parents," who—in contrast to our childhoods when they protected us—are now "fucking scared of us." This apparent rise to power, though, is fundamentally premised on the symbolic importance of one primary element in new ways of being violent: the gun.

The Gun

The symbolic importance of the gun has a long history in America, especially in popular culture: the classic six-shot, single-action revolvers of the wild West; the compact snub-nosed revolvers carried by hard-boiled detectives in *noir* films; Prohibition-era tommy guns; as well as the M-16s and M-60s shot one-handed by action stars in the 1980s. Guns are also both praised and reviled in public discourse, with some believing they are the primary causes of America's high homicide rates, and others believing gun ownership is a fundamental freedom guaranteeing self-defense. The primacy of guns in Biggie's account of violent transformations during the crack era, then, can perhaps be read as another example of rappers being overly sensationalistic, dramatic, or, as is often suggested, simply "nihilistic." Certainly, just as the movie *Scarface* has provided rappers with a ready-made model of gangster heroism, the gun provides an easy way to "be" gangsta. Such seemingly "easy" interpretations, however, neglect the profound moral dimensions that accompany the gun's role in the rise of a new generation.

And, in fact, these moral dimensions of the gun have been examined by a number of writers throughout the years. Employing in-depth interviews with incarcerated juvenile offenders, for example, political scientist Bernard Harcourt has analyzed the "sensual, moral, and political economic dimensions of guns and gun carrying among the youths,"[20] and argues that, while they often have conflicting, paradoxical attractions to guns, the youths value them "for their power, for their ability to control their immediate environment."[21] According to one interviewee, "You feel powerful when you have a gun. You get respect."[22] In the words of another, guns are primarily important for people "when they need to overrule somebody. They need that power over somebody."[23]

A similar sentiment concerning the importance of guns in a new generation's rise to power is also vividly revealed in anthropologist Allen Feldman's ethnography of a Northern Ireland facing increasing levels of violence during the start of its political Troubles in the 1970s.[24] In it, he describes a transition from an ideal of the "hardmen," local street fighters tied to distinct neighborhoods and older codes of violence, to that of the "gunmen," paramilitary fighters who represent a change to "violence as a mechanized component of the gun."[25] He argues that these differences signify two moral orders, and that the folk narratives surrounding them encode a historical change between different "periods, forms, techniques, and intensities of violent practice."[26] The introduction and rapid spread of the gun is key to this change. As one of his interviewees describes, "When the guns came out the hardmen disappeared. . . . I used to love chasing all the hardmen. . . . They all carry fuckin' guns now. . . . The Troubles changed the whole lot."[27] This change from hardman to gunman, then, entailed a new era of deterritorialized violence in which the gunman himself became merely an instrument—"the masked paramilitary holding a weapon is a tool holding a tool."[28] In this sense, the violent code of the hardman depended upon violence as both individual and local expression, while that of the gunman depended upon violence—and the men who do it—as instrument.

Essentially, Biggie, Harcourt, and Feldman all point to the profound symbolic role that guns often play in the rise of a new generation. Most important, however, the gun signals not only a new generation's rise, but one that is predicated on a predatory stance toward the old ways. The pleasure Biggie takes in "lighting" up unsuspecting fools who start "fighting" is little different from Feldman's interviewee who admits he "used to love chasing all the hardmen." Both reflect a stance of disrespect, ridicule, and contempt toward old forms of violence. "Step away" with your old school "ways" is a dismissive warning to the old guard. The gun, hence, represents the degree to which "things done changed"—the old ways are bypassed, cast aside, and taunted. Significantly, though, while Feldman and Harcourt discuss the role of the gun in general terms, rap artists, instead, emphasize the kind of gun used. While Feldman's interviewees discuss "guns," Biggie specifies actual guns—especially Tec-9s and Mac-10s—as do most rappers when recounting gun violence. Thus, the symbolic importance of the gun in crack's violent transformations does not lie in the simple fact that "a gun" is used; rather, the gun's power relies on a fundamental aesthetic of violence that forms around the specific tools, and their designs, that make such violence possible.

Take, for instance, the infamous Tec-9 and Mac-10 mentioned above, which are both notoriously unreliable and inaccurate machine pistols with twenty-plus–round magazines that distort the classic look of a pistol into an awkward, spiked menace. The AK-47, which is another rap favorite, has a distinctive banana-shaped magazine, and is associated in American memory with the trauma of Vietnam and the Soviet threat. Perhaps more than any other gun, however, it is the Glock that comes to symbolize the crack era's transformation of violence most vividly. Developed in Austria, and adopted by many law enforcement agencies around the world in the mid-1980s, the Glock was a truly revolutionary pistol that, in the interest of more efficient combat, did away with two of the most recognizable features of modern semiautomatic handguns—the hammer and the safety. Glocks are hammerless, with an internal firing pin that makes cocking and decocking irrelevant. They also have no external safety, only a "trigger safety" that is disengaged as the trigger is pulled. Instead of having to flick the safety or cock the hammer to shoot, Glock users have to do only one thing: pull the trigger. Glocks are not World War II–era 1911s or six-shot revolvers, with forged steel and smooth contours. They have boxy plastic grips and distinctive blocklike slides. Brutish on the outside, their sophistication—i.e., the increased ease with which they are fired—is hidden inside. And it is precisely the Glock's ugly, lethal simplicity that has become imbricated into an aesthetic of new-era violence more broadly. In analyzing what he called the rise of "paramilitary culture in post-Vietnam American," for example, sociologist James William Gibson argued that it was the ugliness of new-era weaponry—the "pistol grips, flash hiders, bayonet lugs (mounts), folding stocks, and metal parts with dull parkerized finishes that didn't reflect light"[29]—that gave them a "lethal aura,"[30] and, correspondingly, a seductive "power-death aesthetic."[31] And, as Gibson has shown, this aesthetic of ugly simplicity is everywhere apparent in this latest chapter in America's long love affair with guns. Consider the opening lines of a recent book, *Living with Glocks: The Complete Guide to the New Standard in Combat Handguns*:

> I kept my first Glock a secret from my closest friends. It was an illicit love affair. . . . [I] felt compelled to conceal my perverted but irresistible temptation to embrace the exotic lightweight polymer, the mind-boggling reliability, the simple reassurance under stress, and the thoroughly unconventional beauty of this new Austrian siren. . . . I was . . . living in sin with a compact little .40 caliber Glock 23.[32]

For this author, Glocks are far more than pure instrumentality. Described as "illicit," "perverted," "irresistible," "exotic," Glocks provide "mind-boggling reliability" and "simple reassurance under stress," which mark them as especially beautiful. Glocks, thus, announce a new aesthetic of violence that arises from the merger of physical ugliness and a "mind-boggling" ability to remain functionally lethal under pressure. Ugliness and lethality blend in this new era of violence to create a "thoroughly unconventional beauty."

A similar specificity suffuses Harcourt's interviews as well, and his subjects are quite aware of the perverse, functional beauty of new-era weaponry. As one seventeen-year-old gang member describes, "'I had me two baby nines. I fell in love with those. They look beautiful to me.'"[33] Another youth recounts a particularly lethal episode, detailing in his description the numerous weapons of new-era violence:

> "He pulled out one of those [AK-47s] and he shot my homeboy and killed him. Shot him in the throat. . . . And then that's when we came and then I had my .45. I mean I had my nine, the Glock, and I started shooting at them. . . . We were in a Blazer, we're like, five. I only had my nine, my homeboy had two .45s, and my other homeboy had a .357."[34]

Harcourt's description of one interviewee's relationship to guns also reveals a whole arsenal of new-era weaponry: "His cousin gave him a Glock .45 semi-automatic to sell. That cousin had about six other guns, including a 12-gauge sawed-off shotgun, a Tech-9, a couple of 9mms, a .357, and a few others."[35] Significantly, however, the way in which the cousin got the Tec-9—one of rap's favorite symbols of new-era violence—perfects the association with crack violence and new-era weaponry: "[H]e traded crack for the Tech-9."[36]

No longer praised as gleaming, glinting, polished steel, new-era weaponry possesses a brutish, choppy crudeness that exerts an attraction experienced as a perverse desire, the flip side of a "classic" love affair. And it is here, in this perverseness, that a new kind of violence is perceived, and its difference relies primarily on a newfound lethal efficiency. Crack violence, that is, is marked by a change within the gun, literally: in its firing pins, hammers, and elongated magazines. Through its lethally simple design, the Glock, perhaps more than any other handgun, has become a metaphor for the overriding experience of crack's violent changes: the absence of safety.

Crack Makes Violence Automatic

The fact that simplicity and lethality go hand in hand in Biggie's description of crack-era violence does not mean he is making a "simple" connection; like their reliance on the iconography of *Scarface*, rappers' references to specific kinds of guns make a direct correlation between, in Feldman's words, "two moral orders." For Feldman, the gunmen represent "tools holding tools," but for Biggie—and for the many rappers who articulate similarly "perverse" desires—the symbolism of the gun suggests a far deeper association that occurred in crack's violent intensifications: rappers give *life* to the tools of new-era violence. Rappers do not simply "like" guns; they *become* them by naming themselves after such weapons—Tech N9ne, Mac-10, 40 Cal., Beretta 9, 40 Glocc. In that naming, rappers perfect, in essence, their own union with new school violence. In becoming violent instruments, they do not simply fall in love with perverse violence; they come to embody it. Take, for example, Biggie's claim: "My mind's my nine, my pen's my Mac-10."[37] Or, an even clearer statement is Nas's song "I Gave You Power," which is written in the first person from the perspective of a living .50 caliber pistol: "My body is cold steel for real / I was made to kill, that's why they keep me concealed."[38] In their unification with crack, rap, and the tools of new-era violence, many rap artists symbolically address the courier-to-kingpin paradox at the heart of crack's punishment rationale by saying, "If I am to be punished as the kingpin I am not, and blamed for the moral decline I did not create, then I will become precisely that which I have been taken to be: I am crack; I am Mac-10." Like the inherently low-level dealers through which crack moved itself, rappers fuse with the tools of crack violence to become, simply, the means by which ugly, revolutionary lethality expresses itself. The fact that so many rappers have indeed been killed by new-era weaponry—and that, in the words of rap artist MF Grimm, getting shot is "now part of your deal"[39]—attests to this reality. Crack's intensified violence, in other words, has become deeply embedded in the work of rap. In order to "be" successful rap artists, many *work to embody*—labor to become—the living counterparts, the cultural adaptations, the breathing contradictions of our paradoxical and disproportionate drug policies.

In chapter 2, I discussed the broad consensus concerning the degree to which extreme violence became a necessary regulatory mechanism in unstable crack markets, resulting in the intensification of non-drug-related violence, and making such violence the norm. When paired with my discussion of the symbolic importance of the gun in this chapter, crack's intensification of violence becomes even more significant. The violent transformations wrought by the crack era are not only changes from fistfighting to gunplay, which, in Feldman's words, mark "violence as a mechanized component of the gun"; in addition, crack violence marks a change *within* the gun: instead of mechanizing it, the crack era made violence *automatic.* Again, Monster Kody's vivid portrayals of these changes in his autobiography are instructive in this regard. After explaining that the "dope has changed everything," for instance, Monster's friend suggests that the automatic nature of new-era violence can be encapsulated in the notion of the "fullie spray"—the lethal potential of fully automatic weapons.

[E]verybody got fullies, so one ride usually is enough now to drop several bodies at once. . . . [L]et me explain what fullies do . . . they *spray* you. Remember when you were shot back in eighty-one, you were hit six times? Bro, Chino just got sprayed with a fullie and he was hit seventeen times! Sprays are permanent. They ain't no joke. We got shit that shoots seventy-five times. I heard that the Santanas got LAWS rockets. The latest things out here are fullies, body armor, and pagers. . . . This shit is as real as steel.[40]

The fullie spray, that is, represents the spread and permanence—both in material bullets and trust-corroding violence—of crack-era ruthlessness. This era is marked not only by a transition *to* the gun, but also by an even more profound transition *from shooting to spraying* and its associated notions of finality and permanence. The vision of the fullie spray announces a change in culture, violence, tactics, and weaponry. Not only are fullies representative of the new age in crack violence, but their actual designs embody this all-pervasive culture of terror. The "spray" symbolizes the intensification, the normalization, and the inescapable spread of new-era violence. Such violence is "sprayed into" community life at all levels through the encroachment of unstable, heavily punished, market-based relations. As Monster's homeboy put it, these changes are "as real as steel." Fullie sprays, in short, mark permanence in two main senses. First is the finality of death. And second is that things done changed, never to go to back to a time when local crews relaxed on the avenues and young kids pitched pennies on the sidewalk. In this way, rap artists—and the crack generation from which so many are drawn—have come to personify crack's experiential fabric by taking it on themselves to become the equally paradoxical counterpart to crack's impure purity: *living lethality.*

Schooled in New School Violence

New-era violence, to use terms heard often in rap, represents a change from "old school" to "new school" violence. True, "school" more generally evokes a battleground between parents and children that is not unique to rap's representation of the crack experience. School is a world that the young must, by law, inhabit, but, by strength of their own wills, often make their own, for better and worse. Schools are liminal spaces between the home and the labor market and are simultaneously tasked with imbuing not only practical knowledge, but moral guidance as well. Even given these broad associations with "school" generally, the representative power that it exerts in rap is considerable. In one common usage, "school" refers to a perceived break in rap eras whereby the "new school" implies a distinct departure from "old school" styles of rapping and music making. Even more telling, however, "school" is often used as a verb—to "school" people means to teach and guide as well as to better or best them. Both of these aspects of the word are important here, and play crucial roles not only in rap slang, but in the symbolic role of crack in rap's reflexive stance toward its own commercialization.

Consider 50 Cent's education in new school violence as he learned it from Grits and Butter, two members of an early drug crew of which he was a part. As he recounts in his autobiography, "I didn't realize that Grits and Butter played by different rules. . . . [T]here was no arguing, no threatening, no facial gestures. For them, everything was pure target."[41] In due course, 50 "began to realize that that's how it gets done. That's when I realized that as long as you don't broadcast your beefs, you get away cold with murder."[42] Grits and Butter showed him that it is better to talk less and shoot more, and 50 soon felt himself change as a result. "I knew something was changing in me. . . . The price of life was getting cheaper and cheaper. . . . I realized that the people that really mattered didn't say. The serious guys knew better than to have any kind of conversation or let anyone know they had any differences with someone."[43] If Grits and Butter had a problem, "they'd just tear someone's ass up. . . . [T]hey . . . altered my thought process. Shooting someone was now nothing to me."[44] 50, thus, chronicles being schooled in new school violence. And, in an even more powerful juxtaposition between old and new, 50 relates the reaction of Butter, one of his mentors in new school violence, to a night-club security guard with whom 50 was about to fight.

> The security guard was one of those older dudes from back in the day, when a mean knuckle game was everything. . . . The security guard looked over my shoulder. His face went blank, like he was seeing the ghost of someone he really didn't like. I turned around and saw Butter running at me, gun first. . . . Butter was running behind the security guard with his hand outstretched, his finger squeezing. . . . With each shot, the security guard's body jerked and changed direction, until he went down on the steps of a junior high school. Then Butter ran over to the security guard and dumped the rest of the clip into him. . . . Out of seventeen shots, sixteen hit their mark.[45]

The fact that the security guard—"one of those older dudes from back in the day, when a mean knuckle game was everything"—died on the steps of a junior high school is profoundly significant, announcing both a literal and metaphorical death of "old school" violence. Not only are schools themselves liminal spaces, but junior high, especially, is a transitional stage between elementary and high school in which the young are neither children nor "true" teenagers. In addition, Butter killed the representative of old school violence *while he was fleeing*, detailing, forcefully, that not only was the old school *running from* the predatory ruthlessness of the new school, but he was killed anyway, shot repeatedly *in the back*, and finished off while he lay dying. Similarly, Butter shot the man sixteen times, which is simply impossible with a six shot revolver, signaling, again, the symbolic power of specific kinds of guns in the rise of new school violence. The representative of old school violence was also, in fact, a security guard, indicating not just the changing of the guard, but, literally, his "passing." Recall, in this respect, Biggie's depiction of the poor fool who tried to "scrap" and wound up with holes in his back. Recall, also, Feldman's interviewee: "I used to love chasing all the hardmen. . . . They all carry fucking guns now." There is perhaps no clearer account of this transformation in violence than 50's: old school violence is dead and gone forever, shot sixteen times and sprayed out of existence. Things done changed.

Loss

The violence represented in underground-era, New York rap recalls, in lyrical form, what the expert consensus concerning the social impact of crack has specified in argumentative form: that a manifold intensification of violence during the crack era fundamentally altered perceptions, understandings, and expectations of violence that continue to this day. In addition, rap's version often seems to coincide with broader—but statistically unfounded—fears about increasing juvenile violence, expressed most ominously in John DiIulio's notion of superpredators. In rap's version, however, there is a key difference: it also expresses a deep sense of loss as a consequence of these changes.

Take, for example, the covers of Biggie's and Nas's 1994 debut albums, both of which display their baby pictures, suggesting the degree to which New York City's lyrical resurgence was based upon coming-of-age narratives. Biggie's album is perhaps the most pronounced example of the disturbing juxtaposition they present: the joy displayed by the smiling baby boy on the cover is belied by both the title, *Ready to Die*, and the opening song, "Things Done Changed," which indicate the degree to which these coming-of-age progressions are suffused with the perception, experience, and acceptance of new school violence.

Biggie's last verse in "Things Done Changed" is most poignant in this regard. What appears during the first two verses to champion a vision of inner-city homicidal mania also mourns the losses that resulted from crack's lethal wake. Biggie starts bluntly, stating that if it hadn't been for the "rap game," he'd still be lost in the "crack game," stuck on a dead end route. But, Biggie continues, things have gotten even "crazier" since he left the game, with ever younger kids taking their makeshift drug operations on the road in order to get rich and "blow up." Invariably, though, within a few months, the bodies start to "show up." This violent reality, in essence, has intensified even more. And, for Biggie, the fact that kids younger than he are dying after trying to sell drugs out of town makes him "wanna grab" the tools of new school violence—the 9mms, the Tec-9s, the Mac-10s, and the "shotties"—out of pure frustration. But, as Biggie relates, even that frustration is itself frustrated since he's continually being called on to identify bodies. "What happened," he demands, to the neighborhood "cookouts"? Everywhere he looks, his friends are being "took out." So, he says to the listener, don't waste his time asking about his reasons for being "stressed." Anyone who has to ask such questions in the midst of such obvious bloodshed has not comprehended how things done changed. In this fashion, the contrast between the baby boy and the young man trying to accept lethality as a way of life suggests a close connection between loss and childhood. In many ways, then, this association also reveals that, at the heart of these changes lies a loss of childhood— that the necessity of new school violence as a regulatory mechanism in crack's unstable marketplace amounted to a loss of childhood for those raised in it. This is no loss of morality, however; rather, "Things Done Changed" both celebrates and mourns the disrupted social stability that once kept such devastating lethality at bay. The song, thus, displays anger and moral outrage at the inescapable nature of crack-era lethality.

Conclusion: From Loss to Adaptation

In their articulations of having been schooled in new school violence, neither Biggie, 50 Cent, nor Harcourt's interviewees present themselves as the creators of this new school violence. Instead, they convey an urgent sense of having been swept into it by forces out of their control. This loss of control suggests that guns—and, more important, specific kinds of guns—become central organizing symbols of control for those who perceive an overwhelming loss of it. And, in becoming the tools of new school violence, many rap artists celebrate the rise of a new generation out of crack's devastations while mourning their inevitable adaptations to the losses that accompanied that rise. Paradoxically, then, new school violence is experienced as a *crushing freedom*. Biggie's frustration with the dead bodies of kids younger than he showing up after they tried to sell drugs out of town makes him want to reach for the very tools by which the youth were, very likely, killed in the first place. Life, that is, moves outside of their control, and they have been recruited to staff a system in which lethal violence is used as regulation, and for which they provide "a never ending supply of new dealers." In this way, the metaphor of crack in the songs of New York's lyrical resurgence reflects an acute apprehension of the roles youth play within a never-ending supply of violent labor in a market they did not create, and at the bottom of which they remain, even while they are treated—legally and culturally—as if they were the kingpins of global criminal enterprises believed to have caused such massive transformations. And, when rappers begin to intentionally promote themselves as if they were the kingpins they are punished for being, public debate often condemns them, simplistically, as lacking morality.

Crack and old school violence, therefore, are presented as inherently contradictory and incapable of coexisting. Where one dominates, the other is killed, shot in the back while running away. It is not that one is moral and the other is immoral. Nor does new school violence represent a moral order that a new generation of youth have, somehow, "lost." In seeming to "glorify" crack's violence, rappers, instead, have presented detailed accountings of the profound transformations that accompanied crack's market volatility, and the rise of a system that now requires violence in order to function. This supposed lack of morality is shown up for what it is: not just a celebration of gaining power, but a cynical comprehension of the lethal changes that older generations have yet to fully understand. Hence, the old school approaches new school violence as "immoral," and its actors as "superpredators" without conscience, while the new school approaches old school violence as if it were a vestigial wing, a pointless dance around the lethality at the core of heavily punished market-based relationships.

Old school violence, then, can only be seen for what it is: a game fit for a time when violent markets had not yet overwhelmed neighborhood relationships. This is why Monster Kody was at a complete loss when trying to understand such violent changes after only four years in prison. Crack, thus, symbolizes the new generation's insight into and experience of profound change, the old school's refusal to admit to these changes, as well as the U.S. government's irrational attempt to shore up a perceived loss of morality through punishment. What is often misunderstood in this pursuit, however, is that morality is never "absent," as if it were an all-or-nothing affair. Crack calls forth not a lack of morality, but a new moral order that has emerged regardless of anyone's control in which low-level, grinding young people are treated as if they were drug kingpins, and punished by a legislated sledgehammer that cares nothing for their actual individual circumstances, ascribing weights to mental states and pretending that "simple" possession is really complex distribution. Crack recalls the loss of childhood stability and camaraderie that is the price paid by so many young people for the incursion of underground markets and the violence used to regulate them. Their only "power" comes from the fact that they "know" old school violence is dead, and, so, they no longer play the game. Youth in the crack era, simply put, adapted to the structural conditions they were given. The cultural work that crack has come to perform in America's criminological structure of feeling, then, articulates a multilayered, conflicted sensibility about that coerced adaptation. Cosbylike criticisms, no doubt, will continue to promote the notion that old school culture—simplistically referred to as "parenting"—can somehow be resurrected and transplanted wholesale into a new world of systemic violence that has already intensified it into obsolescence. As criminologist Elliott Currie has argued, these kinds of moral-loss explanations are not problematic in and of themselves; rather, the problem lies in their "denial that those [moral] conditions are themselves strongly affected by larger social and economic forces."[46]

Fears of juvenile superpredators suggest a collective insecurity about our own role in the problematic moral orders we have helped create for young people through the targeted sledgehammer of crime policy. That new school violence relies on a widespread, perverse love affair with brutal simplicity in part reflects our own twenty-plus-year reliance on a brutally simple punitive calculus: five grams equals five years. In the wake of this severe logic, many rap artists have articulated an equally simple connection: simple possession and simple lethality go hand in hand. In creatively working out the complicated effects of the crack era, therefore, many rap artists have come to personify forms of *living lethality* moving units of *impure purity* in environments of *crushing freedom*. Unfortunately, all too often, public responses to these connections focus on simplistic policies requiring young people to "pull up their pants."

5

Training and Humiliation

Teenagers turned trick, pimped by pedophile labels.
    —El-P in Company Flow, "Blind," *Funcrusher Plus*, 1997

In all of 1990s New York rap, there is perhaps no better example of its emphasis on lyricism than Nas's song, "One Love,"[1] which came out the same year as "Things Done Changed." Written as a letter to a friend in jail, the song describes changes in the neighborhood since his friend's incarceration, and recounts, for example, who had been shot, who was now selling drugs, and who had been arrested. In the last verse, though, Nas turns to the listener, and details coming back home to the neighborhood after taking a short trip to get away from the pressures of new school violence. Needing "time alone," he takes a "two day stay," leaving his 9mm pistol in order to relax "his dome." When he returns, however, nobody is outside except for a twelve-year-old crack dealer. Nas befriends him, and they hang out together on the youth's drug turf. The boy addresses him, explaining that, since people routinely shoot from the project rooftops, he wears a "bullet proof" and holds a "black trey-deuce." Nas then takes the opportunity to *school* the boy, and provide the young street soldier with a way to reign in the intensified, hard-to-control new school violence that, by necessity, had become so thoroughly imbricated into community life that the boy had to wear a bullet-proof vest. "I had to school him," Nas tells the listener, explaining how he told the boy not to be fooled by those who advocate for blind retaliation. He then goes on to underline the fact that the spray of new school violence can cause profound loss when not reigned in, too easily turning to bad "luck" as whole families get "fucked up." Nas's last bit of advice to the youth, therefore, takes the form of a warning against the spray of new school violence: since bad luck occurs far too often in the crack era, Nas tells him to "take heed," and wait till his target's alone so the "right man bleeds." To be sure, Nas's advice is no beacon of nonviolence; it is still a lethal vision of community life. Indeed, his last words to the youth concern ways of killing someone. Fundamentally, however, the song communicates an effort to restrain the spray even while lethality remains a necessary regulatory mechanism in the crack era. Problematically, though, those who too readily dismiss depictions of violence in rap misrecognize the "fact" of violence as a lack of morality—as cold-hearted predation. Rather, what "Things Done Changed," "One Love," and many other songs suggest is that the death of old school violence has been anything but easy for those who have been forced to take part in its killing, and who have been engaged, instead, in a very serious effort to reign in the wild lethality that the crack era engendered. Thus, Nas's song communicates in lyrical form what many researchers have concluded in academic form: that a significant influence on the steady decline of lethal violence in the United States since the mid-1990s has been the growth of "powerful anti-crack norms" that were "catalyzed first and foremost indigenously—that is, from within the street drug scene itself."[2] In effect, many researchers suggest that the profound difficulty of living with the ever-presence of lethality on a daily basis has helped to "make *crack* a dirty word and vilify those who use it."[3]

All too often, however, debates about rap seem to turn on an assumption that the violence it depicts is somehow just an "easy" gimmick, and that, more than anything, such violence exemplifies the seriously detrimental effects of "bad parenting." Youth, in these assumptions, play little or no role in influencing their own lives for the better. Recall Bill Cosby and Juan Williams, for instance, who have placed almost sole responsibility for the problems of the inner city on this notion of bad parenting. But what is it about parenting that so consumes such critics? And how is it assumed to operate in such a powerful way in combating the criminal proclivities of young people?

In fact, since the latter half of the twentieth century, parenting has figured prominently in academic explanations of crime and criminality. And, in many ways, recent criticisms of rap's role in the acceptance of criminal behavior by those who have been badly parented can be seen as populist versions of control theory, or, more specifically, self-control theory, the most important representative of this kind of explanation. In this chapter, I analyze the ways in which rap's reflexive stance toward its own commercialization has consistently reflected serious efforts to restrain new school violence through training regimens that have been fundamentally self-imposed. Rap's expressions of restraint do not refute such explanations, but do problematize the all-too-easy, reductive notion that self-control is an all-or-nothing affair, dependent wholly upon an ill-defined premise of punitive parenting.

Crime in Waiting

Published in 1990, Michael R. Gottfredson and Travis Hirschi's *General Theory of Crime* posits that parenting is the most important element in helping youth develop the self-control that, in their argument, is the sine qua non of noncriminal behavior.[4] Gottfredson and Hirschi's theory relies on two primary moves. First, they return to Jeremy Bentham's hedonistic calculus—"all human conduct can be understood as the self-interested pursuit of pleasure or the avoidance of pain"[5]—as the first premise in their definition of criminal behavior. Second, they argue that, contrary to the views of the public, who are misled about the real nature of crime, "the vast majority of criminal acts are trivial and mundane affairs that result in little loss and less gain."[6] Gottfredson and Hirschi, therefore, make a connection between routineness and ease, arguing that most crime, even white-collar crime, is simple, and requires barely any skill. In their words, "Crimes result from the pursuit of immediate, certain, easy benefits."[7] For Gottfredson and Hirschi, crime is really an inherent property of acts themselves. Consequently, they have provided a vision of crime in which, again, it lies coiled in waiting, an intrinsic element of fun, easy actions that, strangely, exist prior to anybody actually doing them. In essence, then, anyone who has not developed the proper self-control will naturally gravitate toward such inherently fun actions.

It is, however, their discussion of the cause of impulsive behavior that is most important for my analysis. According to them, "all of the characteristics associated with low self-control tend to show themselves in the absence of nurturance, discipline, or training."[8] In other words, "The major 'cause' of low self-control thus appears to be ineffective child-rearing," which, in order to be effective, requires three primary efforts: "(1) monitor the child's behavior; (2) recognize deviant behavior when it occurs; and (3) punish such behavior."[9] Because of the ever-presence of crime, which always exists in potential, the only thing that can prevent its fulfillment is the monitoring and punishing of youth who gravitate toward such easy activities. If youthful indulgence in inherently fun activities is monitored and punished, the logic goes, young people will eventually develop an internal mechanism of self-control through which they will come to recognize such actions as the easy, short-term fulfillment of their own interests and, instead, opt to engage in activities that provide long-term benefit. Crime, in short, is easy, and criminals are impulsive.

At their core, the recent populist versions of control theory—such as those espoused by Bill Cosby and Juan Williams—that exist in criticisms of the relationship between bad parenting, crime, and rap music rest on a fundamentally "simple" premise: no one is monitoring, punishing, or training the youth. Quite to the contrary, however, what rap, ethnographic literature on crack dealing, and research on the crime drop suggest is that youth have been engaged in very serious efforts to monitor, train, and restrain *themselves*. That these efforts have influenced rates of serious violence in the United States is all the more significant as youth have done so even in the midst of severe family and community disruption caused by excessive punishment and despite the near-constant public condemnation of their supposed lack of morality. Nas's song, hence, represents the fact that so many young people in the crack era took it on themselves to become the "old heads" whom sociologist Elijah Anderson argued have become far less important since then.[10]

The loss articulated in "Things Done Changed" and the schooling of the young crack dealer in Nas's "One Love" both convey a serious effort to restrain new school violence. While clearly not intentionally geared toward lowering crime rates, Nas's advice to the young street soldier is an expression of this larger, collective effort—a counterimpulse—to take up where old school codes were forced to leave off. These efforts to restrain new school violence, therefore, do not reject self-control, for they clearly emphasize its role in community cohesion and stability. They do, however, severely problematize the consistently held belief, in both academic and popular criticisms, that self-control is only something that can be given to children through parenting, and that at the heart of good parenting is monitoring and punishing. Unfortunately, such obsessive reliance on punitive parenting as the only thing that can save youth from the ever-presence of crime—which lies coiled in perpetuity, tempting impulsive people with easy gratification—ignores the roles youth have played in influencing declines in real violence. And so, in crack's lethal logic of work, self-control is understood in its most literal sense—selves controlling themselves. Youth, in fact, have been engaged in some of the most difficult gratification-deferring work of the late twentieth century:

rebuilding a semblance of old school codes of honor in order to restrain the spray, and regain some stability even in the face of coercive mobility.

Training

Many rap artists have expressed a clear view that the ruthless lethality at the core of crack-era violence—which transformed from culturally based and expressive to instrumental and corrosive—must be mitigated somehow. While this violence depended upon a move away from the old school, there is a pervasive sense running throughout rap's expressive media that the only way to mitigate ruthless lethality in the service of business is to return to the old school through training. Because lethality constantly threatens to spill over, sometimes the only thing one can do is train and restrain one's own lethal potential, and make a renewed space for the old school in the midst of social disruption.

Recall, from the last chapter, 50 Cent's education in new school violence during which Grits and Butter taught him to "talk less and shoot more." Interestingly, however, 50 also describes engaging in parallel efforts to take those instruments of new school violence and train in ways similar to Nas's instructions to the young crack dealer. As 50 describes, "I practiced shooting . . . near my grandmother's house. I shot at stationary targets—cans, old toys, basketballs, whatever I could get my hands on."[11] In addition, 50 also boxed, the most important benefit of which was the emotional calmness during street violence that practice and training instilled in him. "That's what boxing did for me. It stopped me from getting angry when I fought."[12] 50, that is, learned that much new school violence has no technique, relying, instead, on a raw lethality, and that emotional control is crucial to success in the streets. While the crack era intensified existing forms of violence, diffusing them throughout community life, training—the hard work of selves controlling themselves—holds the possibility of narrowing such violence back down. 50, in his words, became "like a scientist. . . . Before I boxed, I was more likely to fight mad. . . . The guys on the streets had no technique."[13] And, by merging discipline with his street ethos, he found success. "The calmer and more confident I became, the more I fought. The more I fought, the less I got hit. The less I got hit, the more people got stomped in the head. The more people got stomped in the head, the calmer and more confident I became."[14] For 50, training set up an interesting loop: the wildness of the streets may push one to find a way to restrain such violence, but once started, boxing also becomes the training ground for the streets. In addition, training also helped him understand that the drug game was not "simply" about the lethality of the new school; rather, "Once I got it in my head that the [drug] game was as much psychological as it was physical, things changed. I learned that a large part of anything physical in this world is how you think about it mentally."[15]

The calming effects of violence training suggested by 50 also resonate with recent academic work. In his ethnography of a Chicago boxing gym, for example, sociologist Loïc Wacquant argues that the gym is counterpoised against crack-related changes to community life.[16] He suggests that the gym "stands opposed to the street as order is to disorder," and describes "a climate of pervasive fear, if not terror, that undermines interpersonal relationships and distorts all the activities of daily life," arguing that the club is a sanctuary from this terror.[17] His informants also castigate the neighborhood "in merciless terms," since most have experienced violent, predatory crime first-hand. In this fashion, the gym—especially its order, stability, and self-enclosed nature—helps keep people off the street, but also helps them once they are outside. Just as 50 learned, Wacquant's subjects also realized that, in gradually building up their pain tolerance in the gym, they learned not to flee in street confrontations. The gym, thus, represents the "controlled violence of a strictly policed and clearly circumscribed agonistic exchange"[18] in which sparring—the "serious play" that develops a "common rhythm" at the heart of the gym—is considered essential to the boxer's training. Through the punishment of self, and the eventual reaching of "flow," training becomes its own reward, enabling "one to score a victory over oneself."[19] Monastic, repetitive, monotonous, and self-punishing, sparring represents a "regulation of violence in the ring."[20]

Put differently, the crack era's transformation of violence into an unseated, unattached network turned the "serious play" of sparring—through which the old school violence of the hardman was learned and perfected like a craft—into the deadly serious. Recall, for instance, the juxtaposition between the old school play of children and the wildness of new school violence in Biggie's song "Things Done Changed." Recall, also, how Grits and Butter—in their killing of the security guard on the steps of a junior high school—showed 50 that new school violence bypasses old codes of "serious play" and gets right to the lethal point. Sparring, while serious, was the old school "play" of adult violence; crack, hence, killed sparring. When all confrontations become potentially lethal, they inherently carry more weight and are taken more seriously. People stopped playing in the crack era because interpersonal conflicts of all sorts had been transformed into potentially lethal episodes. Talking "slick," in Biggie's words, might lead to getting your throat "slit." As with the symbol of the Glock pistol discussed in the previous chapter, in the crack era, there is no longer an "external safety"—no control from the outside because the outside is now governed by abstract market relations that have no sense of honor. Like 50, many of Wacquant's subjects believe training—in monastic, repetitive, monotonous ways—makes for a "victory over the self," and, thus, for calmer street fighting. Internal control makes for external calm. In this way, they become like islands unto themselves, able to restrain the spray through self-imposed methods of social stabilization.

The ascetic practice of boxing makes the gym a sanctuary from street terror, and, similarly, becoming an old school hardman is often the only sanctuary from new school violence. Essentially, such training helps to remake a place for the old school in ways that now make sense—at the level of the self. Old school ways cannot simply be transplanted wholesale into relationships that have been thoroughly transformed by the ebb and flow of markets and the intensification of violence. The crazy and unpredictable violence of the new school needs to be mitigated by personal toughness. Violence training reinvigorates this old school mentality, and, ironically, difficulty is a sanctuary from the unpredictable. In short, training not only takes work; it is work.

Learning technique is an attempt to reseat unseated violence—to reattach its simple brutality to a code. Most important, however, is that reigning in new school violence by reintegrating old school codes is, fundamentally, hard, grinding work—a remaking of old school community through the making of the self. Through the training articulated in rap's creative reworkings of the crack era, and as evidenced by the declines in real violence ascribed to cultural stigma, the metaphor of crack in rap's reflexive stance toward its own commercialization has also come to symbolize the possibility of restraining the very violence that the crack era inaugurated. Crack's experiential fabric, then, includes patchworks of seemingly incongruent elements—the terror of a Darwinian lethality; a new generation's rise to power; the grief experienced through the losses of life that accompanied that rise; and the possibility of restraining crack's diffused violence through self-control. Such articulations of self-control sit in stark contrast to the "vacant stares" and decaying morality that so many proponents of punitive parenting have attributed to both rap and youth in environments of social disruption. Instead, many rap artists suggest that, while the "old heads" may be gone, young people have stepped in to fill that vacuum in order to regain some semblance of community cohesion.

Humiliation

It is precisely this effort to reconnect the unpredictable power of new school violence to daily work, however, that forms the core experience of humiliation at the hands of the industry. Training sets up this experience of humiliation because it is often successful for those who engage in it. Recall, in this regard, 50's development of calmness and confidence. If training had not been successful for him, then the humiliation he later experienced at the hands of the industry would not have been so painful. Consider how he describes his initial frustrations with the music business, directly referencing Nas's famous line, "somehow the rap game reminds me of the crack game," in the process. According to 50, his first record deal "was only for sixty-five thousand dollars. After lawyer's fees, I was left with five thousand dollars. I was like, Fuck—sometimes the rap game does remind me of the crack game!"[21] It is the next sentence, though, that reveals the problem at the heart of crack symbolism in rap. "But at least in the crack game," he says, "you can lay on somebody. . . . The music industry has a whole separate set of rules that I had to adjust to."[22] 50's frustration highlights the differences between the streets and the music industry and alludes to the methods of possible redress in each. At least in the streets, 50 suggests, there are new school methods that, no matter how brutal, get things done. As I detailed in chapter 2, new era violence was essential to the functioning of underground markets, and its use can be quite efficient and clearly rational.

This difficulty of transitioning to the industry is perhaps most poignantly recounted in Voletta Wallace's memoir of her son, Biggie.[23] Interestingly, Voletta sets up a juxtaposition similar to the one in Biggie's "Things Done Changed": where he set the stage for a description of new school violence, Voletta sets the stage for the profoundly humiliating violence of the music business. She begins her memoir by describing her childhood in a close-knit family in Jamaica, and her later emigration to the United States, a move about which she admits having daydreamed for years. She then discusses her early years in America during which she came up with a five-year plan to become a teacher, went to night school in order to get her General Equivalency Diploma, and—reflecting the safety of discipline discussed above—ensconced herself in a "safe cocoon" of hard work. Biggie's birth was transformative in many ways as it inspired her to focus on childhood education. She remembers doting on Biggie, and that she unintentionally helped him get his nickname by feeding him too well. It is her emphasis on the importance of school, though, that becomes especially pertinent, echoing the symbolic significance of school discussed in the previous chapter. In her words, Biggie was always a "kind and gentle boy," until high school: "That's when he changed. He went from a sweet little boy who loved school to a rebellious youth who hated school. School became the battleground where we had most of our fights."[24]

Biggie was put in Catholic school and did well, but hated it and dropped out at seventeen. He eventually stopped coming home altogether. In Voletta's words, "the streets kept calling." She thought he was wasting a good mind, and that he was out of control—"all of a sudden he'd turned into a disruptive monster."[25] Biggie, meanwhile, began establishing a reputation as a rapper in his neighborhood. She notes that, while he was always practicing in his room, she thought it was just noise: "What I did know was that my son could not sing. In my book, he had a lousy voice."[26] After hearing Biggie's first song on the radio, though, she admits feeling proud. And, soon, Biggie begins talking to her about the possibility of making money as a rap artist. According to Voletta, however, "things started to go sour. It seemed to happen all of a sudden. Christopher started paying more attention to that rap thing and spending more and more time in the streets."[27]

While things were beginning to go sour, Voletta admits that Biggie was "focused and energized," and, in fairly short order, had a record deal, a manager, and some money. But before long, she saw that Biggie was getting a different kind of schooling in the industry, and one that he described as "worse than a serious drug game on the streets."[28] She recalls telling her son not to trust Sean "Puffy" Combs, his manager and head of Bad Boy Records. She thought that Biggie was being too loyal, and that he did not have enough business knowledge, believing that "Bad Boy [Records] was concerned with its self-interests and not ours."[29] And, in turn, her reservations appeared to be accurate as Biggie "found out that he was grossly

underpaid for his publishing rights." In Voletta's words, "My son was part
of a high-stakes game and didn't know the rules."[30] "Christopher," she says,
"accepted the illusion of a friend and mentor for about $25,000. That's the
amount Puffy lured my son with. . . . It was enough money to make my
son believe that Puffy was ready to do anything for him. It was enough to
buy blind love and loyalty."[31]

After Biggie's murder, Voletta lost her love for teaching and became
the full-time manager of his estate. And it was through this experience
that she came to be schooled herself, coming to understand what her son
had meant about the industry being worse than the drug game. In her
words, "I left school to go to another—Music Business School."

> The world that Christopher had thrived in that I'd purposely kept at
> a distance I was now thrust into. Shortly after Christopher's death, I
> got a crash course in contracts, conflicts, and royalty rip-offs. . . . The
> first thing that I learned in Music Business School is that everyone—
> and I do mean everyone—is out for himself. Everyone is looking to
> take advantage of anyone he can. If money is involved, you can and
> will be raped and robbed of it until you and the money are no more.[32]

Essentially, Voletta's description of being schooled in the ways of the
industry revolves around duplicity in the service of predatory complexity.
Biggie, as she recalled, had been "energized" by the possibility of creating a life for himself through the *work of rap*. And it was this new-found
energy that was preyed upon. Biggie's desire to make himself through the
work of rap was a vulnerability that allowed him to be "lured" into a bad
contract by the "illusion" of a friend, which, eventually, suspended his
productive potential.

In describing her experience of the industry as akin to being "raped
and robbed," Voletta makes no simple connection. Instead, she articulates
a specific kind of humiliation that is often experienced as *worse* than violent victimization. Take, for example, 50 Cent's account of how he was
rebuked by his record label after getting shot nine times. "I get shot," he
remembers. "I'm in the hospital 13 days, after that I call back to Columbia
[Records]. I'm like, 'what's up, I'm ready!' And they don't have no answers
for me. That's *worse* than getting shot. Like getting shot is, to me, after
I'm patched up, I'ma be alright."[33] 50's and Voletta's experiences are not
unique, however. Indeed, similar episodes are at the heart of rap's reflexive turn in the mid-1990s.

Rap's Reflexive Outbursts

In many ways, rap's reflexive stance toward its own commercialization began with A Tribe Called Quest's album, *The Low End Theory*.[34] Frustration with the industry was summed up in one line that has since become famous: "Industry rule number four thousand and eighty / Record company people are shady."[35] By vocalizing the shadiness of record companies, Tribe was setting a trend: knowledge of the industry and the way it "really" works is a kind of capital that, if not gained, understood, and heeded, can be one's downfall.

For Tribe, the best way to deal with that frustration is to "know the deal"—to understand not only the big picture, but also the fine print of the record deal itself. In a different song on the same album, aptly titled "Show Business," Q-Tip, one of Tribe's two main rappers, cautions the listener about "the snakes, the fakes, the lies, the highs" that abound in the industry. Setting the stage for the stress and anger that were to become central to New York City's lyrical resurgence during the mid-1990s, Tribe suggests a number of prominent themes that emerged later: frustration with a business perceived as fundamentally corrupt; duplicity that is worse than physical violence; the necessity of "knowing the deal" as a means of protection and self-defense; and, perhaps most significant, the role of the contract in binding one, in perpetuity, to bad deals. In other words, complexity, duplicity, and the suspension of a productive life figure as central in these accounts. Importantly, though, these feelings of being deceived are almost always accompanied by the promise of revenge.

This theme of frustration continued into New York City's lyrical resurgence and could be heard on numerous songs and records. Take, for example, Large Professor, a highly respected producer and rapper whose career has spanned over twenty years, but whose record label troubles have also been the stuff of legend.[36] To the listener, he describes riding the "train," "trying to maintain / Getting lowered in the hole while the record man gain." The injustice of the situation makes him "wanna sting somebody with the shottie / 'Cause I can't relate to living less than great."[37] Large Professor, that is, expresses that very desire to labor, to make something of himself through the work of rap. Each day, however, while he rides the subway, barely able to "maintain"—to keep his head up in the face of adversity—the "record man" gains from his creations, both causing and ignoring a humiliation and frustration so deep that it makes him want to shoot "somebody with the shottie," the very tools of new school violence.

Likewise, Jeru, another well-respected artist who got his start in the 1990s, articulates a similar notion. "My company fucked up my project's momentum," he says to the listener. "I came to the table with snakes" while executives "put figures on my plates."[38] Similarly, for Company Flow, an influential underground group in the 1990s, the source of label violence is to be found in the backbone of the system itself—paperwork and contracts. For El-P, the group's main producer and one of its two rappers, his past experiences with the industry have been so humiliating that he promises to die before he would ever go through another episode like it. "Never again," he warns, "I let a record label trap me" with "paperwork that leaves me empty / Gas me to dis me / I swear to god you'd have to kill me."[39] Perhaps the most pronounced contempt and frustration, though, came from GZA, a founding member of Wu-Tang Clan, one of the most influential groups of the era, whose music merged the wildness of new school, crack-era violence with a deep respect for both mental and physical training through chess and martial arts. His contempt, while blatantly disrespectful, also suggests the ways in which labels themselves enact their own kinds of violence.

The first line of GZA's verse on Wu-Tang's breakthrough single, "Protect Ya Neck," for example, plays on the famous rap label, Cold Chillin', equating it with probably the most famous legend of duplicity in human history—the biblical story of Cain and Abel.[40] After claiming that record labels "be doing artists in like Cain did Abel," GZA goes on to describe the current situation in which the industry finds itself: "Now they money's getting stuck to the gum under the table." GZA's experience of pain, therefore, is never far from angry contempt. His stance, like that of new school violence toward old school fighting, is one of ridicule. He mocks a system of duplicity that—despite its callous tactics—still "ain't had hits." Labels might treat artists like Cain treated Abel, but they still lose money. So what's the use? In the end, GZA suggests, it will all fall apart, and deservedly so. This sense of labels deserving to lose money precisely because of their duplicity is forcefully evoked in the next line, suggesting that the industry's appropriation of rap for duplicitous ends will be its downfall: "That's what you get when you misuse what I invent / Your empire falls and you lose every cent." Put simply, these ruthless labels that treat people as Cain did Abel do not even know what they are doing, what rap is, or what to do about it; they are both corrupt and clueless, and, like old school violence, will become, simply, obsolete.

GZA's contempt is also palpable in the ways he denigrates foolish aspirants to music industry fame, calling them "non-visual niggas with tapes and a portrait," who all "flood" the same old venues and music seminars staged by record companies in efforts "to orbit this industry." Such people are nonvisual and unable to see—they lack both self-respect and innovation. For GZA, tapes and portraits—which suggest things that are soft focused, weak, and touched up—have no place in real, raw, street rap. He belittles the methods of marketing and promotion created by and for the industry.

While most of his contempt is saved for labels and the fools who follow them, he also attacks the more sinister aspects of the industry in "Labels," a song that plays on the names of no fewer than thirty-nine different record labels.[41] The song's intro, spoken by the group's famous producer, RZA, is one of the more explicit statements of label violence up to that point, suggesting, as RZA does, that the industry's actions are clearly intentional.[42] "Lot of people, they be getting misinformed," RZA begins, "thinking . . . that you could just get yourself a little deal, you gonna get on, you gonna get rich." Importantly, RZA indicates that, by preying on that initial vulnerability, "all these labels be trying to lure us in like spiders into the web." The next line, however, captures the essence of rap's reflexive stance toward its own commercialization, as RZA sees it as his *duty* to school those who do not yet understand. "So sometimes people gotta come out and speak up, and let people understand . . . if you don't read the label, you might get poisoned."

In addition, by using no fewer than thirty-nine labels as lyrics, GZA, in fact, *schools the industry*, a reversal of what's normally done to artists. In the first line of the song, for example, he begins by making fun of Tommy Boy, a well-known hip hop record label, saying "Tommy ain't my motherfucking Boy" since it "fakes moves" against those it "employs." GZA also shows that labels are not what they seem; often they are owned by other, larger labels while pretending to be independent, with their ears to the street: "Cold Chillin' motherfuckers are still Warner Brothers." Whatever their incompetence and ineptitude, though, labels are still, first and foremost, described as snakes. In rap's conflict with its own commercialization, labels *are* violent; their lies are damaging, and can be, to repeat 50 Cent, "worse than getting shot." The core of the industry's violence, however, lies in its humiliating effects.

Contractual Humiliation

Since sociologist Jack Katz's book *Seductions of Crime*, the concept of humiliation has played an increasingly important role in explanations of criminal behavior.[43] Katz was interested in replacing an emphasis on individual and economic backgrounds that had, so far, framed most explanations of crime, with an emphasis on the "foregrounds" of the criminal act itself—the "experiential dynamics" by which people come to feel compelled toward murder or robbery, for instance. He proposed a "theory of moral self-transcendence," whose central feature was a family of "moral emotions," and argued that "the attraction that proves to be most fundamentally compelling is that of overcoming a personal challenge to moral—not material—existence."[44] Many have since borrowed from Katz's work, often depending upon a specific reading of his arguments. For example, cultural criminology—an important and ever-growing orientation within the discipline, which has been described as "an emergent array of perspectives linked by sensitivities to image, meaning, and representation in the study of crime and crime control"[45]—has adapted Katz's notion of experiential foregrounds to a concept of "edgework": "a developing area of interest in criminology [that] explores the sensual motivations and experiential frameworks for illicit social action, and investigates the associated moments of marginality, recuperation, and resistance."[46] For many cultural criminologists, then, edgework's focus on "moments of voluntary risk taking" holds the promise of studying "transgressive practices," and can "offer a glimpse of alternative nomadic ways of being that emerge and become visible inside, but to some degree outside, an actuarial order."[47] Interestingly, however, in shifting emphases from backgrounds to foregrounds, Katz appeared to articulate a vision of sensual determinism whereby the mundane world is intensified, not escaped. In his words, "A sense of being determined by the environment, of being pushed away from one line of action and pulled toward another, is natural to everyday, routine human experience."[48] Similarly, in analyzing the moral emotion of rage that moves people to "righteous slaughter" in order to avenge humiliation, Katz argued that "we should not err by treating rage as an escape from humiliation."[49] Crime, risk, and edginess, therefore, do not necessarily create zones outside the social order, but, instead, hot spaces right in its belly. Moral transcendence does not escape order; it makes and remakes it through fire and fury. Consequently, rap's reflexive stance toward its own commercialization—in which humiliation and moral outrage figure as key—does not reflect an attempt to get out, but, rather, to get in.

In discussing the role of humiliation in "righteous slaughter," for example, Katz argued that, "[w]hen the assailant suddenly drops his air of indifference, he embraces his own humiliation."[50] And, importantly, in doing so,

> He then makes public his understanding, not only that he was hurt by the victim, but that he was falsely, foolishly, and cowardly *pretending* not to care. In this double respect, the once-cool but now enraged attacker acknowledges that he has already been *morally* dominated just as he moves to seek *physical* domination. He becomes humiliated at the same time and through the same action in which he becomes enraged.[51]

Katz goes on to contend that "[h]umiliation may be experienced when there is a revelation to you about the conduct of others. Thus, you may become humiliated at the sudden revelation of the misleading and immoral acts by which others have long treated you as a fool."[52] Humiliation, in short, lies in the perception that others' "help" is offered in an "aggressive, demeaning spirit,"[53] and is felt in the "overt intention by others to degrade me."[54]

For Katz, rage, humiliation, and the effort to redress degradation occur simultaneously. In becoming enraged, one's humiliation is made public at the same time that one moves to avenge it. Importantly, though, in rap's reflexive stance toward its own commercialization, humiliation is not simply made public; it is *recorded for, distributed to, and consumed by millions.* In their moral outbursts, rappers are often admitting their own vulnerabilities on a vast public scale, betraying a significant amount of pain even while they brag and boast about their own success. These moral outbursts, while seemingly random, take on far more significance when viewed as a whole, expressing, collectively, humiliation, rage, and violent redress. Recall, for instance, Large Professor, whose constant humiliation at the hands of the record man makes him want to "sting somebody with the shottie." The actions of the industry are experienced as misleading and immoral, and their duplicity is felt as even more degrading because it intentionally preys on vulnerability.

Rap artists, even in their most violent promises of revenge, do not call for an escape, but, instead, signal a moral attack on the ways in which the music industry intentionally suspends artists' productive lives. Rap's promises of violent revenge are, in Katz's words, in defense of the "Good"—the "sacred core of respectability."[55] Rappers are honoring "values typically labeled as middle class or bourgeois: the sanctity of the marital union, respect for property rights, and the importance of being a responsible debtor."[56] Rap artists—like anthropologist Philippe Bourgois' crack-dealing subjects—are "frantically pursuing the American dream," and their anger cannot simply be read as efforts to escape the current order, examples of mere reflection, potential political resistance, or gimmicky sensationalism.

In expressing their moral outrage, vulnerability, and desire for vengeance, many rap artists since the 1990s have articulated themes that have long been deeply intertwined with what criminologists—as I outlined briefly in chapter 3—call white-collar crime. Edwin Sutherland's classic statement of "White-Collar Criminality" in 1940 was a watershed in the discipline, reorienting, as it did, criminology away from its focus on biological and intelligence-based theories of criminal behavior.[57] Writing just after the Depression, Sutherland's concept of white-collar crime was premised primarily on the massive consequences of duplicity and broken trust on a large scale. In his view, "white-collar crimes in business and the professions consist principally of violation of delegated or implied trust, and many of them can be reduced to two categories: misrepresentation of asset values and duplicity in the manipulation of power."[58] Sutherland was quite concerned with arguing that "[w]hite collar crime is real crime," and that its social costs far outweigh its financial ones.[59] In his words, "The financial loss from white-collar crime, great as it is, is less important than the damage to social relations. White-collar crimes violate trust and therefore create distrust, which lowers social morale and produces social disorganization on a large scale."[60] As criminologist David O. Friedrichs has argued, Sutherland's "personal sense of outrage at corporate criminality was clearly a strong motivating factor in his work."[61] And it is precisely this sense that duplicity in business "lowers social morale and produces social disorganization on a large scale" that continues to animate scholarship to this day. It is the widespread belief among both academics and popular critics that the most damaging effect of business-related manipulation is that, in criminologist Gil Geis's words, it sets examples that tend to "'erode the moral base of the law'" since many "'corporations and their managers'" are often well-respected leaders.[62] Put differently, "When the rules of the game by which the free enterprise system operates . . . are disregarded, the entire system is endangered."[63]

To be sure, rap artists since the 1990s have not contributed to scholarship on white-collar crime. As their efforts to train and restrain new school violence, however, mix with the music industry's business-as-usual duplicity, rappers' reflexive stance toward their own commercialization signifies very real, serious, and collective indictments of the *moral base* of *the work* of the industry, effectively communicating that the young people who have become "energized," as Biggie had, by the prospect of remaking themselves through the work of music simply should not be treated with such disdain. Recall, in this regard, the similar experiences of humiliation articulated by rock-and-roll artists discussed in chapter 3. Tom Waits, for instance, said it was a "nightmare to be trapped" in the corporate music system. Rap's conflict with its own commercialization, though, is different from these expressions because it promises violent redress, and—in the process of articulating its humiliation—adopts the *predatory stance* of new school violence toward this newly experienced form of white-collar duplicity. In rap, expressions of pain, rage, revenge, ridicule, and contempt go together. And, in conveying such emotions, rap artists evoke both Sutherland's "personal sense of outrage at corporate criminality" and Susan Shapiro's reformulation of his original status-based definition around the fundamental importance of duplicity.

While Katz's arguments concerning the moral emotion of humiliation provide alternative ways in which rap might be understood, the music industry effects an even greater form of humiliation in the form of the contract: while public rage exposes the fact of one's vulnerability, in the contract—which suspends one's productive potential without providing a physical means of redress—one's humiliation becomes *inescapable*. In chapter 3, I suggested that rap's conflict with its own commercialization articulated anger at, in Shapiro's words, the lies that "abound in the ordinary world of work."[64] It is duplicitous, in other words, when white-collar agents operate with the knowledge that their principals do not understand the true consequences involved with the deal. In such situations, the implied consent of the "contract" becomes, simply, a proxy for intentional obstruction, if not outright duplicity. Rappers' claims about the rap game reminding them of the crack game, thus, stem not from efforts to sound sensational but from the accumulated experiences—personal and second-hand—of being duped, or repeatedly being lied to, for example, by one's drug suppliers, who claim product is pure when it has actually been adulterated, or who use rigged scales when distributing weight. The problem is that the record contract explicitly eschews the trappings of a "drug deal" and, instead, is presented as its antithesis—similarly situated individuals voluntarily coming together to create mutually beneficial agreements. Rappers do not articulate simple naiveté, but emotional outrage at a drug deal—a complex business agreement fraught with serious consequences—being dressed up as if it were a fair game.

The industry's violence, then, is experienced as "worse than getting shot" because it suspends one's productive potential through contract, postponing the possibility of normalizing the modicum of stability that had been achieved through victories over the self. Through the contract, one's vulnerability is not simply shown up and made public; *it is preserved*, perhaps indefinitely. Contractual language fossilizes one's humiliation by preserving the double-cross as well as the initial vulnerability that made it possible. The attempt to reign in new school violence through the work of rap—making rap into a nonhumiliating space of self-creation—is not only denied, but suspended in contract, and made untouchable by violent means alone. In the industry, one's humiliation exists in a fundamentally different realm. Note, in this regard, the actual language used by rappers to express their humiliation. "Lured" and "trapped" in "webs" of disrespect. "Never again," El-P warns, "I swear to god, you'd have to kill me." The violence of the industry is worse than getting shot, as 50 remarks, precisely because, after getting physically "patched up," one will be "alright." The physical is repairable; flesh and blood provide boundaries; they indicate when injuries have healed. The violence of contractual suspension gives no such advantage, and no sign of healing. Rap artists relate experiences of being duped, jerked, fucked, lied to, surrounded by snakes, and locked in contractual webs that threaten to suspend their productive potentials in perpetuity. It is the humiliation of being made the fool and the violence of being locked in one bad decision. While the lethality of the streets lies in the finality of physical death, the violence of the industry results in a special form of lethality: the death of a productive life left to rot in perpetuity on the shelf in someone's office. The humiliation of the industry is doubled by the contract, and further compounded because it completely negates the efforts to reseat new school violence through training. "[A]t least in the crack game," 50 explains, "you can lay on somebody." In the contractual game, however, the language that now preserves one's humiliation requires the help of professionals to decode, which recruits others into the knowledge of one's vulnerability. The humiliation of being duped must now be explained, patronizingly and expensively, by others, like a joke that everyone but you seems to understand. Recall, hence, RZA's sense of duty to "come out and speak up, and let people understand . . . if you don't read the label, you might get poisoned."

Conclusion

For many rap artists, stabilizing new school violence through training comes into conflict with a different kind of violence—that of the industry. While violence practice may help mitigate the lawlessness of the street, in order for one to transition into the rap game, industry training itself becomes essential. This knowledge, though, is usually harder to get and, most often, can only be gained by being taken advantage of first. In addition, the training that reseated unpredictable violence is found to be useless in transitioning to the industry. And, the inability of violence training to translate to the white-collar world is often felt as humiliation.

All of this pain amounts to a kind of exploitation for which violence is sometimes seen as the only redress. It is not the simple fact of duplicity, but that such duplicity becomes far worse when rap artists are trying to make a moral switch from unpredictable lethality to more stable forms of work. In transitioning out of new school violence by remaking a place for the old school, many rap artists find themselves in a new world of white-collar duplicity whose effects are, in every way, experienced as violent. At bottom, through this experience of humiliation, new school violence becomes seen as a necessary form of regulation to be brought back into the music business. Such exploitation at the hands of the industry provokes promises of revenge—to never let it happen again and to make things right.

The symbolism of crack in rap's reflexive stance toward its own commercialization concerns the remaking of a world around a moral order in which hard, grinding work figures as key. The violence that comes to be associated with the rap industry—especially in the figure of Suge Knight, the subject of the next chapter—often revolves around attempts to disrupt humiliation from its contractual state of frozen animation, and to return the possibility of a productive life.

%⁄ 6 %⁄

Facing the Corporation

Pay us like you owe us.

—Jay-Z, "Izzo," *The Blueprint,* 2001

On September 6, 1996, Tupac Shakur was shot four times as he sat in the passenger side of a car while Suge Knight—the head of Tupac's label, Death Row Records—was driving both of them to a club in Las Vegas after attending a Mike Tyson fight. Tupac died six days later. His passing was deeply felt by fans, fellow rap artists, and the entertainment community. On March 9, 1997, Biggie was also shot four times in the passenger side of a car after leaving a party in Los Angeles. He died that night. His passing was similarly mourned by fans and colleagues. And, in September 1997, Suge Knight was arrested and imprisoned for a parole violation stemming from his participation in a fistfight in the lobby of a Las Vegas hotel less than an hour before Tupac was killed. Since then, Suge has been in and out of jail on numerous charges, and has filed for bankruptcy.

The deaths of Biggie and Tupac remain significant, defining events for the rap industry as a whole. But the story of Death Row Records—which has been described as having "set the framework for a whole new way of doing business in the music business"[1]—is just as defining, providing, as it did, a bridge between the two violences addressed in this book: new school violence and industry exploitation. And it is the mythology that has grown around the figure of Suge Knight that sits at the core of this intersection. In fact, Suge's mythology grew concomitantly with New York rap's reflexive turn, both of which came to stand for the real possibility of avenging the industry's humiliating effects. Both, that is, adopted the predatory stance of new school violence toward the asymmetrical nature of the music business. Because of the East Coast versus West Coast conflict with which the murders of Biggie and Tupac will always be associated, however, Suge and underground New York rap are often seen as enemies. The two, though, cannot be separated; they both depended on each other. In short, the promises of revenge that accompanied the lyrical rage analyzed in the last chapter find their symbolic satisfaction in the figure of Suge Knight. In reality, Suge only dealt with a handful of artists, but his actions have come to represent the possibility of redressing the humiliation that many others expressed only lyrically. Suge's mythology, therefore, gives lyrical warnings physical weight, and reveals the moral battles at the center of much industry-related violence. His myth is "not just legal," as one journalist put it, but it *makes the legal personal*, reminding the suits in the suites that there are consequences to their actions.[2]

In this chapter, I analyze the complicated mythology of Suge Knight as it has evolved into a composite picture through multiple popular sources. In both criticism and praise, Suge's story is an important re-creation myth for crack-era rappers as it exemplifies the possibility of *success without subservience*, a possibility that continues to operate as a core element in rappers' own life stories even if Suge himself has retreated from the spotlight.

Suge as Hero

Suge, like Biggie and Tupac, has come to be more myth than man. And, also like Biggie and Tupac, his mythology provides the rap industry—and the many aspiring artists and executives that strive to succeed in it— with an exemplary and cautionary tale. As journalist Ethan Brown has shown, the migration of street hustlers into the music business—which has become a defining feature of the rap industry as a whole—is almost invariably believed to be personified most powerfully by Suge. In Brown's words, tales of "bat-wielding thugs working over music industry execs took on mythical status within the hip-hop industry. Budding hip-hop impresarios studied Suge's hardball tactics with great envy."[3] Suge did not begin his career as a myth, however. According to many, in the early years of Death Row Records, Suge was "just a big kid," "totally nobody."[4] The famous rapper Snoop Dogg—who was an original artist on Death Row— described him as being quiet, humble, behind the scenes: "he was invisible, the invisible man."[5]

Although Suge was to become a larger-than-life character, he is most often described as having had an innocent, even "idyllic" childhood, and, as a result, is somewhat of a liminal figure in the rap industry. "Suge Knight's childhood was idyllic compared to that of most youngsters in his Compton neighborhood. He had two gainfully employed parents. . . . [H] e was an athlete."[6] As Dick Griffey, one of his former partners, said, "Suge wasn't a gangsta. Suge came from a family; his mother and father are still together. He was a college football player."[7] Consequently, the first element of Suge's composite emphasizes his liminality—a child of the ghetto who, nevertheless, was cushioned from some of its most destructive forces.

Because of his size and athletic ability, Suge was able to attend the University of Nevada–Las Vegas on a football scholarship. By many accounts, Suge was a nice guy during his time at UNLV. By his senior year, however, Suge is believed to have gone through significant changes. "On campus, he was regarded as a big, friendly guy who slapped backs, told jokes, and indulged with remarkable moderation in drugs, sex, and alcohol. . . . During his senior year, though, Suge became a more remote and mysterious character."[8] Suge began working as a bouncer and, eventually, as a bodyguard for singer Bobby Brown, a job he described, interestingly, as a form of industry schooling, and to which he attributed his eventual rise in the music business. "[B]eing a bodyguard," Suge explained,

> is probably one of the best music industry schools you can go to because you're gonna learn everything about the business. . . . I was out there looking and learning and I seen the different people complain, I seen artists, I seen people trying to be artists, I hear people talking about songs, I'm just listening, hearing it all.[9]

Suge soon became an industry consultant, and, with his early artists, "practiced what would prove his greatest skill as a businessman, exploiting an artist's vulnerability."[10] The second element in Suge's myth, then, builds on his liminality, and foreshadows the primary role he was to play as a bridge between street violence and industry exploitation. And Suge's first mythmaking event in the development of this role was his "punking" of the popular white rapper Vanilla Ice.

As Suge made further inroads into the business as an industry consultant, he started managing an artist named Mario Johnson who had written a number of songs for Vanilla Ice, as Johnson claims, "on the kitchen table at his [Vanilla Ice's] house."[11] According to Johnson, however, while he had gotten credit for his work, he never received any money for it, which—after Vanilla Ice's biggest hit, "Ice, Ice Baby," began making money—became a serious problem. Johnson claimed that Vanilla Ice tried to pay him off, but that Suge wasn't having it. Ice recalls that, one night, Suge came to see him in a restaurant: "'And I was sitting there, eating a nice meal, and all of a sudden these huge guys—it looked like a football team—showed up.'"[12] Vanilla Ice claimed that later, in his hotel room, Suge demanded he pay Johnson a percentage of the publishing rights, and hung him over the balcony until he agreed. In Vanilla Ice's words, "You can look at it as I was an investor in Death Row Records with no return on my money."[13] Vanilla Ice later denied the story, however, claiming that there was no bad blood between them, and that the balcony incident never happened. Despite legal records showing that Suge had to sue Vanilla Ice's record label, EMI, in order to receive any money, the story of the balcony incident stuck, solidifying Suge's growing reputation in the industry. And, as word of Suge's ability to cut through industry complexities and take care of his artists spread, he began to get other clients who needed similar help. The most famous of them was Dr. Dre, who, according to a former partner, "had the worst contracts I'd ever seen in the history of the record business."[14] Dre's story, though, begins with his attempt to leave the most famous and genre-defining gangsta rap group of all time, Niggas With Attitude (N.W.A.).

According to legend, N.W.A. was originally put together and financed by Eazy-E, a local crack dealer from Compton who decided he wanted to make records. As Jerry Heller—a well-known rock-and-roll agent who eventually became Eazy's business partner—put it, "If Eazy made N.W.A., then rock made Eazy. Not rock 'n' roll, but rock cocaine."[15] Eazy—who "never intended to be a rapper," but, instead, "wanted to be a financier"[16]— met Dre through Lonzo, a local music promoter, who had originally introduced him to Heller. As Dre would later describe the Eazy-Heller partnership, "The white boy came in and kind of fucked it all up."[17] As money started coming in from different projects, relationships between group members began to sour. For example, Eazy's solo album, *Eazy Duz It*, was written by fellow N.W.A. member Ice Cube and produced by Dre, but the money generated from its sales, according to many, was never split up fairly. Eazy allegedly wanted to keep all the money from his solo record and share only the proceeds generated from the N.W.A. project. In addition, N.W.A. had no written contracts until Heller came into the picture and demanded that the group sign in order to receive their checks. In characterizing his own view about contracts in the industry, Heller, bluntly, says this: "Locking an artist into a recording contract might resemble some form of medieval patronage, but that's the way things are done."[18] As the story goes, Ice Cube was the only one who did not sign the contract and "was soon telling band mates they were being robbed."[19] Eventually, Cube says, Eazy and Heller told him to "fuck off."[20] Cube's departure and the success of his subsequent solo career generated one of the rap industry's biggest conflicts. As Kevin Powell, a journalist who has covered rap since the 1990s, said, the on-record arguments between NWA and Cube "upped the ante" for all dis records, introducing serious threats of violence into the industry, which has become, in the opinions of many, an integral element of the current rap game.[21]

Before long, the remaining members of N.W.A. wanted out of the group as well. In order to secure his release from Eazy and Heller, Dre sought out Suge, both of whom then decided to form their own label, Death Row Records, in the process. Eazy did not want to let go of Dre, however, and had to be persuaded "to make some moves."[22] As the story goes, Suge went to see Eazy and Heller with friends and baseball bats and "convinced" them that Dre no longer worked for them. As Heller recounts, "Suge Knight walks into the studio through the control room door, and he brings along muscle. A pair of them, big-shouldered guys, each carrying a Louisville Slugger, handling the maple bats as if they are toothpicks."[23] Essentially, Suge's composite serves as a re-creation myth of sorts in which his liminal nature was transformed into his greatest strength. Neither experiencing the worst of ghetto life nor breaking into the music business in the usual way, Suge merged elements of both the streets and the suites to develop his own specific method of success. In his words, "I feel I got a whole, whole lot of street credibility and street smarts. And at the same time, I graduated from college . . . I hit the books and I put both of them together."[24]

As I have tried to show in previous chapters, rap's conflict with its own commercialization has never been "simply" about business. And Suge, who is a central figure in this reflexive turn, is symbolically powerful not only because he made money. Suge is significant, instead, because he is a morally charged figure who stands for the redress of an immoral system, and his actions cannot be explained away as business strategies executed in the service of making money alone. Recall, for example, that his career in the industry began, tellingly, at the intersection of the corporeal and the corporate. That is, as a bodyguard for artists, Suge was schooled in the business of industry exploitation through the protection of bodily capital. Where Biggie, Nas, and 50 Cent were schooled in the ways of the industry through personal humiliation, Suge never set out to be an artist; instead, he learned by "just listening, hearing it all." In other words, Suge learned the corporate by protecting the corporeal, and, in protecting flesh and blood commodities from possible corporeal violence, he was able to develop a key skill: using physical violence to extricate people from the violence of contractual suspension.

In fact, Suge specialized precisely in extricating his clients not only from bad business deals, but from deals that had become *intolerably humiliating*, which had *suspended* his clients in a state of *perpetual humiliation* into which—to borrow a phrase from the last chapter—they had been lured "like spiders into the web" and trapped in contract. Suge had come to understand—in his role as bodyguard, not as artist—that the violence of the industry is not impenetrable. And he proved it by breaking contractual ties with baseball bats, and securing publishing points by threats of death, effectively negating the lies that "abound"—as Susan Shapiro famously put it—"in the ordinary world of work."[25]

For the generation of rap artists raised in the crack era, then, Suge's mythology shows that the often humiliating conditions created by an industry predicated on asymmetrical relationships are not necessarily binding. While 50 Cent and others suggest that violence training can calm street lethality, Suge's story highlights the degree to which it can also simplify suite complexity. While bringing discipline to the streets is calming, bringing the streets to the industry is simplifying, focusing, and ruthlessly effective. New school violence cuts through violent complexity. Sometimes the streets need a little technique, the suites a little violence. Suge, therefore, signals a reversal of power through a fundamental disrespect of business as usual. Just as the rise of new school violence was based on a predatory stance toward the old school, Suge's rise became a symbolic reference for the way the work of rap has been conceived of since the crack era, which takes a contemptuous position toward music industry practice. Suge—like GZA and Biggie—articulates contempt for the old ways that he sees as useless.

Consider, in this regard, Suge's discussion of the key problems he sees in the industry. The "older guys" in the business, Suge says, only want to "sit you down and say, 'Look, ok Suge, you say you're a young entrepreneur, this is what we're going to do: Give me all the stuff you got—give me your tapes, give me your masters, give me your groups—and I'm going to go over there and make you a deal.'" Suge's response, however, was to say "look, I ain't no punk. You ain't got to talk for us. We're going to go in there and speak for ourself. Instead of getting a dollar, we want five. *And our masters, and our ownership*."[26] Suge's mythology, thus, announces a crucial break with the industry's methods of humiliation, which relied, chiefly, on the ignorance and vulnerability of artists who had yet to understand the two key imperatives discussed in chapter 3: keep ownership of your master recordings, and never give up your publishing rights. In the process of *punking the industry*, Suge used a new school stance toward violence to bring the complexity of the industry back down to earth.

Criminal Violence as Productive

To be sure, Suge's mythology is not the first to imply that criminal violence is an efficient means of resolving conflicts in the business world. Take, for instance, the classic scene in *The Godfather* in which the boss of a movie studio who has denied Don Corleone's request to cast his godson in a role is given an "offer he can't refuse." The studio boss only agrees to the request after waking up beside the severed head of his favorite horse the next morning. While only fiction, the scene suggests the degree to which the myths surrounding the Mafia have relied on a perceived willingness to use extreme violence to solve otherwise legal disputes. And, as music journalist Frederic Dannen has shown, a similar atmosphere of menace also played a key role in the "new payola," a record industry scandal during the late 1970s and early 1980s in which record companies were all but forced to hire "independent promoters" who paid radio station managers to play specific artists.[27] Simply put, the threat of violence is often depicted as being a productive force in the legitimate economy.

Indeed, the notion that crime and violence are socially productive forces has been articulated many times before. In chapter 1, for instance, I discussed the degree to which paradox figures as an essential element in many writers' understandings of the punitive turn in American criminal justice since the 1970s. And, it is often precisely in these paradoxical functions that crime and violence are believed to be most productive. In *The Rich Get Richer and the Poor Get Prison*, for example, philosopher Jeffrey Reiman argues that the criminal justice system's supposed "failures" to reduce crime actually function as successes, both perpetuating the myth that we are helpless in preventing crime, and masking what Reiman sees as its true source: economic disparity.[28] In Reiman's conception, the inherently coercive realities of wage labor in a capitalist society are masked by a rhetoric of choice that contributes to the fundamentally damaging belief that predatory acts of interpersonal violence on the part of the poor are far more blameworthy and threatening to social stability and justice than the predatory acts of mass thievery and violence on the part of the rich and powerful. While the criminal justice system is believed by many to function in the service of reducing crime, in reality, according to Reiman, the system operates to project the image that crime is a threat from below, perpetrated by a criminal class made up of the undeserving poor, and is, therefore, quite productive.

Similarly, criminologist Nils Christie's *Crime Control as Industry* charts the many ways in which crime has become a large-scale industry employing corporations and thousands of workers, thereby complicating common beliefs that the system is focused solely on preventative functions.[29] Sociologist Howard Becker has also described the degree to which the failure of criminal justice operations actually aids in their continuation: "First they [enforcement organizations] say that by reason of their efforts the problem they deal with is approaching a solution. But, in the same breath, they say the problem is perhaps worse than ever (though through no fault of their own) and requires renewed and increased effort to keep it under control."[30] While very often associated with Marxist, critical, or labeling perspectives in criminology, the paradoxically productive function of crime, in fact, has been most explicitly articulated by Durkheim. In his famous formulation, not only has crime existed in all societies in all times and places, it has everywhere served an essential function in keeping societies from stagnating into morbidity. If not for the criminal's ability to push against moral strictures, societies would no longer progress.[31] And in positing that crime is not a pathological element of biology or a throwback to a savage evolutionary stage, but, instead, can be understood as a normal, rational, innovative response to a broken system, sociologist Robert Merton similarly demonstrated that crime could be a productive force in providing alternative means of achieving the culturally prescribed goal of wealth accumulation.[32] Likewise, the entire tradition of learning theory in criminology—from the Chicago School to the subcultural theories that revised them—evokes a similar sense, as crime is understood to provide entire ways of life that allow for both money and respect for those who face few legitimate prospects.[33]

Perhaps the notion that crime is multiply productive, though, can best be seen in Foucault's notion of the "carceral archipelago" in which, he famously argued, the disciplinary techniques of the penitentiary have become so completely diffused throughout every social institution that at the very heart of modern punishment is the creation and detailed delineation of the criminal, not his eradication.[34] And in a similar vein—although presented as an inversion of aspects of Foucault's argument—anthropologists Jean and John Comaroff contend that crime in postcolonial South Africa "has come to be represented . . . as *a means of production* . . . for those alienated by new forms of exclusion."[35] They suggest that "the criminal obsessions of both rulers and subjects" have become even more important to the functioning of the state in recent years, and that popular melodramas of crime "are founded on a dialectic of production and reduction—on the productive conjuring of a world saturated with violence and moral ambiguity, the threat of which" law enforcement agents "alone are able to reduce to habitable order."[36] In short, they argue that "a metaphysics of *disorder*—the hyperreal conviction, rooted in everyday experience, that society hovers on the brink of dissolution—comes to legitimize a physics of social order to be accomplished through effective law enforcement."[37]

Thus, the perception that crime can be productive on multiple levels pervades analyses of crime at every turn. And it is here, in the apparent productivity of crime, that the importance of Suge Knight's *villainy* lies. While a huge swell of educated opinion—from conflict to consensus theory—attributes paradoxical functions to both criminal actions and the system's response, public debate, more often than not, casts figures like Suge as monstrous aberrations, rather than rational actors responding to broken systems. This is akin to the "bad apples" theory so often invoked to explain complex problems with systemic sources. Suge, however, signals a key difference in the productivity-of-violence argument: the mythology surrounding Suge Knight is an indication of the degree to which the seemingly efficient, instrumental use of direct street violence to simplify the humiliating complexity of industry manipulation fell back on itself. This cautionary element is crucial to Suge's mythology, which problematizes his status as hero, and begins, according to multiple sources, shortly after the success of Dr. Dre's groundbreaking solo album, *The Chronic*.[38]

Suge as Villain

After securing Dre's release from Eazy, and in order to finance a studio for their new record label, Suge turned to Michael "Harry O" Harris, a major cocaine trafficker who grew up as a member of the Bounty Hunter Bloods gang in South Central Los Angeles. Known as "godfather" to his street associates, Harry O also had numerous legitimate business ventures, one of which was a Broadway play, *Checkmate*, which starred a young Denzel Washington. In order to fight a number of serious drug trafficking charges, Harry O hired David Kenner, a long-time Los Angeles criminal lawyer specializing in federal drug cases, and the two became close friends. Harry O eventually offered Kenner's services to Suge. As Harry O recalls, "Suge had about five or six pending cases which David Kenner was able to control and get rid of. . . . David Kenner was the guy who made Suge secure."[39] Suge, in turn, was able to offer Kenner's skills to the artists on Death Row. Together, Harry O and Suge decided to create Godfather Entertainment, of which Death Row Records was to be one entity. Harry O, however, wanted to stay behind the scenes, with no official attachment. With Harry O's help, Suge upgraded their studio and Dre began working on *The Chronic*, which would eventually become one of the most famous rap albums of all time, securing Dre's reputation as one of rap music's most important producers.

Before finding success with it, though, Suge and Dre had tried to shop *The Chronic* at several record labels in order secure a distribution deal. Sony, for instance, was interested, but declined, according to some, out of fear, believing that Suge had "robbed" Eazy of his artists. As one journalist described it, "Part of their fear in dealing with rap bands is that some of these gangster rappers might turn out to be real gangsters."[40] Death Row eventually made a deal with Jimmy Iovine, head of Interscope Records, and went "triple platinum," selling over three million copies of *The Chronic*. Because of the success of both *The Chronic* and Snoop's debut album, *Doggystyle*,[41] "Death Row became the core of Warner Brothers Music's [Interscope's parent company] money-making machine."[42] Importantly, however, it is the success of *The Chronic* that marks the beginnings of Suge's downfall, which, as a number of former associates remember, he precipitated by embracing his growing celebrity status.

After a while, Suge started to appear on magazine covers and became a celebrity himself; in the eyes of many, he was getting lost in the fame. As Harry O recalls, "Originally I told him that he should never put himself on the front of magazines. Always stay in the cut, always stay in the background. That's how you have more power."[43] Suge's lawyer, David Kenner, also seemed to get caught up in the lifestyle, getting more involved with the music business, and, allegedly, treating Harry O's cases as secondary. Kenner and Suge eventually created their own separate company without Harry O's knowledge.

For many of the artists, however, working in Death Row became, in their words, like working "in a prison." According to one former employee who also recounted an episode in which Suge beat her up, "He ran that company like it was his gang."[44] Death Row operated under a demerit system that RBX, one of its former artists, described thus: "Say something wrong, you get smacked. If you come late, you get smacked. If you do this, you get smacked. . . . To me it was like pimps and hoes."[45] And Snoop recalled that, "after a while, Suge was unapproachable."[46] In addition, according to a number of former artists and employees, beatings in the Death Row offices had become regular occurrences, and people auditioning for record deals would often be caught unawares. "'They would famously lock the doors on you,'"[47] "the infamous door locking where they take you in a room and touch you up and down."[48] Kenner, by some accounts, would often watch, and people would sometimes videotape. Harry O remembers that "[i]t was funny to him [Suge]. It made him feel good to have that kind of power or to instill that type of fear."[49] Perhaps not surprisingly, many of the artists began to have serious problems with this turn. Both DOC—another instrumental figure in gangsta rap's early years—and "RBX grew unhappy with the label's direction."[50] Eventually, as Snoop put it, "through the grace of god and through good attorneys, they were able to leave. Everybody else was forced in a chokehold after that."[51]

This darker side of the intersection of street and suite violence that Death Row represented came to its most visible form in the murders of Biggie Smalls and Tupac Shakur. Suge's rise to success, and the methods through which it was accomplished, put him in direct competition with Sean "Puffy" Combs, the New York City–based label owner who, some claim, had modeled his own company, Bad Boy Records, on Death Row. What had started as a competition between music rivals took, in the words of journalist Kevin Powell, "this violent turn that hadn't happened before."[52] The ensuing conflict between the two camps would involve death threats, and accusations of violence all around. While the tragedies that followed appeared to be unsurprising results of that conflict, the actual events have not been resolved and, despite numerous theories, there is no clear evidence of criminal responsibility in any direction.

Undoubtedly, his is a dramatic story of business and money; but Suge's primary significance lies in his dual role as *both hero and villain*. As a result, his mythology does double duty in rap's confrontation with its own commercialization, providing a model to emulate as well as a path to avoid. Where Suge's use of street violence to negate the humiliating effects of the industry provides rap artists raised in the crack era with a heroic figure, Suge's villainy also suggests that enjoyment of violence for its own sake—rather than its instrumental use—can lead to one's downfall. By letting his own violence overtake him, Suge, according to his composite picture, authored his own demise. His early instrumental urge to own the masters and get his artists their due became a personal desire for violence, which, in the words of Harry O, was "funny to him." The monster image of Suge, hence, serves as a cautionary tale for the crack generation: when the line between violence in the service of business and violence for its own sake blurs, the transformation of violence from its formerly circumscribed nature in the old school to the unattached, unpredictable networks of the crack era can become the fetishization of violence for its own sake. As I discussed in chapters 2 and 4, new school violence became socially disruptive because it ebbed and flowed according to impersonal, uncontrollable, abstract forces, rather than being anchored by codes of respect and honor. Suge's mythology, therefore, shows that, when violence becomes an end in itself, it can lose its functionality, becoming unraveled and undisciplined. Violence for its own sake, in other words, no longer functions as an instrument in the regulation of markets.

Violence in the crack era was unseated from its cultural moorings in the community; it became terrifying because its only attachment was to profit, bypassing traditional methods that once controlled it. Suge's later violence, then, illustrates that instrumental violence can double back and terrorize itself, becoming a closed system attached to the production of violence rather than the production of profit through the efficient use of new school methods. Put simply, instrumental violence gone too far is *inefficient*. Neither culturally attached nor driven by profit, it becomes counterproductive. The very simplicity that made Suge's use of bodily violence so effective in the short run ultimately led to his own demise in the long run.

In sum, Suge Knight is a powerful symbol in the rap industry because he exemplifies two sides of the use of violence: when used in disciplined bursts, it provides freedom from humiliation and a suspended life; when an end in itself, however, it can become a thoroughly unproductive element that signals the demise of one's productive potential. Consequently, Suge's mythology reveals a key balancing act that many in the current rap industry often must navigate: (1) be just violent enough to (a) stimulate a voyeuristic public ever eager for tales of inner-city violence, and

(b) deter white-collar agents from the more egregious forms of deception and manipulation; but (2) not so violent that one is actually killed or jailed—like so many have been—as a result. The ultimate lesson of Suge's villainous mythology, therefore, is to be found in one depressing fact: while Tupac and Biggie are dead, Harry O is in prison, and Suge is in bankruptcy, Interscope Records was able to sell its share in Death Row for $400 million. This is the case even though it was Death Row's violent escapades that had made Interscope so much money in the first place, turning it into "the core of Warner Brothers Music's money-making machine." In addition, Interscope executives, according to a number of industry insiders, were well aware of Death Row's violent activities since, for one thing, the two companies sat, literally, across the hall from each other. As one writer put it, "Interscope Records decided to turn a blind eye to the violence. . . . Many people connected to Interscope felt, since Death Row was earning the label millions of dollars, Interscope could not afford to risk damaging the relationship."[53] Interscope's ability to avoid any guilt by association, actually, was due, in large part, to the specific structure of corporate music, which can hide its own ties to violence behind the many artists who become, in essence, its visible *face*. While white-collar violence is often hidden, physical violence is inherently messy, visceral, and visible to all. In turning to such violence as a means to create spaces of nonhumiliating work, many in the rap game, like Suge, hasten their own demise.

Facing the Corporation

If, as I tried to show in the last chapter, the industry's violence is perceived as worse than street violence because it suspends, in contract form, one's humiliation in perpetuity, and, thereby, compounds it, then avenging that humiliation would require erasure of that suspension, and a breaking of the binds. Often, though, redressing that humiliation is made all the more difficult because of the corporate nature of the music business, which—because of the corporation's structure—makes it difficult to locate sources of blame, allowing for a diffusion of responsibility. This structure, as legal scholar Joel Bakan has shown, includes at least three interrelated elements: (1) the separation of ownership from management; (2) corporate "personhood," whereby corporations are protected by the Fourteenth Amendment's rights to due process; and (3) the corporation's mandate to increase shareholder wealth at all costs.[54] Indeed, collectively, these elements are often described by those it affects as *facelessness*. Recall from chapter 3, for example, musician Steve Albini's vision of the corporate music making process in which "a faceless industry lackey" stands at one end of a trench "filled with runny, decaying shit," waiting for a band to swim across and sign a recording contract. Recall, also, singer Tom Waits's notion that "corporations don't have feelings," suggesting that facelessness and lack of compassion go hand in hand.

In fact, many recent critics contend that facelessness—in both corporate and international governance—lies at the very heart of social justice today. In the first pages of *Globalization and Its Discontents*, for instance, economist Joseph Stiglitz describes the degree to which perceptions of facelessness have risen to global prominence: "International bureaucrats—the faceless symbols of the world economic order—are under attack everywhere. Formerly uneventful meetings of obscure technocrats discussing mundane subjects such as concessional loans and trade quotas have now become the scene of raging street battles and huge demonstrations."[55] Similarly, in an analysis of community trauma in the aftermath of technological disasters, sociologist Kai Erikson traces how perceptions of facelessness exacerbate such experiences for the victims.[56] He argues that technological catastrophes are experienced quite differently from natural disasters, and "provoke outrage rather than resignation" precisely because "[t]hey generate a feeling that the thing ought not to have happened, that someone is at fault."[57] Unfortunately for the victims, Erikson explains, "the company draws into its own interior spaces and posts lawyers around its borders like a ring of pickets."[58] He goes on say that "[t]hose who manage corporations" then talk about the people who have been hurt "as if they were *things*, bloodless and inorganic."[59] Those hurt, however, "rarely forget . . . that corporate decisions are made by human beings and that corporate policies reflect the views of human beings. And it can be profoundly painful when the people in charge of a company . . . deny responsibility, offer no apology, express no regrets, and crouch out of sight behind that wall of lawyers and legalisms."[60]

These widespread beliefs about the duplicity and deceitfulness of faceless companies are personified in Bakan's book and documentary film, *The Corporation*. In both, he argues that, if real human beings had performed many of the same actions in which corporations regularly and legally engage, they would be defined as sociopaths without compassion, feelings, or regard for human life. Essentially, what many of these recent criticisms of corporate facelessness reveal is the fundamentally paradoxical nature of corporate responsibility: the modern corporation is an organization that, by law, is given fictitious personhood, yet its structure of diffused, public ownership simultaneously allows it to remain faceless. The corporation is a person without a face, and a body that has no body to attack, allowing the real human actors who run it to "crouch out of sight behind that wall of lawyers and legalisms." And, as so many critics suggest, it is exactly this inability to hold real people accountable that makes corporate humiliation so painful.

In addition, these problems of accountability become even more diffused when these faceless persons take ownership—as they have come to do on a grand scale—of intellectual and cultural properties. Legal scholar Rosemary Coombe, for example, has argued that the conception of authorship undergirding intellectual property law denies "the social conditions and cultural influences that shape the author's expressive creativity," thereby investing him or her with "a power that may border on censorship in the name of property."[61] She argues that, "[w]hether the law recognizes an original work understood to embody the personality of a unique creator, as it does when affirming copyright, or acknowledges a signifier and its meanings to be creations of a singular and unique source of origin, as it does in protecting trademarks, the power of the author is reinforced."[62] Consequently, "Both frameworks depend for their intelligibility upon the assertion of a unitary point of identity," what Coombe calls "a metaphysics of authorial presence," which, problematically, "denies the investment of others" in the creative process.[63]

In a strange turn, then, when corporations take possession of cultural properties, there occurs a paradoxical merger of facelessness and authorial presence in which individual sources of origin—which deny the "investment of others" in the creative process—are grafted onto fictitious persons who are protected by walls of lawyers and legalisms. While reaping the benefits that accrue through individual ownership, faceless corporations are difficult to hold accountable—symbolically and materially—for the creations they own. And through this very facelessness, corporations are better able to spread the accountability that, historically, has undergirded intellectual property law's individual point of origin. For example, where early copyright law—which I discussed in chapter 3—held individual authors accountable for creating obscene, blasphemous, and seditious works, in the twenty-first century this same legal structure now allows corporate persons to disown responsibility for the violent effects the creations they own may have caused. Corporations can lay claim to the cultural products they do not create, preventing others from trespassing on those creations, while simultaneously denying their own embeddedness in the real flesh and blood communities that provide their labor.

In other words, much of the pain experienced by people affected by facelessness revolves around the corporation's ability to *own without having to own up*. And, most important, when analyzed in the context of crack's paradoxical punishment, corporate facelessness stands in a strange relationship to rap's reflexive stance toward its own commercialization: while crack dealers were ascribed a form of culpability without intentionality, faceless corporations have been ascribed a form of intentionality—the creativity and ownership claims of individuals—without a commensurate level of culpability. In the rap industry, the rationale underlying crack's punishment (which takes couriers as if they were kingpins) converges with the accountability structure of authorship (by which the music industry benefits) to create a system in which rappers are taken as the sole points of origin generating their criminal creations, while the corporate bodies that underwrite and profit from them continue to diffuse their own responsibility and remain faceless. Since crack dealers are mistakenly seen as the sole "authors"—and, hence, "owners"—of new school violence, rappers are viewed as the mouthpieces for the moral decay that crack dealers are believed to have created. And it is precisely in this strange inversion that the significance of Suge Knight is to be found, a significance that also defines the balancing act that so many in the rap industry must now constantly navigate.

Take, for example, West Coast rap pioneer Ice-T's description of the rap industry: "Most rap crews are made up of fifty percent businessmen and fifty percent thugs. Fifty percent of your crew is made up of homeboys that just came home from jail."[64] As a result, Ice-T asks, "What can he do, what can he actually do but say 'yo, Joe Blow was dissin' you and I knocked him out in the club?'" In his words, "That thug element is always ready to reach out and touch anybody, whether it's a cameraman, whether it's an interviewer, whether it's somebody on the radio." According to Ice-T, many participants in the rap industry "do not have any other way of showing the rapper that they they man other than busting somebody in they head. And that's where they get their stripes." In short, "That thug element is always available" precisely because the productivity of crime has become so thoroughly integrated into the work of rap. The "thug element" is far more than gimmick; it is, instead, *a means of production* for those who are useful only as long as they can put themselves in the middle of violent situations that they can then handle. They are, that is, necessary only as long as they are violently productive.

Take, also, a quote from 50 Cent, which reveals a similar element at work. As he explains, "Any nigga that you got with you that roll with you that's supposed to be a real nigga, if he's your support, if he's the nigga the streets look to and say 'don't fuck with them because of this nigga,' he needs an altercation to take place for him to be there, for him to be necessary."[65] According to 50, "He needs you to have problems for him to be necessary, and then you need to give him something for handling it for you. So all he wants is situations that can come and he can deal with for you." It is, however, 50's next line that reveals the key to the balancing act that is often seen as a necessity in the rap industry: "But when the shit really hit the fan, he ain't going to want to be part of that neither. . . . At the end of the day, what the money mean? Nice flowers at your wake?"

Essentially, in having to negotiate the productive role of violence—which holds the promise of redressing humiliation as well as the potential for precipitating one's downfall—participants in the rap industry face double-edged swords. New school violence is only productive as long as it can be kept in line. But for those whose productive lives have become completely united with their criminal potentials, that violence constantly threatens to spill over and become unproductive. The training and restraining of new school violence—as Nas's song "One Love" expresses—has become, therefore, an indispensable part of the work of rap, and it is Suge's dual mythology that communicates this necessity. Consider the following quotation from famous rap manager Russell Simmons:

> When you first come out of the 'hood . . . and you were a drug dealer, your friends were drug dealers, and your friends is thugs, and you were just a poet that hung out with thugs—you might have been a thug too—and you got a record. People around you are very protective, they're very violent, they don't really believe they have anything to live for, and you are the centerpiece of their lives, and you're trying to train them as you learned. It's tough.[66]

So it is that the successful rapper is one who has mastered both worlds—one who has come to successfully embody this merger of street violence and industry predation and who can negotiate and restrain the new school violence that constantly threatens to spill over and precipitate the demise of one's productive life. This convergence is never fully reconciled, however, and is—to recall a phrase from chapter 4—a *crushing freedom*.

Indeed, the fulfillment of this consolidation can be seen in Jay-Z's plainly titled song, "Rap Game / Crack Game,"[67] which brings us back, full circle, to the equation with which this book began: "somehow the rap game reminds me of the crack game." Significantly, the song begins, "We treat this rap shit just like handling weight," indicating that the rap-crack connection is no longer a critique, or a critical flash point; it is now an explicit advantage, *a way to do it ourselves*. In addition, Jay's use of "we" instead of "they" to describe the relationship between the rap game and the crack game is important, as it symbolically merges the artists who strive to restrain the new school violence of the crack era with the record labels who lie, cheat, and seduce naïve rappers into webs of broken promises underwritten and reinforced by the humiliating suspension of a productive life. The song signals a crucial shift in the way that relationship had been rapped about before. The crack game is now the structural logic, the prime mover, the grammar of business. The work of crack is no longer reminiscent of the work of rap; it *is* the work of rap. Jay does not articulate a duty to "speak out"; rather, he is making it clear how *we*, not just those sleazy executives, treat the industry. Jay-Z perfects the union of crack work and rap work, claiming about his songs, "I got that uncut raw to make a fiend's body jerk." And, like the crack trade, the fiend's addiction is our profit. Because we are real, street hustlers, we can do what the executives do, but better. "We" have become just as exploitative as the labels; the difference is that we now revel in, rather than hide from, that exploitation. We embrace it. If used correctly, anger and frustration become another school of hard knocks, allowing one to learn about the business—the ins, the outs, as well as the ways to exploit others. In this respect, fighting the beast turns you into one. To quote, again, Biggie's first line in "The Ten Crack Commandments": "I been in this game for years, it made me a animal / There's rules to this shit, I made me a manual."

In sum, Suge's mythology symbolizes the possibility of combating the industry's humiliating violence by cutting through the suspension of a productive life with the hard violence of the new school. Just as old school patterns of violence were disrupted by the lethal regulation of volatile crack markets, so, too, can old school industry practices be altered by new school methods. Suge demonstrated that contractual humiliation can be neutralized. He also showed that, if left unchecked and undisciplined, those very same means of redress can lead to one's downfall.

Conclusion

Paradoxically, while crack dealers never have been kingpins, in taking them as such, the punishment structure for crack downplays their intentionality while upgrading their culpability. And, similarly, while faceless corporations are never the sole points of origin of creative works, the legal fiction that treats them as such upgrades their authorial presence while downplaying their culpability in perpetuating humiliation and compromising the moral base of law. Although swept up by crack-related transformations out of their control, and taken as representatives of a new era of violence they denounce as well as celebrate, rap artists are now in a position to be the faces of otherwise faceless corporations, and to be taken as wholly responsible for their own "immoral" cultural properties.

Sometimes taken as harbingers of moral decay, or superpredators without conscience, rap artists are often desperately trying to make spaces of nonhumiliating work in worlds of lethal, market-driven violence that they did not create, but now must staff, balancing their own criminal potential with the possibility of death, and standing as the faces of their own criminal brands, positioned to take the fall when the balancing act swings too wildly. The profound misrecognition that changed couriers to kingpins has also come to misrecognize industry-related violence in rap as "only" the incursion of "codes of the street" into an otherwise nonviolent practice.

While record labels that model themselves on drug gangs sometimes mimic corporate structures because their diffusion of responsibility protects the top players, there is one fundamental feature that real street organizations all share: moral and material wrongs are avenged physically. While lower-level soldiers experience the worst of it all, leaders must also remain vigilant because "termination" is taken literally and does not include golden parachutes.

Violent redress seems to relevel the playing field by making consequences real. And, for a while, it does. Yet, as the mythology of Suge Knight illustrates, the very thing that, at first, seems to equalize asymmetrical relationships, results, paradoxically, in the vastly unequal outcomes of physical death and financial ruin. The metaphor of crack in rap's conflict with its own commercialization, thus, recalls an era in which flesh and blood people became necessary sources of flexible, violent labor in market conditions they did not create, but—through the twin forces of disproportionate punishment and coercive mobility—were propelled into staffing. New school violence is multiply productive: in the streets, it effects both power and loss; in the suites, it redresses contractual humiliation; and, for the collective experience of crime and punishment in twenty-first-century America, it continues to provide easy, visceral "proof" that crime is still—despite over a decade of declining violence rates—a problem requiring punitive toughness to combat.

Conclusion

Livin' in the world no different from a cell.
—Inspectah Deck in Wu-Tang, "C.R.E.A.M.," *Enter the Wu-Tang*
(36 Chambers), 1993

On February 23, 2008, an article in the *New York Times* alerted audiences to a new drug "scourge" in Argentina that has an eerie resemblance to the history of crack cocaine in the United States.[1] The article charts the "irrepressible spread of paco, a highly addictive, smokable cocaine residue that has destroyed thousands of lives in Argentina and caused a cycle of drug-induced street violence never seen before." In the early 2000s, the article reports, "crude yellowish crystals" began to show up in impoverished neighborhoods across the country. The narcotics officers who are quoted throughout the article claim that much of the spread is due to the large, porous border Argentina shares with Bolivia, which "[f]ewer than 200 federal police officers patrol," thereby "leaving traffickers free rein." Most interesting, though, is the connection made between paco's "highly addictive" nature and the way in which it is made. According to the article, "Paco is even more toxic than crack because it is made mostly of solvents and chemicals like kerosene, with just a dab of cocaine." This highly addictive toxicity, the article relates, has driven young addicts into "drug-induced hysterias," and has galvanized local communities around efforts to stop the "plague." Recalling the ways in which the crack era transformed violence from a culturally based, honor-bound form to an unpredictable, entrepreneurial force, one local woman explains, "'Before there were codes. . . . Now there are no codes. We need to stand up and stick it to two or three dealers.'"

With a few minor alterations, this article could be an exact copy of those written at the height of the crack panic. To those of us who have lived through that panic, the article—which relies primarily on quotations from narcotics officers—sounds like the not-so-distant drumbeat of another variation on a drug war. As with crack, the danger of paco seems to rely on a similarly paradoxical form of reasoning. Paco's supposedly addictive danger lies in the fact that it is *even more* impure than crack. According to the article, paco is primarily composed of chemicals, with just a "dab" of cocaine. Yet, as in America's response to crack, paco is presented as a social problem that can and should be punished away. The suggestion, however, that the criminal justice system could ever do anything of substance about a "scourge" of crystallized kerosene being smoked by impoverished youth is profoundly problematic. And, in fact, it is a young paco user's own explanation of his addiction that throws the irrationality of such an approach into full relief. In his words, it was the "'desperation and depression'" of Argentina's severe economic crisis— and the "'pressure that it causes in a person'"—that led him to addictively inhale a cocaine-infused chemical cocktail.

If this book communicates only one larger notion about the cultural lives of crime and punishment, I hope it is this: no matter who calls for its use, modern punishment, in the words of criminologist Todd Clear, is, without question, "a blunt instrument. It does not offer a panorama of finely calibrated experiences designed to surgically counteract the forces of evil."[2] While criminal justice has an important part to play in social justice generally, this role is overstated by those—whether on the Right or on the Left—who advocate for increased punitiveness, regardless of how obvious or just their ultimate cause may seem. In truth, the brutally complex nature of real-world suffering can only be addressed by the criminal justice system the one way it has ever addressed anything—through reductive efforts to separate the guilty from the innocent, the predators from the victims. Social complexity is incomprehensible to criminal justice, which is structured against it. Pure victims and pure offenders rarely exist in the real world, and, instead, reflect artificial, narrow abstractions that must fit into the only dichotomy that is ever allowed: right and wrong. This ruthlessly unreal logic is ill suited for healing the multifaceted effects of real-world trauma, which require healing and help beyond the anger stage of state retaliation. None of this is the fault of either criminal justice agents or their agencies, however. Indeed, the system has done precisely what we've asked it to do—put people away. And it continues to do so quite well.

Consider, for example, how felony cases go from arrest to prosecution to punishment. Nationally, our clearance rates—a case is cleared when an arrest is made by police and turned over for prosecution[3]—are 27 percent for robbery cases, 40 percent for rape, 55 percent for aggravated assault, and 64 percent for murder, which always has the highest rate because there is usually a dead body and often many witnesses (property cases have clearance rates in the teens).[4] With those arrests, prosecutors must then decide whether to file formal charges and proceed with prosecution. Even with slight variations across jurisdictions, pretty much across the board, prosecutors file charges around 50 percent of the time.[5] While there are numerous reasons for dropping cases, prosecutors do so primarily because of victim noncooperation or lack of evidence. Once official charges are filed, however, rates for conviction—i.e., the percentage of cases brought for prosecution that lead to a judgment of guilt—are overwhelmingly high, around 70 percent for all felonies.[6] A full 94 percent of those convictions never go to trial, and are obtained through guilty pleas (i.e., defendants admit guilt and waive their right to a trial).[7] Of those convicted, nearly 70 percent are sentenced to jail or prison.[8] Despite conviction and incarceration rates in the seventy-plus percentile, the criminal justice system is continually portrayed as "soft" on this or that crime by advocates across the political spectrum, with seriously damaging—and often unintended—results.

Many black leaders, for example, initially supported tough-on-crime positions against crack cocaine in the 1980s on exactly the same grounds as those who now advocate for hate crime statutes: equal protection before the law. Black communities felt the brunt of crack-related destructiveness, and called on the state to intervene. Of course, the conditions of this epidemic were only created in the first place by the structural dislocations of deindustrialization that made drug entrepreneurs from Latin America some of the only re-employers in the inner city.[9] After a few years, though, when it was found that over 90 percent of those sentenced under the laws were black, these same leaders then rightly condemned the laws, calling for their repeal. They have called for their repeal every year since. In short, many of those who once supported seemingly righteous punitive policies have since become their most vocal critics precisely because the onus has fallen overwhelmingly on poor communities of color, the very groups originally intended, by some activists, to be protected in the first place.

Calls for increased punitiveness arise alongside heightened social insecurity and almost always have racialized effects, leading to declines in social spending on those who are criminalized and increases in privatization, so that pleas for serious structural equality—the core of any critical position—become ever more narrowly channeled into the few available state-funded projects: the punitive apparatus. Claimants to state help must then reformulate their entire lives around theories of victimization, which places them in positions of increasing dependence on state-sanctioned definitions of their lives and relationships. This increased state surveillance does not—cannot, by nature—accept the complex, often contradictory emotions, beliefs, and experiences that many real people bring along with them. These messy realities are then compounded even further when state agents and community members interact in the heat of real-life confrontations. While calling on the state for help in domestic violence cases, for instance, many poor women of color—partly because of mandatory arrest policies originally intended to protect women from their batterers—have found themselves arrested for complicity in child maltreatment, or for possessing whatever illegal paraphernalia might be strewn about their homes since many of them depend, at least in part, on the underground economy for survival.[10] In addition, stringent public housing requirements can lead to the eviction of entire families for the possession of minuscule drug amounts. In fact, young women in general have fared poorly in our punitive climate. For example, even though young women's actual criminal behavior has been fairly stable for the past decade, during this same period "girls' arrests for simple assault continued to climb, increasing by 18.7%, while boys' arrests for the same offense declined by 4.3%."[11] These arrests often occur "because of arguments with their parents . . . or for 'other assaults' for fighting in school because of new zero-tolerance policies enacted after the Columbine shootings."[12] Even more troubling, girls' "commitments to facilities increased by an alarming 88% between 1991 and 2003, while boys' commitments increased by only 23%."[13] Such statistics are painful reminders that tough-on-crime positions on anything, anywhere, rarely operate in the interest of those they purport to help. In the case of many young women, this punitive reality has meant substituting the violence of the patriarchal family with that of the patriarchal state.

It is, therefore, a severe mistake—one that many left-of-center advocates often make—to explain away America's experiment of mass incarceration as if it were only the result of a conservative, Reagan-era backlash. A more than 500 percent increase in imprisoned populations cannot be accomplished in a democratic state—even one riven with profound structural inequality—without a broad-based consensus. As criminologist Elliott Currie wrote over ten years ago, this reality "reflects a stunning degree of collective denial."[14] The problem lies neither with the left-of-center nor the right-of-center, but with the center itself, what sociologist David Garland has called the "dog that did not bark": "the professional middle classes, an otherwise powerful and articulate group, who have done little to oppose the drift towards punitive policies."[15] Put simply, to "overcome mass incarceration requires that we incarcerate fewer people,"[16] which can only happen, in criminologist Michael Tonry's words, after we're first able to "admit what happened . . . and then set about the task of learning to restrain our collective emotions"[17] and reduce our reliance on punitive policies to assuage every conceivable social anxiety.

Take, as a comparison, Scandinavia, which has displayed a consistent philosophical unwillingness to incarcerate significant proportions of its population for anything. Finland, for instance, has no one on death row (which is obvious, since, like most of the developed world, it does not have the death penalty), and fewer than one hundred people serving life sentences, the majority of whom will only wind up spending twelve to fifteen years behind bars.[18] Over 90 percent of sentences in Finland are monetary fines, calculated according to the offender's income.[19] Less than 10 percent of those sentenced in Finland are given prison terms, and the median sentence for all offenses is below four months.[20] Average sentences for robbery—which, along with murder, rape, and aggravated assault, constitute the most serious forms of violence in any criminal justice system—are around one year.[21] In Sweden, robbery sentences are twenty-three months, just below two years.[22] In the United States, they are eighty-nine months, or a whopping seven-plus years.[23] For another comparison, sentences imposed for homicide—the most serious crime of violence in any system—are seventy-seven months in Sweden, and 244 months in the United States, or six and twenty years, respectively.[24]

Finland, in fact, has engaged in one of the most concerted decarceration efforts in the twentieth century, reducing its population behind bars from nearly 200 per 100,000 in the 1950s to around 60 per 100,000 currently, constituting a 300 percent decrease.[25] During roughly this same period, the United States embarked on one of the largest imprisonment experiments in human history, increasing its population behind bars by over 500 percent and solidifying its place as the undisputed punitive champion of the universe, standing atop a pyramid of state violence with an incarceration rate of 750 per 100,000, which is over ten times that of any Scandinavian country.[26] Finland now has fewer than three thousand people locked up on any given day;[27] we have over two million. At around 60 per 100,000, Scandinavian countries, along with Japan, have some of the lowest incarceration rates in the world, and stand virtually alone among the international community in their humane approach to punishment.

In many ways, though, in the early decades of the twenty-first century, it seems the United States is at a crossroads in criminal justice. While stimulated, in large part, by a struggling economy in which the massive expenditures required by our imprisonment boom seem at least problematic—if not outright irresponsible—to a growing number of politicians and professionals on either side of the political aisle, this crossroads also shows signs that deeper changes are afoot. To quote, again, the words of Senator Jim Webb, "America's criminal justice system is broken," and "[o]ur failure to address these problems cuts against the notion that we are a society founded on fundamental fairness."[28] Similarly, the repeal of the mandatory minimum for simple possession of crack, and the reduction of the 100-to-1 crack-powder ratio to 18-to-1—while still empirically flawed and irrationally disproportionate—indicates at least a basic collective willingness to admit fault and move forward with positive, more evidence-driven policies. And, perhaps most promising of all, in 2009, state prison populations declined for the first time in thirty-eight years, dropping by nearly five thousand people, a 0.3 percent change.[29]

Even if these changes become normalized over the long term, however, one inescapable fact remains: a near-forty-year experiment in mass incarceration will have sociocultural effects unbounded by the timelines of official decision making. Indeed, one of the central premises of this book is that even the most obviously "instrumental" policies have cultural lives that extend far beyond their intended targets in ways and in degrees to which neither their original designers nor their most strident opponents could ever have controlled, predicted, or, as is often the case, even perceived. My premise implies that crime has cultural lives, that culture has criminal lives, and that the policies affecting both never start and end with passage and repeal. Instead, crime and punishment get woven into existing webs of meaning, creating, in the process, patchworks of cultures and policies that violently overlap and work at cross-purposes. Laws intended to target the same things wind up trumping each other, and policy efforts aimed at supporting community cohesion wind up systematically picking it apart, all of which, all the while, become absorbed—often imperceptibly—into social practices as seemingly insignificant as lyrical flows.

In addition, the promising drop in state prison populations noted above is tempered by other findings, which show that, while twenty-six states did see reductions, another twenty-four *increased* their prison populations, some substantially so.[30] Even more problematic, the federal prison population has continued to increase, having doubled since 1994 and showing no signs of slowing.[31] This continuous growth has been spurred in the past few years by one primary factor: a concentration on immigration offenses, which accounted for just 12 percent of federal sentences in 1996 but now constitute 32 percent, nearly triple the 1996 number.[32] And, since almost 90 percent of those sentenced under federal immigration laws are Hispanic, Latinos now account for 40 percent of everyone sentenced at the federal level, over three times their proportion of the general population.[33] And so it is that crack's place as the lethal core of our emotional sociality has been subsumed under new concatenations of criminological fervor in which fears of terrorism, illegal immigration, "super" gangs, and cross-border drug cartels are coalescing to form new structures of feeling. Given our experiences with mass incarceration over the past thirty-plus years, it is unclear how the social complexities inherent in this emerging nexus could ever be served by the punitive efforts to which we have already been turning. These changes well underway will undoubtedly have their own lasting cultural consequences, radiating outward and inward in unforeseen ways. The staggering level of lethality in Mexico's drug war, for example, has already reshaped the everyday lives of citizens as well as their cultural creations, coloring everything from the way people interact in public space to the popularity of *narcocorridos*, the ballads written and sung by aspiring musicians that praise the exploits of specific drug cartels.[34] As in America's experience of crack cocaine, though, Mexico's hyperaggressive, militaristic enforcement efforts, without question, have only fueled the violence.[35]

"I feel," then, in the words of Raymond Williams, "a direct continuity with these works and experiences I've emphasised"[36] in this book, and believe the problems to which they speak "are still close and difficult, and that whatever we may do in other directions we are still driven, necessarily, to what is possible in that area in the way of creative response."[37] My own creative response to the devastations of the crack era has been to write this book—to show how the lethal core of America's criminological structure of feeling has been creatively reworked through rap's confrontation with its own commercialization. Crack has connected a vast array of social experiences into a shared language that expresses a "new sense of society as not only the bearer but the active creator, the active destroyer, of the values of persons and relationships."[38] Crack is a complex experiential fabric that has been patched together from often contradictory drives, desires, and impulses but which, in Williams's words "speaks from its own uniqueness and yet speaks a common experience."[39] In my premise, the crack era is a "vital area of social experience"[40] that "entered lives, to shape or to deform; a process personally known but then again suddenly distant, complex, incomprehensible, overwhelming."[41] And, as the child of this "sense of crisis," rap's conflict with its own commercialization was a "response to a new and varied but still common experience"[42] in which "a different moral emphasis has become inevitable."[43]

Crack is symbolic of a break in historical periods, moral codes, ways of violence, and patterns of work. It marks a key turning point in community relations as well as in ways of making a living, reflecting the degree to which market relations have suffused all aspects of social life as well as the violence necessary to regulate them. Crack put lethality to work in ways and at levels not seen since, leaving lasting impacts on communities and broader cultural trends. Communities had to adapt to the vicissitudes of a predatory marketplace that diffused ruthless violence throughout many forms of social interaction. Once diffused, such adaptations became normalized, affecting the mood of whole neighborhoods even after actual violence declined. Crack is market logic shorn of all complexity, its bare fact of regulation made plain and simple. If the punitive turn, in large part, depended upon a collective impulse to "get down to brass tacks" and simplify the complex social dislocations of deindustrialization, then lethal violence in the regulation of the underground economies that increasingly came to dominate social relations and community life is that simplified logic reduced even further. A simplified logic of market competition is, simply put, killing one's competition.

Crack represents ever more precarious patterns of work, and the lethality that is often necessary to regulate them. It is a historical marker that is grounded in a logic of business, a new method of violence that entails new aesthetics and moral adaptations, as well as the efforts to train and balance those changes. And, in rap's conflict with its own commercialization, crack serves as a means to indict a seemingly nonviolent business, exposing its pretensions to fairness and equality before the law.

The punishment structure for crack cocaine has never been anything but a self-contradiction. It can absorb any new finding or drug quantity ratio because, as a paradox, it is itself infinitely elastic. It is a law that searches for kingpins where none will ever be found, that squeezes purity out of a process that depends on the introduction of impurities, and that treats an inanimate substance as if it had more intelligence than the flesh and blood people who move it. In this way, the infinite elasticity of the crack laws reflects an unintentional, but no less powerful, collective effort to pin down and punish away a pervasive, free-floating sense of unease, instability, and formless predation. In treating low-level dealers moving inherently impure forms of cocaine *as if* they were the masterminds of global criminal enterprises, the punishment structure for crack signifies an attempt to manufacture a form of *pure culpability*. Even though the 100-to-1 ratio has been reduced, our emerging criminological structure of feeling—dependent, as it is, on an anti-immigration hysteria that grows more energetic by the minute—reveals a reinvigorated effort to enucleate a kind of raw culpability through which real people can be punished *as if* they had authored the social dislocations for which the United States has diffused its own responsibility. Since punishing culpability itself is inherently impossible, the flesh and blood people who must, by force of law, inhabit the cultural spaces of this impossibility will take it on them-selves to become the living, breathing counterparts to our contradictory efforts—forms of *living lethality* moving units of *impure purity* in environments of *crushing freedom*. It is a brutal, ruthless logic indeed.

Methodological Essay

Many years back, one of my mentors told our seminar he thought *Moby Dick* was one of the best books of scholarship he'd ever read. He was convinced that scholarship was a literary genre in its own right, and laughed when one of my classmates told him *Moby Dick* wasn't scholarly because it didn't have footnotes. He was sincerely concerned that the scholarly apparatus had become too easily mistaken for good scholarship, and set about trying to convince us that the most important thing we could do on our way from being knowledge consumers to becoming knowledge producers was to start caring about the *process* of scholarly work—of coming up with good ideas that interest one's colleagues and taking pleasure in putting arguments together on the page. In short, scholarship—I learned and still believe—concerns saying something both true and interesting about the world that might challenge others to think differently about it. That vision of scholarly work has stayed with me and continues to inform everything I do. Even if those who have helped shape this vision do not recognize their influence in these pages, this book, in every way, is a defense of that sensibility. Rather than depending on creed-like statements bluntly professing allegiances to this or that "theoretical orientation" along a still-here positivist-post-everything epistemological continuum to which almost no one in practice actually adheres, this sensibility, instead, is grounded in one primary notion: that one's scholarly process—and not just the "methods" by which one chooses and sorts data—is a way of being in the world. Scholarship is, first and last, about craft—daily processes of layered work that move pages out the door.

Given this sensibility, I've come to believe that, before colleagues ask each other about methods, they should first ask about philosophies of scholarship. Such orienting questions might save us from talking at cross-purposes or, worse, from dismissing each other's claims out of hand. As part of job announcements, for instance, we routinely require applicants to submit teaching philosophies, a practice that reflects a realistic understanding of the business we are in: regardless of how much we publish, a substantial portion of our lives will be spent in classrooms and office hours, prepping, lecturing, discussing, and grading. Because of this reality, we know that how we approach those activities matters a great deal more than the specific content we try to relay through them—that we are not, in other words, just the vehicles through which information is transmitted, or the mouthpieces for textbook corporations, but conveyers of sensibilities who hope to stimulate an appreciation for knowledge through the achievement of hard-won perspectives. Just as teaching is a way of being in the world, accounting for thousands of interactions across our careers, so, too, is scholarly process a daily, yearly practice of being. Some see scholarship only as an extension of scientific method—the recording of observable facts in order to make generalizable truth claims about cause and effect. Others see scholarship as I do: a multilayered process of systematic brainstorming and intellectual bridge making—from personal to professional, and sources to argument—within which method stands as but one element in larger efforts to say interesting things about the world around us. It is not enough for me to know how one chooses and sorts data. I want to know how often you write, how broadly you read, and if you care about turning a phrase.

Unfortunately, the artificial divorcing of method from its inherent moorings in larger contexts of scholarly process is reinforced at the graduate level where incredibly useful writing workshops are often approached as mere addenda to training, after the discipline has been absorbed, methods internalized, and data collected—when it is time, in other words, to "write it all up." But this emphasizes method at the expense of process, mistaking drift for bedrock. My scholarly process—within which method, with a lowercase "m," figures as an iterative subprocess—starts, therefore, from one bedrock activity: daily, uncensored journal writing, a practice I had developed as a youth in order to work out the world. In this forum for raw thought, patterns, problems, and themes emerge, develop, and reappear. Some die out, others stick. The ones that stick matter. They grow in depth and breadth. They become frameworks around which other themes build themselves. Some themes gather enough force to become self-sustaining; a "topic" is formed. Through this process, one takes ownership of one's work since it was one's own from the start, even while constantly being infused with the thoughts of others—friends, colleagues, mentors, and writers living and dead. It is, at every stage, a layered process that grows ideas, rather than excerpting "research questions" from "the literature" as if other people's work led directly to one's own. And this is precisely how this book took shape.

It started simply, with a ten-word phrase that would not go away: "Somehow the rap game reminds me of the crack game." In that lyric I saw a circuitry of meaning—connections between crime and culture, mainstreams and undergrounds, industries of crime and crimes of industry. To see something interesting in this phrase, though, already required a certain cultural literacy, a personal connection. To even ask, as I've done in this book, What are the products themselves saying about being products, the process of becoming products, and their relationship to their producers? requires, first, that one notice the products are, in fact, talking back—that one listen closely enough so that a ten-word phrase sandwiched between bass-heavy brags stands out as meaningful. Second, it requires that one notice the phrase is connected to other disjointed interjections buried in the interstices of sound and rhythm. These are sensibilities that can never emerge "from the literature." There are no data sets from which random samples of disjointed interjections can be drawn. There are, to be sure, representative cases, but in hip hop, being representative does not mean being interchangeable with others who have an equal chance of being chosen. *Respect* ensures representation, not randomness. And respect is earned through showing and proving—by putting oneself to the test and coming out on top. Representatives are champions who stand for the highest level of skill that a community holds for itself. In subcultures of heavily policed tastes, of which hip hop is one, there will always be disagreements about which artist, song, or album is the most definitive. But no one with real ties to rap in 1990s New York could ever seriously argue that, say, Wu-Tang or Nas did not define—i.e., represent—the period. Similarly, no one could ever seriously argue that Suge Knight did not play a formative role in reshaping how rap artists approached the music business. More than media hype, Suge was part of everyday conversations on trains and stoops and was integrated into other discussions about contract points or how to chop samples, all of which were crucial elements in the period's experiential fabric. I know this because I was there, sharing stages and studios with many important artists of the time, and the sources I've used in this book reflect that firsthand experience—the communal knowledge of who really represents what. In this book, therefore, I draw from many of the classic albums that defined New York rap in the 1990s, including Wu-Tang's *36 Chambers*, Nas's *Illmatic*, Mobb Deep's *The Infamous*, O.C.'s *Word . . . Life*, the

Notorious B.I.G.'s *Ready to Die*, Organized Konfusion's *Stress*, and Company Flow's *Funcrusher Plus*, to name only a few. In addition, I draw from the numerous DVDs and books that constitute the cottage industry surrounding the murders of Biggie and Tupac, most of which fall into three general categories: journalistic efforts at discovering the "truth" behind their murders; more reverent biographical portrayals written and produced by friends, family members, and former employees; and opportunistic exposés made by former enemies. I also use autobiographies written by those still in the rap industry, whether artists, executives, or both. Together, these sources stand as the key public forums through which rap artists have confronted their own commercialization, airing their grievances to the world, and standing as products that talk back to their producers while actively taking part in their own production.

In general, my process of working through sources roughly follows a three-tiered method of systematic brainstorming, cobbled together from my own processual temperament and the tradition of "grounded theory,"[1] which allows me—since "findings" never speak for themselves, and intellectual bridges between data and argument are only made by human ingenuity—to be systematic without compromising inventiveness, rigor and spark. The first stage revolves around "line-by-line coding," which, as the phrase suggests, depends on reading each line of text—after first transcribing all nontextual sources—and giving it a short, descriptive keyword summary in the margin. This accomplishes two main goals simultaneously: it transforms a large amount of material into a much smaller form, and—by reading, rereading, and rewriting the material—one actively engages with the sources, making them one's own. While my goal at this first level is to create a basic "nuts-and-bolts" summary of every source, it is also, and importantly, a time of nonstop free writing during which anything and everything that stands out as striking—a word, a metaphor, an image—is pursued, queried, broken down, and rebuilt. It is about accuracy and play, description and invention, with all ideas traceable to their origins in the source.

The second stage of intellectual bridge making revolves around searching for patterns and themes in the first set of codes—coding the codes. At this stage I remove all of the original text by printing out my handwritten notes sans sources. It is another layer of playful process that builds to a higher level of abstraction as I connect the dots across sources, looking for points of both consensus and conflict—shared expressions and experiences as well as the key factors about which sources agree to disagree.

It is about free writing to connect sources, and layering description with invention.

Last is organizing what has been connected into hierarchal arguments. Some connections may be enfolded into others, described anew, and fleshed out further. Others stand tall, refusing to be subsumed, and pull the rest into their orbit through allegorical dominance. This was crack, which emerged as the key metaphor through which rap's conflict with its own commercialization was articulated. But crack wasn't a simple analogy; it bespoke a great deal of pain, being a primary conduit through which forceful accusations of betrayal were relayed. Crack had a social logic to it, a specific kind of reasoning that drew from a vast well of common experience for its symbolic resonance. Crack stood for pain and power, chaos and order, the truth behind the lie. Crack was a sociolegal logic grounded in blood.

I approach my material, then, with the assumption that all sources—whether official documents, published autobiographies, personal letters, or song lyrics—are the products of complicated social practices that say something, but not everything, about the contexts from which they emerged. Unfortunately, suspicion about the worthiness of "popular" sources still—despite many decades of vigorous cultural analysis—permeates much of the social sciences. This suspicion is often undergirded by a stubborn assumption that sources are corrupted—and, therefore, less "reliable"—when they are made for a market. But to follow that same logic, we should dismiss, en masse, the products of academia since almost everything it produces is in furtherance of career, which is itself determined by market conditions. Before judging the merit of an academic publication, for example, we would not only have to know how it was enabled by a specific grant, but also what role this grant and publication have had in the scholar's tenure and promotion reviews. Just as graduate students finish dissertations in order to get jobs, and junior faculty publish in order to get promoted, so, too, do artists and musicians record songs in order to keep food on the table and a presence in the industry. Dismissing popular sources because they were done "for money" conveniently overlooks the degree to which almost all academic labor is done, at least in part, for similarly instrumental purposes.

Because of these assumptions, scholars who want to take rap—or any other commercially bound social practice—seriously have often felt the need to defend it, arguing that rap is really another form of poetry, literature, oral history, or postmodern expression and, by nature of such distinctions, is worthy of study. But rap always has been and always will be its own phenomenon, sharing elements of the above, but recombining them with other forms until what is left is, simply put, rap. Like academia, rap is a complex, commercially bound social practice, which can neither be divorced from its professional aspirations nor reduced to them. And, like novels, plays, government documents, or interview transcripts, rap's expressive media contain traces of authorial intent, structural forces, and the contextual interplay of subject and object. In the end, since I am a scholar of crime and punishment, my work with rap—in legal theorist Robert Cover's famous phrase—"takes place in a field of pain and death."[2] It has been my goal, then, to use rap in order to say something both true and interesting about that field of pain, and to speak to the men and women—whether strangers, friends, relatives, or colleagues—for whom it has mattered most.

Notes

INTRODUCTION

1. As of this writing, the most recent text of *The Fair Sentencing Act of 2010*, which became Public Law 111-220, can be read in the final version as approved by both the Senate and the House on January 5, 2010, 111th Cong., 2d sess.

2. *The Anti–Drug Abuse Act of 1986*, Pub. L. No. 99-570, 100 Stat. 3207 (1986) (hereinafter 1986 Act); *The Anti–Drug Abuse Act of 1988*, Pub. L. No. 100-690, 102 Stat. 4181 (1988) (hereinafter 1988 Act).

3. United States Sentencing Commission (hereinafter USSC or commission), *Special Report to the Congress: Cocaine and Federal Sentencing Policy* (Washington, DC: U.S. Sentencing Commission, February 1995), http://www.ussc.gov/crack/exec.htm (accessed August 15, 2010) (hereinafter 1995 USSC Report), 123.

4. See USSC, *Report to the Congress: Cocaine and Federal Sentencing Policy* (Washington, DC: U.S. Sentencing Commission, May 2007), http://www.ussc.gov/r_congress/cocaine2007.pdf (accessed August 15, 2010) (hereinafter 2007 USSC Report), 12.

5. In 1992, this number was 91 percent. See 2007 USSC Report, 15. For demographic trends in cocaine use, see 1995 USSC Report, 34: "The [National Household Survey on Drug Abuse] found that of those reporting cocaine use at least once in the reporting year, 75 percent were White, 15 percent Black, and 10 percent Hispanic. And of those reporting crack use at least once in the reporting year, 52 percent were White, 38 percent were Black, and 10 percent were Hispanic."

6. Lynn d. Johnson, "Hip-Hop's Holy Trinity," *Pop Matters*, August 8, 2003, http://www.popmatters.com/music/features/030808-50cent.shtml (accessed August 16, 2010).

7. Raymond Williams, *Marxism and Literature* (Oxford: Oxford University Press, 1977), 131.

8. Ibid., 132.

9. Ibid., 131.

10. For national homicide rates and yearly totals, see James Alan Fox and Marianne W. Zawitz, *Homicide Trends in the United States* (Washington, DC: Department of Justice, Office of Justice Programs, Bureau of Justice Statistics, 2007). One hundred and twenty-nine per 100,000 is the rate for Precinct 41 in the South Bronx, New York, in 1991. See Andrew Karmen, *New York Murder Mystery* (New York: New York University Press, 2006), 71.

11. Raymond Williams, *The English Novel* (New York: Oxford University Press, 1970), 192.

12. Williams, *Marxism and Literature*, 132.

13. David Garland, *The Culture of Control: Crime and Social Order in Contemporary Society* (Chicago: University of Chicago Press, 2002), 142. In phrasing his argument thus, Garland clearly differs from others who argue that crime policy is driven primarily by manipulative politicians and, instead, suggests far more collective complicity in policy measures, even while recognizing that such complicity is never complete, wholly planned, or even intentional. For a somewhat contrasting analysis, see sociologist Katherine Beckett, who argues—against what she calls the "democracy-at-work" thesis—that "support for punitive anticrime measures has waxed and waned throughout American history, coexists with support for less punitive policies, and is only loosely related to the reported incidence of crime-related problems." *Making Crime Pay: Law and Order in Contemporary American Politics* (New York: Oxford University Press, 1997), 5.

14. Often influenced by the work of David Garland, a growing number of writers are analyzing the degree to which crime and punishment have come to suffuse social life generally. See, for example, Garland, *Culture of Control*; David Garland, *Punishment and Modern Society: A Study in Social Theory* (Chicago: University of Chicago Press, 1993); Philip Smith, *Punishment and Culture* (Chicago: University of Chicago Press, 2008); and Michelle Brown, *The Culture of Punishment* (New York: New York University Press, 2009).

15. Pew Center on the States, *One in 100: Behind Bars in America, 2008* (Washington, DC: Pew Charitable Trusts, February 2008).

16. Pew Center on the States, *One in 31: The Long Reach of American Corrections* (Washington, DC: Pew Charitable Trusts, March 2009).

17. Together, offenses known to the police and unknown victimizations represent the "true" total of crime—what criminologists call the "dark figure" of crime—which is actually unknowable since the only means by which we can access it are through crimes reported to police and victimization surveys, both of which, although much improved over the years, remain, understandably, imperfect.

18. Of around fourteen million annual arrests (not including traffic violations), those for drug abuse violations are the most frequent, accounting for nearly two million. Around 80 percent of those drug arrests are for possession, rather than for sale or manufacturing. See United States Department of Justice, *Crime in the United States, 2008* (Washington, DC: Federal Bureau of Investigation, September 2009), http://www.fbi.gov/ucr/ cius2008/arrests/index.html (accessed August 15, 2010).

19. I discuss the statistics for these processes more fully in the conclusion, but a full 94 percent of convictions are obtained through guilty pleas and never go to trial. See Sean Rosenmerkel, Matthew Durose, and Donald Farole Jr., *Felony Sentences in State Courts, 2006: Statistical Tables* (Washington, DC: U.S. Department of Justice, Office of Justice Programs, Bureau of Justice Statistics, December 2009), section 4.

20. As stated earlier, one in every thirty-one U.S. adults is under some form of correctional supervision, including over two million in jail or prison, and over five million on probation or parole. See Pew Center, *One in 31*.

21. Analyzing how common sense gets to be common in the first place has long been a pillar of critical scholarship in every discipline, whether inspired by the work of Marx, Marcuse, Foucault, or Gramsci, to name only a few. The influence of such

work on my own scholarly process has been far too deeply internalized to disentangle and profess easily. Without question, however, one of the most important early works looking at the symbolic power of crime in modern politics is Stuart Hall and others, *Policing the Crisis: Mugging, the State, and Law and Order* (New York: Palgrave Macmillan, 1978).

22. *California Penal Code* § 186.21 (West Supp. 1996).

23. Williams, *English Novel*, 11.

24. I've borrowed the phrase "language of exploitation" from Loïc Wacquant, "Whores, Slaves, and Stallions: Languages of Exploitation and Accommodation among Boxers," *Body & Society* 7, nos. 2-3 (2001): 181-94.

25. Williams, *English Novel*, 186.

26. For a more in-depth discussion of my scholarly process, see the methodological essay at the end of the book.

CHAPTER 1

1. See, for example, *Apprendi v. New Jersey*, 530 U.S. 466 (2000); *Blakely v. Washington*, 542 U.S. 296 (2004); *Cunningham v. California*, 549 U.S. 549 (2007); *Kimbrough v. United States*, 552 U.S. 85 (2007); *Rita v. United States*, 551 U.S. 338 (2007); *United States v. Booker*, 543 U.S. 220, 224 (2005).

2. *Sentencing Reform Act of 1984*, Pub. L. No. 104-38 (1984).

3. USSC, *Guidelines Manual*. (Nov. 2007), § 1A1.1, p.3.

4. In the *Booker* decision, the Court excised the statutory provisions 18 U.S.C. § 3553 (b) (1) and 18 § 3742 (c), which made the guidelines advisory only.

5. The issues concern the determinate sentencing structures at both the state and the federal levels, which often *require* judges to increase sentences beyond the maximum allowed by statute based on finding aggravating facts that have not been pled before a jury, thereby violating defendants' Sixth Amendment rights. California's sentencing structure, however, is interesting because it does not provide a true range; instead, it requires judges to impose the middle of three terms unless aggravating facts are found. In the wake of the *Cunningham* decision, therefore, California passed an emergency bill removing the middle term as the presumptive statutory maximum. The Court's decisions, then, suggest that sentencing structures which allow for enhancements based on facts not proved beyond a reasonable doubt to a jury are unconstitutional. In *Kimbrough*, however, the Court decided that judges could consider the unjust disparity between crack and powder in going *below* the statutory minimum.

6. 1995 USSC Report; USSC, *Special Report to Congress: Cocaine and Federal Sentencing Policy* (Washington, DC: U.S. Sentencing Commission, April 1997), http://www.ussc.gov/r_congress/NEWCRACK.PDF (accessed August 15, 2010) (hereinafter 1997 USSC Report); USSC, *Report to Congress: Cocaine and Federal Sentencing Policy* (Washington, DC: U.S. Sentencing Commission, May 2002), http://www.ussc.gov/r_congress/02crack/2002crackrpt.htm (accessed August 15, 2010) (hereinafter 2002 USSC Report); 2007 USSC Report.

7. 2007 USSC Report, 8.

8. As noted in the introduction, over 80 percent of those sentenced under the federal crack laws have been black. For an in-depth focus on the role of race in the laws' passing, see Michael Tonry, *Malign Neglect: Race, Crime, and Punishment in America* (New York: Oxford University Press, 1995); and Doris Marie Provine, *Unequal under Law: Race in the War on Drugs* (Chicago: University of Chicago Press, 2007). For a contrasting analysis of race's role in the passage of the laws, see Randall Kennedy, *Race, Crime, and the Law* (New York: Pantheon Books, 1997), 351-86.

9. Sen. Jim Webb, "Why We Must Reform Our Criminal Justice System," *Huffington Post*, June 11, 2009, http://www.huffingtonpost.com/sen-jim-webb/ why-we-must-reform-our-cr_b_214130.html (accessed August 16, 2010). On March 26, 2009, Webb introduced the National Criminal Justice Commission Act of 2009, S. 714, which is the companion to House bill H.R. 5143, which was introduced, collectively, by Democratic representatives Bill Delahunt, Marcia Fudge, and Robert C. "Bobby" Scott and Republican representatives Darrel Issa and Tom Rooney on April 27, 2010. As of August 2010, the House bill still needs to pass the Senate, having passed the House in July 2010.

10. See, for example, Adam Liptak, "Right and Left Join to Challenge U.S. on Criminal Justice," *New York Times*, November 24, 2009, http://www.nytimes. com/2009/11/24/us/24crime.html (accessed August 16, 2010).

11. Bruce Jacobs, *Dealing Crack: The Social World of Streetcorner Selling* (Boston: Northeastern University Press, 1999), 5.

12. Ibid., 6.

13. See, for example, Craig Reinarman and Harry G. Levine, *Crack in America: Demon Drugs and Social Justice* (Berkeley: University of California Press, 1997).

14. 1995 USSC Report, 129 n.163.

15. George Rusche and Otto Kirchheimer, *Punishment and Social Structure* (New York: Columbia University Press, 1939), 65.

16. William J. Chambliss, "The Law of Vagrancy," *Social Problems* 12, no.1 (Summer 1964): 77.

17. Richard Quinney, *Class, State, and Crime* (New York: David McKay, 1977), 136.

18. Garland, *Punishment and Society*, 282.

19. Smith, *Punishment and Culture*, 1.

20. Brown, *Culture of Punishment*, 12.

21. Ibid., 212.

22. George L. Kelling and others, *The Kansas City Preventive Patrol Experiment: A Technical Report* (Washington, DC: Police Foundation, 1974).

23. George L. Kelling and others, *Newark Foot Patrol Experiment* (Washington, DC: Police Foundation, 1981).

24. All quotations attributed to this work can be found here: George L. Kelling and James Q. Wilson, "Broken Windows," *Atlantic Monthly*, March 1982, http://www. theatlantic.com/doc/198203/broken-windows (accessed August 16, 2010).

25. See, for example, the strong praise of New York's success in George L. Kelling and William J. Bratton, "Declining Crime Rates: Insiders' Views of the New York City Story," *Journal of Criminal Law and Criminology* 88, no. 4 (Summer 1998): 1217-32. But see also the critique of this praise in Judith A. Greene, "Zero Tolerance: A Case Study of Police Policies and Practices in New York City," *Crime and Delinquency* 45, no. 2

(April 1999): 171-87. Perhaps the strongest critique, however, is Bernard E. Harcourt, *Illusion of Order: The False Promise of Broken Windows Policing* (Cambridge, MA: Harvard University Press, 2005).

26. In a large field, see the concise discussion in Norval Morris, "The Contemporary Prison: 1965–Present," in *The Oxford History of the Prison: The Practice of Punishment in Western Society*, ed. Norval Morris and David J. Rothman, 202-31 (New York: Oxford University Press, 1998).

27. Garland, *Culture of Control*, 147.

28. Samuel Walker, *Taming the System: The Control of Discretion in Criminal Justice, 1950-1990* (New York: Oxford University Press, 1993).

29. Robert Martinson, "What Works? Questions and Answers about Prison Reform," *Public Interest* 35 (Spring 1974): 25.

30. See, for example, a concise critique of Martinson in Francis T. Cullen, "Rehabilitation and Treatment Programs," in *Crime: Public Policies for Crime Control*, ed. James Q. Wilson and Joan Petersilia, 253-89 (Oakland: Institute for Contemporary Studies, 2002). For a cultural analysis of Martinson's role in prison science, see Brown, *Culture of Punishment*, 153-89.

31. See, for example, Paula M. Ditton and Doris James Wilson, *Truth in Sentencing in State Prisons* (Washington, DC: U.S. Department of Justice, Office of Justice Programs, Bureau of Justice Statistics, January 1999).

32. "The popularity of mandatory minimum sentences," according to drug law historian David F. Musto, "had been gathering strength at the state level since the enactment of the so-called Rockefeller Laws in New York in 1973." *The American Disease: Origins of Narcotic Control*, 3rd ed. (New York: Oxford University Press, 1999), 273.

33. See, for example, Alexander Smith and Harriet Polack, "Curtailing the Sentencing Power of Trial Judges: The Unintended Consequences," *Court Review* (Williamsburg, VA: American Judges Association, Summer 1999). For an economic critique, see Jonathan P. Caulkins and others, *Mandatory Minimum Drug Sentencing: Throwing Away the Key or the Taxpayers' Money?* (Santa Monica, CA: Rand, Drug Policy Research Center, 1997). For a discussion of the prosecutor's rise in power over the latter half of the twentieth century, see Jonathan Simon, *Governing through Crime: How the War on Crime Transformed American Democracy and Created a Culture of Fear* (Oxford: Oxford University Press, 2007), 33-74.

34. Quoted in Mark Martin, "Maximum Insecurity: California's Prison System Produces Bizarre and Dangerous Results Harmful to Inmates and Public," *San Francisco Chronicle*, August 27, 2006, http://articles.sfgate.com/2006-08-27/opinion/17308491_1_corrections-system-prison-parole (accessed August 16, 2010).

35. For example, see, in a very large field, James Austin and John Irwin, *It's about Time: America's Imprisonment Binge*, 3rd ed. (Belmont, CA: Wadsworth, 2001).

36. Take, for example, the following quotation from Christine Ward, director of the Crime Victims Action Alliance: "We understand that this is a move by the Legislature to help relieve prison overcrowding and save money in the budget. But we're very disappointed that public safety seems to have taken a back seat to other issues." Sam Stanton, "California Inmate Release Plan Begins," *Sacramento Bee*, January 25, 2010, http://www.sacbee.com/topstories/story/2486280.html?storylink=omni_popular (accessed August 16, 2010). Consider, also, the words of Paul M. Weber,

president of the Los Angeles police union: "We are concerned about victims these felons will leave in their wake before being rearrested for committing new crimes." Randal C. Archibold, "California, in Financial Crisis, Opens Prison Doors," *New York Times*, March 23, 2010, http://www.nytimes.com/2010/03/24/us/24calprisons. html?hp (accessed August 16, 2010). Assemblyman Ted Lieu states his views even more plainly: "Inmates are being released early, it's happening now and it's going to increase crime." Sam Stanton, "Early Jail Releases in California Worry Former Violent Offender," *Sacramento Bee*, February 6, 2010, http://www.sacbee. com/2010/02/06/2517364/early-releases-worry-former-violent.html (accessed August 16, 2010).

37. For the relevant cases, see the Prison Law Office's website, http://www.prison-law.com/cases.php.

38. Morris, "The Contemporary Prison," 229.

39. Philippe Bourgois, *In Search of Respect: Selling Crack in El Barrio*, 2nd ed. (Cambridge: Cambridge University Press, 2003), 143.

40. Jacobs, *Dealing Crack*, 120.

41. Ibid.

42. Bourgois, *In Search of Respect*, 198.

43. Ibid., 172 (brackets in original).

44. Ibid., 266.

45. Sudhir Venkatesh, *Gang Leader for a Day: A Rogue Sociologist Takes to the Streets* (New York: Penguin, 2008), 89, 101.

46. Loïc Wacquant, "Deadly Symbiosis: When Ghetto and Prison Meet and Mesh," *Punishment and Society* 3, no. 1 (January 2001): 116 (original emphasis).

47. Jean Comaroff and John Comaroff, "Millennial Capitalism: First Thoughts on a Second Coming," *Public Culture* 12, no. 2 (2000): 307.

48. Jock Young, "Merton with Energy, Katz with Structure: The Sociology of Vindictiveness and the Criminology of Transgression," *Theoretical Criminology* 7, no. 3 (2003): 410-11.

49. Jeff Chang, *Can't Stop Won't Stop: A History of the Hip-Hop Generation* (New York: Picador, 2005), 208.

50. Tricia Rose, *The Hip Hop Wars: What We Talk about When We Talk about Hip Hop—and Why It Matters* (New York: Basic Civitas Books, 2008), 47.

51. Jeffrey Ogbar, *Hip-Hop Revolution: The Culture and Politics of Rap* (Lawrence: University Press of Kansas, 2009), 144.

CHAPTER 2

1. 1995 USSC Report; 1997 USSC Report; 2002 USSC Report; 2007 USSC Report. To be sure, federal law is not the only law of the land, and many states did not adopt the exact same punishment structure. Without question, however, statutes and decisions at the federal level have material and symbolic effects that reverberate nationally in significant ways, many of which are directly stimulated by federal funding given to those states that follow suit, whether in the area of education or in the area of punishment. In Marie Provine's words,

Taking a "tough" stand on crack cocaine has been a bipartisan commitment in Washington since President Ronald Reagan spearheaded the war
on drugs. Legislation criminalizing the possession and sale of crack
cocaine quickly passed both houses of Congress in 1986 and 1988, with
huge margins of both parties in support. The states were urged to follow
the federal example and given inducements to do so. (*Race in the War on
Drugs*, 92)

By the 1990s, thirty-two states had mandatory minimums for drug offenses, and fourteen states differentiated between crack and powder. See 1995 USSC Report, 129-36.
See, also, generally, Musto, *American Disease*.

2. 1995 USSC Report, 121 n. 130.

3. Ibid.

4. Ibid.

5. Ibid.

6. Ibid., 121. National security has routinely been invoked throughout the history
of America's war on drugs. As researcher Peter Dale Scott and journalist Jonathan
Marshall have shown, President Ronald Reagan's response to the threat of commu-
nism in the "Third World" was to "invent a new threat, closely associated with com-
munism and even more frightening to the public: narcoterrorism. The term, rarely
well defined by its users, encompasses a variety of phenomena: guerilla movements
that finance themselves by drugs or taxes on drug traffickers, drug syndicates that
use terrorist methods to counter the state's law enforcement apparatus, and state-
sponsored terrorism associated with drug crimes." Crack's historical uniqueness,
however, lies in the speed with which its punitive scaffolding was erected, and the
community-level lethality that grew with it. Peter Dale Scott and Jonathan Marshall,
Cocaine Politics: Drugs, Armies, and the CIA in Central America, updated ed. (Berkeley: University of California Press, 1991), 23. For the history of drug enforcement in
the United States generally, see, again, Musto, *American Disease*.

7. 1995 USSC Report, 116.

8. Ibid., 124.

9. Ibid., 117.

10. Ibid., 122.

11. Ibid., 123.

12. See the collection in Reinarman and Levine, *Crack in America*.

13. Jacobs, *Dealing Crack*, 4.

14. On making powder, base, and crack, see 1995 USSC Report, 9-14.

15. John P. Morgan and Lynn Zimmer, "The Social Pharmacology of Smokeable
Cocaine: Not All It's Cracked Up to Be," in *Crack in America*, ed. Reinarman and
Levine, 133.

16. Ibid., 134.

17. Jacobs, *Dealing Crack*, 4.

18. Craig Reinarman and Harry G. Levine, "Crack in Context," in Reinarman and
Levine, *Crack in America*, 2.

19. Ibid.

20. 1995 USSC Report, 13.

21. Ibid., 91.

22. 2007 USSC Report, 5.

23. 1995 USSC Report, 123.

24. Ibid.

25. Ibid., 128.

26. Ibid., 129, quoting the Strategic Management System, which outlines the key responsibilities of the Drug Enforcement Agency (DEA).

27. Ibid., 125 (my emphasis).

28. Ibid., 120 (emphasis in report).

29. Ibid., 118 (my emphasis).

30. Ibid., 119.

31. Ibid., 67.

32. Ibid., 66.

33. Ibid., 63 (my emphasis).

34. Ibid., 64.

35. Ibid., 66, quoting research by Bruce Johnson.

36. Ibid.

37. Ibid., 68.

38. See, for example, the discussion in James Lynch, "Crime in International Perspective," in Wilson and Petersilia, *Crime*, 5-41.

39. See, for example, Franklin E. Zimring and Gordon Hawkins, *Crime Is Not the Problem: Lethal Violence in America* (Oxford: Oxford University Press, 1997).

40. Alfred Blumstein and Joel Wallman, "The Recent Rise and Fall of American Violence," in *The Crime Drop in America*, ed. Alfred Blumstein and Joel Wallman (Cambridge: Cambridge University Press, 2000), 4.

41. Ibid.

42. Ira Glasser and Loren Siegel, "When Constitutional Rights Seem Too Extravagant to Endure: The Crack Scare's Impact on Civil Rights and Liberties," in Reinarman and Levine, *Crack in America*, 235.

43. Bruce Johnson, Andrew Golub, and Eloise Dunlap, "The Rise of Hard Drugs, Drug Markets, and Violence in Inner-City New York," in Blumstein and Wallman, *Crime Drop*, 183.

44. Herbert L. Packer, *The Limits of the Criminal Sanction* (Stanford, CA: Stanford University Press, 1968), 279.

45. See, for example, Jerome Skolnick, "Gangs and Crime as Old as Time, but Drugs Change Gang Culture," reprinted in *The Modern Gang Reader*, ed. Malcolm Klein, Cheryl L. Maxson, and Jody Miller (Los Angeles: Roxbury, 1995), 222-27, from "Commentary," originally published in *Crime and Delinquency in California, 1980-1989* (Sacramento: California Department of Justice, Office of the Attorney General, Bureau of Criminal Statistics and Special Services), 171-79.

46. See, for example, Robert J. Sampson, Stephen Raudenbush, and Felton Earls, "Neighborhoods and Violent Crime: A Multilevel Study of Collective Efficacy," *Science* 277 (1997): 918-24.

47. Todd Clear, *Imprisoning Communities: How Mass Incarceration Makes Disadvantaged Neighborhoods Worse* (Oxford: Oxford University Press, 2009), 73.

48. Elijah Anderson, *Code of the Street: Decency, Violence, and the Moral Life of the Inner City* (New York: Norton, 1999).

49. Legal scholar Tracey Meares, for example, has argued that many community members—when dealing with the day-to-day realities of drug and gang violence—often welcome increased police presence, even at the expense of their own civil liberties. Seemingly supporting this argument is the fact that many black leaders initially endorsed the federal crack laws, calling on the state for help in addressing crack-related issues. After it became clear that black community members were shouldering the worst of increased policing, however, these same leaders then condemned the laws and called for their repeal. Similarly, legal scholar Randall Kennedy, in defending the rational basis of the crack laws, has argued that "[o]ne of the strongest reasons *favoring* the crack-powder distinction is precisely that crack is more accessible and, for that reason alone, more dangerous. . . . [Because a cheaper drug] is less expensive it is more affordable to more people and thus more potentially accessible." Kennedy's analysis, however, is deeply flawed, completely ignoring, as it does, evidence-based approaches to rational policymaking. Serious arguments about "potential" problems—i.e., things that have not yet happened—must provide, if they are to drive rational policy, empirical *evidence* for their claims and projections, rather than abstract possibilities based on nothing more than unsupported wheel spinning. Neither the USSC reports, the research on which they've been based, nor annual self-reports of drug use statistics have ever supported such projections, thereby nullifying any rational basis for "fearing" what has never been shown to have existed. Kennedy's defense, therefore, rests solely on yet another paradoxical assumption: fears that have no basis in reality—which, by definition, are irrational—are adequate and appropriate bases for rational policies. In addition, Kennedy's argument completely ignores the foundational doctrine of drug enforcement in the late-twentieth-century United States: the Kingpin Strategy, which, by law, *requires* enforcement officials to focus primarily on high-level suppliers, a strategy that, at every step of the way, is undermined by a fear-based structure that punishes street-level dealers moving minuscule drug amounts. See Tracey L. Meares and Dan M. Kahan, *Urgent Times: Policing and Rights in Inner-City Communities* (Boston: Beacon, 1999); and Kennedy, *Race, Crime, and the Law*, 383 (original emphasis).

50. Paul J. Goldstein and others, "Crack and Homicide in New York City: A Case Study in the Epidemiology of Violence," in Reinarman and Levine, *Crack in America*, 118 (original emphasis).

51. 1995 USSC Report, 95.

52. Ibid., 83.

53. Ibid., 97.

54. Ibid., quoting other researchers.

55. Ibid., 105.

56. Barry Bluestone and Bennett Harrison, *The Deindustrialization of America: Plant Closings, Community Abandonment, and the Dismantling of Basic Industry* (New York: Basic Books, 1982).

57. William Julius Wilson, *When Work Disappears: The World of the New Urban Poor* (New York: Vintage Books, 1996), 4, 21.

58. See, for example, Katherine S. Newman, *No Shame in My Game: The Working Poor in the Inner City* (New York: Vintage Books, 2000); Jay MacLeod, *Ain't No Makin' It: Aspirations and Attainment in a Low-Income Neighborhood* (Boulder, CO: Westview, 1995).

59. Skolnick, "Gangs and Crime," 222.

60. Philippe Bourgois, "In Search of Horatio Alger: Culture and Ideology in the Crack Economy," in Reinarman and Levine, *Crack in America*, 64-65.

61. Ibid., 69 (original emphasis).

62. 1995 USSC Report, 103.

63. William B. Sanders, *Gangbangs and Drive-Bys: Grounded Culture and Juvenile Gang Violence* (New York: de Gruyter, 1994).

64. Ibid., 68.

65. Ibid., 83.

66. Lisa Maher, *Sexed Work: Gender, Race, and Resistance in a Brooklyn Drug Market* (Oxford: Oxford University Press, 1997).

67. Ibid., 133.

68. Ibid., 83-107.

69. Ibid., 134: "Many women who held out for $10 as their lowest price for a blowjob were heroin users, with $10 corresponding to the market price for a bag of heroin."

70. Ibid., 195.

71. Ibid., 137.

72. Ibid., 139.

73. Ibid., 144.

74. Ibid., 148-55.

75. 1995 USSC Report, 82-83.

76. Felix Padilla, *The Gang as an American Enterprise* (New Brunswick, NJ: Rutgers University Press, 1993), 12.

77. Skolnick, "Gangs and Crime," 224.

78. In a growing genre, see, for example, Reymundo Sanchez, *My Bloody Life: The Making of a Latin King* (Chicago: Chicago Review Press, 2000); Colton Simpson with Ann Pearlman, *Inside the Crips: Life Inside L.A.'s Most Notorious Gang* (New York: St. Martin's, 2006).

79. Sanyika Shakur, *Monster: The Autobiography of an L.A. Gang Member* (New York: Grove, 1993), 367.

80. Ibid., 365-67.

81. Ibid., 365.

82. 1995 USSC Report, 65.

83. Quoted in Michael Woodiwiss, *Gangster Capitalism: The United States and the Globalization of Organized Crime* (New York: Carroll and Graf, 2005), 111 (emphasis added).

84. 1995 USSC Report, 78.

85. 2007 USSC Report, B-6.

86. Ibid.

87. The literature that has grown around and through this reconceptualization process—which has paralleled and been intertwined with notions of flexible labor and post-Fordist economic restructuring—is quite substantial, and has redefined almost every field it has touched, academic and popular. I cannot, therefore, do it full justice here. But Manuel Castells's work in the 1990s is a key example. See, for instance, Manuel Castells, *Rise of the Network Society* (Oxford: Oxford University Press, 1996).

88. Indeed, this is what Benjamin Barber called "Jihad vs. McWorld." Benjamin Barber, *Jihad vs. McWorld: How Globalization and Tribalism Are Reshaping the World* (New York: Random House, 1996).

89. Neal Stephenson, *Snow Crash* (New York: Bantam Books, 1992).

90. Of course, the difficulty here lies in deciphering who, in fact, is mimicking whom. Take sociologist Jack Katz's discussion of gangs as sovereign nations. "Street elites," he contends, "use violence innovatively to elaborate the theme of sovereignty. . . . With task forces and spy activities, police departments—big groups of serious, tough-looking, gun-bearing, flesh-and-blood adult men—organize their work lives along units that are dictated, in effect, by metaphors designed by the ghetto adolescents. What greater proof of sovereignty than the ability to draw official maps of urban geography!" In this way, Katz has argued for an interesting game of follow the leader: gangs first mimic sovereignty, then law enforcement responds to their innovative mimicry. But others, such as political scientists Peter Andreas and Ethan Nadelmann, for example, argue that the game of follow the leader works the other way round—that American law enforcement agencies have, in fact, aggressively worked to "export" their own versions of crime around the world in furtherance of national interests, and that underground networks adapt to them. Importantly, these kinds of arguments find their opposite in the work of many terrorism experts such as Walter Laqueur, who clearly suggests that American efforts need to adapt to increasingly extremist groups. To put it simply, trying to find a kingpin in a network is like trying to find a needle in a haystack. Perhaps the most important aspect of these reorientations around the concept of networks, however, is that, regardless of the "actual" leader, law enforcement agencies almost always justify—in order to ensure that they are accomplishing what they've been tasked with doing—their actions as necessary in order to follow increasingly nebulous criminal groups, which is precisely what occurred in the crack era as well. See Jack Katz, *Seductions of Crime: Moral and Sensual Attractions in Doing Evil* (New York: Basic Books, 1988), 135; Peter Andreas and Ethan Nadelmann, *Policing the Globe: Criminalization and Crime Control in International Relations* (Oxford: Oxford University Press, 2006); Walter Laqueur, *No End to War: Terrorism in the Twenty-First Century* (London: Continuum, 2004).

91. Thomas Frank, *One Market under God: Extreme Capitalism, Market Populism, and the End of Economic Democracy* (New York: Anchor Books, 2001).

92. "Handbook of the Business Revolution—Manifesto," *Fast Company*, October, 1995, http://www.fastcompany.com/magazine/01/edpage.html (accessed August 16, 2010). All quotations attributed to this work can be found here.

93. Notorious B.I.G., "The Ten Crack Commandments," *Life after Death* (Bad Boy, 1997).

CHAPTER 3

1. Rubber bands around the wrist suggest that one is a drug dealer who uses them to hold cash. The acronym "MBA" refers to the Master in Business Administration degree.

2. See Robert K. Merton, "Social Structure and Anomie," *American Sociological Review* 3, no. 5 (October 1938): 672-82.

3. See Clifford R. Shaw and Henry D. McKay, *Juvenile Delinquency in Urban Areas* (Chicago: University of Chicago Press, 1942).

4. See Bourgois, *In Search of Respect*; Jacobs, *Dealing Crack*.

5. Supremes verse in Boot Camp Clik, "Welcome to Bucktown U.S.A.," *Chosen Few*.

6. Jay-Z, "Rap Game/Crack Game," *In My Lifetime, Vol. 1* (Rock-a-Fella, 1997).

7. Jay-Z, "U Don't Know," *The Blueprint* (Rock-a-Fella, 2001). A "g-pack" is slang for a one-thousand-dollar-bundle worth of crack that is bagged up and ready to sell "hand-to-hand" on the street.

8. Pusha T's verse in the Clipse, "Grindin," *Lord Willin'* (StarTrak, 2002).

9. Raekwon, *Cuban Linx*. See, also, his 2009 sequel, *Only Built for Cuban Linx . . . Pt. II* (Ice H2O/EMI).

10. Ghostface Killah, *Fishscale* (Def Jam, 2006).

11. Fat Joe in Terror Squad, "Lean Back," *True Story* (Umvd Labels, 2004).

12. Juelz Santana, "I Am Crack," *What the Game's Been Missing!* (Def Jam, 2005).

13. For a recent discussion of rap's hustler mythology and its roots in black vernacular traditions, see Eithne Quinn, *Nuthin' but a "G" Thang: The Culture and Commerce of Gangsta Rap* (New York: Columbia University Press, 2005), chapters 5 and 6. While elements of rap's badman mythology are clearly rooted in such traditions, "Nevertheless," as historian Robin Kelley argues, rap—especially gangsta rap—has an "identifiable style of its own, and in some respects it is a particular product of the mid-1980s." Or, as cultural theorist Paul Gilroy asks, "How can rap be discussed as if it sprang intact from the entrails of the blues?" Robin D. G. Kelley, "Kickin' Reality, Kickin' Ballistics: Gangsta Rap and Postindustrial Los Angeles," in *Droppin' Science: Critical Essays on Rap Music and Hip Hop Culture*, ed. William Eric Perkins (Philadelphia: Temple University Press, 1996), 119. Paul Gilroy, *The Black Atlantic: Modernity and Double Consciousness* (Cambridge, MA: Harvard University Press, 1993), 34.

14. Advertisement in *XXL*, March 2004, 178.

15. "Rapper C-Murder Sentenced to Life in Prison," *USA Today*, August 14, 2009, http://www.usatoday.com/life/people/2009-08-14-cmurder-sentencing_N.htm (accessed August 11, 2010).

16. *The Source*, March 2004.

17. Simmons quoted in "Russell Simmons Presents: Hip Hop Justice," *Business Wire*, July 22, 2004, http://www.allbusiness.com/crime-law-enforcement-corrections/law/5200009-1.html (accessed August 17, 2010).

18. In fact, the list of slain rappers is staggeringly depressing, and includes young men from all over the United States: Scott La Rock (NY) in 1987; MC Rock (MA) in 1990; Charizma (CA) in 1993; Mr. Cee (CA) in 1996; Stretch (NY) in 1995; Tupac Shakur (NY and CA) in 1996; Notorious B.I.G. (NY) in 1997; Fat Pat (TX) in 1998; Big L (NY) in 1999; Freaky Tah (NY) in 1999; Jam Master Jay (NY) in 2002; Mac Dre (CA) in 2004; Proof (MI) in 2006; and Stack Bundles (NY) in 2007, to name but a few.

19. See, for example, Geraldine Baum, "Rapper's Upbeat Spirit Recalled," *Los Angeles Times*, November 6, 2002; Geoff Boucher and Paul Lieberman, "Fatal Shooting of Rap Pioneer in Studio Jolts Fans and Peers," *Los Angeles Times*, November 1, 2002; Alan Feuer, "Rap World Baffled by Killing of Star with Peaceful Image," *New York Times*, November 1, 2002; Andy Newman and Al Baker, "Was It a Bad Business Deal

or a Music Industry Feud?" *New York Times*, November 1, 2002; John Pareles, "Latest Violence Is Not Typical of Previous Gunplay," *New York Times*, November 1, 2002.

20. See, for example, Michele McPhee, "Bullets Riddle Busta Ride," *New York Daily News*, February 24, 2003; Chuck Philips, "Rap Feud Prompts Universal to Cancel Party, Sources Say," *Los Angeles Times*, February 4, 2003;William K. Rashbaum, "Investigating Murder of a D.J., Police Use Detectives Specializing in the World of Hip-Hop," *New York Times*, January 25, 2003.

21. Derrick Parker and Matt Diehl, *Notorious C.O.P.: The Inside Story of the Tupac, Biggie, and Jam Master Jay Investigations from NYPD's First "Hip-Hop Cop"* (New York: St. Martin's, 2006).

22. *Grand Upright Music, Ltd v. Warner Bros. Records, Inc.*, 780 F. Supp. 182 (S.D.N.Y. 1991).

23. Mike Davis, *City of Quartz: Excavating the Future in Los Angeles* (New York: Vintage Books, 1992), 87.

24. Paul Gilroy, "'After the Love Has Gone': Bio-Politics and Etho-Poetics in the Black Public Sphere," *Public Culture* 7, no. 1 (Fall 1994): 50.

25. Paul Gilroy, "It's a Family Affair," in *That's the Joint!: The Hip-Hop Studies Reader*, ed. Murray Forman and Mark Anthony Neal (New York: Routledge, 2004), 90.

26. Ibid.

27. Gilroy, *Black Atlantic*, 32.

28. See, for example, David Toop, *Rap Attack 3*, 3rd ed. (London: Serpent's Tail, 2000); Dick Hebdige, *Cut 'n' Mix: Culture, Identity, and Caribbean Music* (London: Routledge, 1987). For more recent histories, see Chang, *Can't Stop Won't Stop*; Alan Light, ed., *The Vibe History of Hip Hop* (New York: Three Rivers, 1999).

29. See, for example, Perkins, *Droppin' Science*; Houston A. Baker Jr., *Black Studies, Rap, and the Academy* (Chicago: University of Chicago Press, 1993); Tricia Rose, *Black Noise: Rap Music and Black Culture in Contemporary America* (Middletown, CT: Wesleyan University Press, 1994).

30. Rose, *Black Noise*, 144.

31. As an example, see, among many, Tony Mitchell, ed., *Global Noise: Rap and Hip Hop outside the USA* (Middletown, CT: Wesleyan University Press, 2002).

32. KRS-One, "Hip Hop vs. Rap," on "Sound of the Police," vinyl single (Jive Records, 1993).

33. Many also add a fifth element: "beatboxing"—the art of making beats solely with one's own voice.

34. See, for example, Chang, *Can't Stop Won't Stop*, 228; and Greg Dimitriadis, *Performing Identity/Performing Culture: Hip Hop as Text, Pedagogy, and Lived Practice* (New York: Peter Lang, 2001), 14-34.

35. Todd Boyd, "Intergenerational Culture Wars: Civil Rights vs. Hip Hop (interview by Yusuf Nuruddin)," *Socialism and Democracy* 18, no. 2 (2004): 50. Similar sentiments are also expressed in Todd Boyd, *The New H.N.I.C.: The Death of Civil Rights and the Reign of Hip Hop* (New York: New York University Press, 2002).

36. George Martinez, "The Politics of Hip Hop (interview by Ron Hayduk)," *Socialism and Democracy* 18, no. 2 (2004): 196.

37. Imani Perry, *Prophets of the Hood: Politics and Poetics in Hip Hop* (Durham, NC: Duke University Press, 2004), 10.

38. Kristine Wright, "Rise Up Hip Hop Nation: From Deconstructing Racial Politics to Building Positive Solutions," *Socialism and Democracy* 18, no. 2 (2004): 15 (original emphasis).

39. Ibid., 17.

40. Gwendolyn Pough, *Check It While I Wreck It: Black Womanhood, Hip-Hop Culture, and the Black Public Sphere* (Boston: Northeastern University Press, 2004), 11.

41. Ibid., 4.

42. Rose, *Hip Hop Wars*, xii.

43. Ibid., 1. See, also, Joan Morgan, *When Chickenheads Come Home to Roost: A Hip-Hop Feminist Breaks It Down* (New York: Touchstone, 1999).

44. Rap has long been the focus of moralistic crusaders. For a discussion of this history, see Quinn, *Nuthin' but a G" Thang*, starting 149.

45. Juan Williams, "Banish the Bling: A Culture of Failure Taints Black America," *Washington Post*, August 21, 2006, http://www.washingtonpost.com/wp-dyn/content/article/2006/08/20/AR2006082000527.html (accessed August 11, 2010).

46. Ibid.

47. Text and MP3 of Bill Cosby's speech can be found at http://www.american-rhetoric.com/speeches/billcosbypoundcakespeech.htm.

48. Williams, "Banish the Bling."

49. Juan Williams, "What Bill O'Reilly Really Told Me," *Time*, September 28, 2007, http://www.time.com/time/nation/article/0,8599,1666573,00.html (accessed August 16, 2010).

50. Jon Caramanica and others, "Victim," *XXL*, March 2005, 132.

51. T. Denean Sharpley-Whiting, *Pimps Up, Ho's Down: Hip Hop's Hold on Young Black Women* (New York: New York University Press, 2007), 82.

52. Between 1993 and 2005, for example, rates for robbery declined by 57 percent, aggravated assault by 64 percent, and rape by 67 percent. Property crimes as a whole also declined by 52 percent during this period. See Shannan M. Catalano, *Criminal Victimization, 2005* (Washington, DC: U.S Department of Justice, Office of Justice Programs, Bureau of Justice Statistics, September 2006), 5.

53. Sharpley-Whiting, *Pimps Up, Ho's Down*, 84.

54. See Timothy C. Hart, *Reporting Crime to the Police, 1992-2000* (Washington, DC: Department of Justice, Office of Justice Programs, Bureau of Justice Statistics, March 2003).

55. Put yet another way, "[A]ntisocial behavior in children is one of the best predictors of antisocial behavior in adults, yet most antisocial children do not grow up to be antisocial adults. In retrospect, high-rate adult offenders will almost always be drawn from the pool of high-risk children, but looking forward from high-risk children, we cannot distinguish well who will persist or desist as adults." Robert J. Sampson and John H. Laub, "A Life-Course View of the Development of Crime," *Annals of the American Academy of Political and Social Science* 602 (November 2005): 20-21 (citation omitted).

56. See, for example, Alan M. Dershowitz, *The Abuse Excuse: And Other Cop-Outs, Sob Stories, and Evasions of Responsibility* (Boston: Back Bay Books, 1994).

57. Sampson and Laub, "Life-Course View," 38.

58. Jody Miller, *Getting Played: African American Girls, Urban Inequality, and Gendered Violence* (New York: New York University Press, 2008), 34.

59. Ibid.

60. Maher, *Sexed Work*, 156.

61. Miller, *Getting Played*, 240 n.10.

62. Bourgois, *In Search of Respect*, 88.

63. Eddie's own troubles demonstrate the horrific depths of this violence continuum even further: "By seven years of age, he [Eddie] had already tried to commit suicide; and at nine, he attempted to throw himself out of a third-floor school window when a teacher 'roughed me up for not paying attention in class.'" Ibid., 183.

64. Ibid., 184.

65. Ibid., 182-83.

66. Ibid., 190.

67. Ibid., 24.

68. Ibid., 23.

69. Ibid.

70. Ibid., 24.

71. Ibid., 208.

72. The term "imprisoning framework" is borrowed from legal scholar Susan Shapiro, and is discussed in more detail later in this chapter.

73. See, for example, Cheo Hodari Coker, "N.W.A.," and Tony Green, "The Dirty South," in Light, *Vibe History*, 251-63, 265-75. See, also, Quinn, *Nuthin' but a "G" Thang*, starting 67.

74. See, for example, David Bry, "New York State of Mind: The Resurgence of East Coast Hip Hop," in Light, *Vibe History*, 327-37.

75. The liner notes in the group Company Flow's first record, for example, proudly proclaimed being "Independent as Fuck!" Company Flow, *Funcrusher Plus* (Rawkus, 1997).

76. Some of these darker elements can be seen in the "horrorcore" rap that began around the mid-1990s. The Gravediggaz, a group led by Wu-Tang Clan producer RZA, is an example.

77. Ghostface Killah in "Shark Niggas (Biters)," on Raekwon, *Cuban Linx*.

78. Redman, "Basically," *Dare Iz a Darkside* (Def Jam, 1994). This quotation also illustrates the degree to which "underground" and "hardcore" rap in mid-1990s New York were inextricably linked.

79. O.C., "Time's Up," *Word . . . Life* (Wild Pitch, 1994).

80. Nas, "Represent," *Illmatic* (Sony, 1994).

81. The outline of the industry that follows clearly reflects the state of the music business in the 1990s, which had yet to see the development of online sales or ringtones, to name only a few industry innovations since then. But many of the same issues persist, especially when it comes to key contract points. In the words of music law experts William Krasilovsky and Sydney Shemel, in *This Business of Music: The Definitive Guide to the Business and Legal Issues of the Music Industry*, 10th ed. (New York: Billboard Books, 2007),

> In the music business old habits are reinforced by long-term contracts
> and complex ownership issues, and participants in the music business

have to contend daily with issues resulting from decisions made long ago. . . . The resistance to reexamining these terms and the willingness to accept terms presented as "standard" are both elements of what can be described as "contractual inertia": the perpetuation of "industry standard" terms long after the original justification for them has ceased to exist. Clauses like this should be as rare as the Coelacanth, but they persist." (*This Business of Music*, 458)

82. There has grown a very large "self-help" literature around the music industry. See, among many, Moses Avalon, *Secrets of Negotiating a Record Contract: The Musician's Guide to Understanding and Avoiding Sneaky Lawyer Tricks* (San Francisco: Backbeat Books, 2001); Donald S. Passman, *All You Need to Know about the Music Business* (New York: Simon & Schuster, 2000); Krasilovsky and Shemel, *This Business of Music*.

83. The history of copyright is also a large and growing field. Perhaps the classic is Lyman Ray Patterson, *Copyright in Historical Perspective* (Nashville, TN: Vanderbilt University Press, 1968). For a more recent account that emphasizes international legal aspects, see Paul Goldstein, *International Copyright: Principles, Law, and Practice* (Oxford: Oxford University Press, 2001). My historical summaries rely on both authors' work, and, especially, on Russell Sanjek's three-volume work, *American Popular Music and Its Business: The First Four Hundred Years* (New York: Oxford University Press, 1988).

84. As Mark Rose, scholar of literature and intellectual property, has argued, modern conceptions of authorship and ownership have developed together and cannot be understood apart from each other. Mark Rose, *Authors and Owners: The Invention of Copyright* (Cambridge, MA: Harvard University Press, 1993).

85. The challenges that digital domains pose to intellectual property law are perhaps the most important issues for intellectual property scholars and critics today. Among many, see James Boyle, *Shamans, Software, and Spleens: Law and the Construction of the Information Society* (Cambridge, MA: Harvard University Press, 1997); Lawrence Lessig, *The Future of Ideas: The Fate of the Commons in a Connected World* (New York: Vintage Books, 2002).

86. As Sanjek describes,

A master, two wardens, and a Court of Assistants were elected to govern the [Stationers' publishing company], assign tasks and obligations to members, and mete out punishment for infractions of trade rules and practices. Agents were recruited to seek out and report the printing and sale of seditious books and ballads. Confiscated material was burned in a large fireplace in the kitchen of Stationers' Hall. . . . Several persons were executed for violation of the law and of company regulations, and others were imprisoned in the hall's cellars. Publishers of unlicensed ballads were fined fourpence for each copy seized and occasionally were held for a short period in the basement cells. (*American Popular Music*, 1:42)

See, also, Goldstein, *International Copyright*, 5; and Donald Thomas, *A Long Time Burning: The History of Literary Censorship in England* (New York: Praeger, 1969).

87. As musicologist Joanna Demers argues, "[M]ost authors do not own the copyrights to their work; they sell them to a publisher for a share in the royalties and

a guarantee that their work will be distributed commercially." Joanna Demers, *Steal This Music: How Intellectual Property Law Affects Musical Creativity* (Athens: University of Georgia Press, 2006), 11.

88. On Tin Pan Alley, see Sanjek, *American Popular Music*, 2:401-20.

89. As one music industry lawyer put it, "When I use the term 'artist,' I am talking about the person who performs the song, whether live or on a record, regardless of whether or not they wrote the song. When I use the term 'songwriter,' I am talking about the person who wrote the song, whether or not they perform it." David Naggar, *The Music Business (Explained in Plain English): What Every Artist and Songwriter Should Know to Avoid Getting Ripped Off!* 2nd ed. (San Francisco: DaJe´ Publishing, 2000), 12.

90. For the complex royalty structures, see authors cited in note 82 above. Again, this overview does not take into account ringtones, for example; mechanical royalties still figure centrally in industry deals, however.

91. According to Passman,

> Record deals used to be for a term of one year, with options to renew for additional periods of one year each. The artist was usually obligated to deliver two albums each year. This worked terrifically in the days when records were banged out like pancakes, since most of the time artists just showed up, sang, then went back to the beach. . . . But all this has gone the way of the dinosaurs. (*All You Need to Know*, 119)

92. Avalon, *Secrets*, 248.

93. See, for example, Edna Gunderson, "Rights Issues Rocks the Music World," *USA Today*, September 16, 2002, http://www.usatoday.com/life/music/news/2002-09-15-artists-rights_x.htm (accessed August 11, 2010); Chuck Philips, "Musicians Urge N.Y. Rights Reform," *Los Angeles Times*, November 1, 2002; Chuck Philips, "State Senate to Examine Music Firms," *Los Angeles Times*, August 26, 2002; California State Senate, *Personal Service Contracts: Seven-Year Rule; Exception for Recording Artists*, Hearing before the Select Committee on the Entertainment Industry, September 5, 2001; California State Senate, *Record Label Accounting Practices*, Joint Hearing of the Committee on the Judiciary and Select Committee on the Entertainment Industry, July 23, 2002; California State Senate, *Record Label Accounting Practices*, Joint Hearing of the Judiciary Committee and the Select Committee on the Entertainment Industry, September 24, 2002.

94. Steve Albini, "The Problem with Music," http://www.negativland.com/albini. html (accessed August 11, 2010).

95. Gundersen, "Rights Issues."

96. Ibid.

97. Ibid.

98. Susan Shapiro, "Collaring the Crime, Not the Criminal," *American Sociological Review* 55, no. 3 (June 1990): 350.

99. Edwin Sutherland, *White Collar Crime* (New York: Holt, Rinehart, and Winston, 1949), 9.

100. Shapiro, "Collaring the Crime," 362.

101. Ibid., 350.

102. Marc Galanter, "Why the 'Haves' Come Out Ahead: Speculations on the Limits of Legal Change," *Law and Society Review* 9, no. 1 (Autumn 1974): 95-160.

103. Ibid., 97.

CHAPTER 4

1. Quoted in Bethany Thomas, "La. Proposes Crackdown on Belly-Baring Pants," *NBC News*, May 13, 2004, http://www.msnbc.msn.com/id/4963512/ (accessed August 12, 2010).

2. Quoted in Laura Parker, "Several Cities Snapping over Baggy Pants," *USA Today*, October 15, 2007, http://www.usatoday.com/news/nation/2007-10-14-Baggy_N.htm (accessed August 12, 2010).

3. Laurie Segall, "New York Politician Hopes to End Youths' Pants-Sagging Trend," *CNN*, March 29, 2010, http://www.cnn.com/2010/LIVING/03/29/new.york.baggy. pants/index.html?iref=allsearch (accessed August 17, 2010).

4. Ibid.

5. Lawrence M. Friedman, *Crime and Punishment in American History* (New York: Basic Books, 1993).

6. See also Barry C. Feld, *Bad Kids: Race and the Transformation of the Juvenile Court* (Oxford: Oxford University Press, 1999).

7. Friedman, *Crime and Punishment*, 415 (original emphasis).

8. Ibid., 165.

9. Nicole Hahn Rafter, "Criminal Anthropology in the United States," reprinted in *The Criminology Theory Reader*, ed. Stuart Henry and Werner Einstadter (New York: New York University Press, 1998), 86.

10. Ibid.

11. John J. DiIulio Jr., "The Coming of the Super-Predators," *Weekly Standard*, November 27, 1995, 23. All quotations attributed to this article can be found here.

12. For a more in-depth presentation of the theory of moral poverty, see William J. Bennett, John J. DiIulio Jr., and John P. Walters, *Body Count: Moral Poverty . . . and How to Win America's War against Crime and Drugs* (New York: Simon & Schuster, 1996).

13. Text and MP3 of Bill Cosby's speech can be found at http://www.american-rhetoric.com/speeches/billcosbypoundcakespeech.htm.

14. Williams, "Banish the Bling." See, also, Juan Williams, *Enough: The Phony Leaders, Dead-End Movements, and Culture of Failure That Are Undermining Black America—and What We Can Do About It* (New York: Three Rivers Press, 2007).

15. Williams, "Banish the Bling."

16. Williams, "Bill O'Reilly."

17. The Notorious B.I.G., "Things Done Changed," *Ready to Die* (Bad Boy, 1994).

18. "East vs. West," *Beef* (Image Entertainment, 2003).

19. For sobering descriptions of just how hectic things did get for many youth in late-eighties and early-nineties New York, see the first-hand accounts collected in Youth Communication, *Things Get Hectic: Teens Write about the Violence That Surrounds Them*, ed. Philip Kay, Andrea Estepa, and Al Desetta (New York: Touchstone, 1998).

20. Bernard E. Harcourt, *Language of the Gun: Youth, Crime, and Public Policy* (Chicago: University of Chicago Press, 2006), 7.

21. Ibid., 10.

22. Ibid., 8.

23. Ibid., 85.

24. Allen Feldman, *Formations of Violence: The Narrative of the Body and Political Terror in Northern Ireland* (Chicago: University of Chicago Press, 1991).

25. Ibid., 52.

26. Ibid., 47.

27. Ibid., 47-48.

28. Ibid., 53.

29. James William Gibson, *Warrior Dreams: Paramilitary Culture in Post-Vietnam America* (New York: Hill and Wang, 1994), 243.

30. Ibid., 244.

31. Ibid., 254.

32. Robert H. Boatman, *Living with Glocks: The Complete Guide to the New Standard in Combat Handguns* (Boulder, CO: Paladin, 2002), 1.

33. Harcourt, *Language of the Gun*, 8.

34. Ibid., 48.

35. Ibid., 41.

36. Ibid., 65.

37. Notorious B.I.G. in Junior M.A.F.I.A, "Player's Anthem," *Conspiracy* (Big Beat, 1995).

38. Nas, "I Gave You Power," *It Was Written* (Columbia, 1996).

39. See note 50, chapter 3.

40. Shakur, *Monster*, 366-67 (original emphasis).

41. 50 Cent with Kris Ex, *From Pieces to Weight: Once upon a Time in Southside Queens* (New York: MTV Books, 2005), 109.

42. Ibid., 111.

43. Ibid., 113-15.

44. Ibid., 115-18.

45. Ibid., 117-18.

46. Elliott Currie, *Crime and Punishment in America: Why the Solutions to America's Most Stubborn Social Crisis Have Not Worked—and What Will* (New York: Owl Books, 1998), 113.

CHAPTER 5

1. Nas, "One Love," *Illmatic*.

2. Jacobs, *Dealing Crack*, 129. In the words of Elliott Currie, who uses a brief quotation from lyrics by Wu-Tang Clan as an illustration, "The falling rates of urban violence may have more to do with these changing attitudes than all the new police tactics put together." Currie, *Crime and Punishment*, 189. Sociologist Robert Garot also makes similar arguments, suggesting that—through complex deployments of various avoidance strategies, including clothing modifications, linguistic diffusion, and not claiming gang ties when faced with bad odds—many youth, even in the most hectic environments, consistently find ways to avoid serious violence without losing face. Robert Garot, *Who You Claim: Performing Gang Identity in School and on the Streets* (New York: New York University Press, 2010). See, also, Johnson, Golub, and Dunlap, "The Rise and Decline."

3. Jacobs, *Dealing Crack*, 128.

4. Michael R. Gottfredson and Travis Hirschi, *A General Theory of Crime* (Stanford, CA: Stanford University Press, 1990).

5. Ibid., 5.

6. Ibid., 16.

7. Ibid.

8. Ibid., 95.

9. Ibid., 97.

10. See Anderson, *Code of the Street*.

11. 50 Cent, *From Pieces to Weight*, 74.

12. Ibid., 55.

13. Ibid., 56-57.

14. Ibid., 58.

15. Ibid., 56.

16. Loïc Wacquant, *Body and Soul: Notebooks of an Apprentice Boxer* (Oxford: Oxford University Press, 2004).

17. Ibid., 22.

18. Ibid., 56-57.

19. Ibid., 68.

20. Ibid., 143.

21. 50 Cent, *From Pieces to Weight*, 174.

22. Ibid.

23. Voletta Wallace, *Voletta Wallace Remembers Her Son, Christopher Wallace, AKA Notorious B.I.G.* (New York: Atria Books, 2005).

24. Ibid., 57.

25. Ibid., 58.

26. Ibid., 65.

27. Ibid., 91.

28. Ibid., 130.

29. Ibid., 140.

30. Ibid., 143.

31. Ibid., 141.

32. Ibid., 136.

33. 50 Cent, Interview on Bonus DVD, *Get Rich or Die Trying* (Shady/Aftermath/Interscope, 2003), 50's emphasis.

34. A Tribe Called Quest, *The Low End Theory* (Jive, 1991).

35. Tribe, "Check the Rhime," *Low End Theory*.

36. Songs from his long-awaited debut album, for example, were widely circulated via bootlegged copies in the mid-1990s. While the album was slated to come out on Geffen Records around 1996, it was "shelved" by the label and never released. Large Professor's "debut" album—called, simply, *The LP*—was officially released by his own company in 2009, almost fifteen years later.

37. Large Professor in Organized Konfusion, "Stress (Remix)," vinyl single (1994).

38. Jeru The Damaja, "Too Perverted," *Wrath of the Math* (Fontana London, 1996).

39. El-P in Company Flow, "Definitive," *Funcrusher Plus*.

40. Wu-Tang Clan, "Protect Ya Neck," *Enter the Wu-Tang (36 Chambers)* (Loud/RCA, 1993). "Gza" is pronounced "Jiza," with a short "i."

41. Genius/GZA, "Labels," *Liquid Swords* (Geffen/MCA, 1995).

42. "Rza" is pronounced "Riza," with a short "i."

43. Katz, *Seductions of Crime.*

44. Ibid., 9.

45. Jeff Ferrell, "Cultural Criminology," *Annual Review of Sociology* 25 (1999): 396.

46. Jeff Ferrell, Dragan Milovanovic, and Stephen Lyng, "Edgework, Media Practices, and the Elongation of Meaning," *Theoretical Criminology* 5, no. 2 (2001): 178.

47. Ibid., 180.

48. Katz, *Seductions of Crime,* 4.

49. Ibid., 23 (original emphasis).

50. Ibid.

51. Ibid. (original emphasis).

52. Ibid., 24.

53. Ibid., 27.

54. Ibid.

55. Ibid., 35.

56. Ibid., 45.

57. Edwin Sutherland, "White-Collar Criminality," *Annual Review of Sociology* 5, no.1 (February 1940): 2-10, with excerpts reprinted in *Classics of Criminology*, 3rd ed., ed. Joseph E. Jacoby (Long Grove, IL: Waveland, 2004), 13-18.

58. In Jacoby, *Classics of Criminology,* 14.

59. Ibid., 15.

60. Ibid.

61. David O. Friedrichs, *Trusted Criminals: White Collar Crime in Contemporary Society* (Belmont, CA: Wadsworth, 2006), 3.

62. Quoted in Marshall B. Clinard and Peter Yeager, *Corporate Crime* (New York: Free Press, 1980), 15.

63. Ibid.

64. Shapiro, "Collaring the Crime," 351.

CHAPTER 6

1. "Chapter 17," *Welcome to Death Row* (hereinafter WDR) (Xenon Pictures, 2001).

2. "Chapter 3," WDR.

3. Ethan Brown, *Queens Reigns Supreme: Fat Cat, 50 Cent, and the Rise of the Hip-Hop Hustler* (New York: Anchor Books, 2005), 114-15.

4. "Chapter 3," WDR.

5. "Chapter 4," WDR.

6. Randall Sullivan, *LAbyrinth: A Detective Investigates the Murders of Tupac Shakur and Notorious B.I.G., the Implications of Death Row Records' Suge Knight, and the Origins of the Los Angeles Police Scandal* (New York: Grove, 2002), 49. In addition, as the story goes, Suge's name, which is short for "Sugar Bear," was given to him "by his

father due to a gracious disposition." Ronin Ro, *Have Gun Will Travel: The Spectacular Rise and Violent Fall of Death Row Records* (New York: Broadway Books, 1998), 10.

7. "Chapter 12," WDR. According to another journalist, "Suge's home life, though characterized by struggle, was a stable one. Unlike many neighbors, he had two parents in the household. . . . While his friends stirred up trouble, Suge focused on sport and earned a reputation as an athlete, which kept him out of the line of fire." Ro, *Have Gun Will Travel*, 13-14.

8. Sullivan, *LAbyrinth*, 50.

9. "Chapter 3," WDR.

10. Sullivan, *LAbyrinth,* 51.

11. "Chapter 3," WDR.

12. Quoted in Ro, *Have Gun Will Travel*, 37.

13. "Chapter 3," WDR.

14. Ibid.

15. Jerry Heller with Gil Reavill, *Ruthless: A Memoir* (New York: Simon Spotlight Entertainment, 2006), 70.

16. "Chapter 2," WDR.

17. "Boyz N the Hood," *Beef.*

18. Heller, *Ruthless*, 42.

19. Ro, *Have Gun Will Travel*, 45.

20. "Boyz N the Hood," *Beef.*

21. Ibid.

22. "Chapter 3," WDR.

23. Heller, *Ruthless*, 15.

24. "Chapter 12," WDR.

25. Shapiro, "Collaring the Crime," 351.

26. "Chapter 8," WDR.

27. Frederic Dannen, *Hit Men: Power Brokers and Fast Money inside the Music Business* (New York: Vintage Books, 1991).

28. Jeffrey Reiman, *The Rich Get Richer and the Poor Get Prison: Ideology, Class, and Criminal Justice*, 6th ed. (Boston: Allyn and Bacon, 2000).

29. Nils Christie, *Crime Control as Industry: Towards Gulags, Western Style*, 3rd ed. (London: Routledge, 2000).

30. Howard S. Becker, *Outsiders: Studies in the Sociology of Deviance* (New York: Free Press, 1963), 157.

31. Emile Durkheim, "The Normal and the Pathological," in *The Rules of the Sociological Method*, trans. Sarah A. Solovay and John H. Mueller, ed. George E. G. Catlin (Glencoe, IL.: Free Press, 1938, 1966).

32. Robert K. Merton, "Social Structure and Anomie."

33. See, for example, Shaw and McKay, *Juvenile Delinquency*; Edwin H. Sutherland, *Principles of Criminology*, 4th ed. (Philadelphia: Lippincott, 1947); Albert K. Cohen, *Delinquent Boys: The Culture of the Gang* (Glencoe, IL: Free Press, 1955); Walter B. Miller, "Lower Class Culture as a Generating Milieu of Gang Delinquency," *Journal of Social Issues* 14, no. 3 (1958): 5-19; Richard A. Cloward and Lloyd C. Ohlin, *Delinquency and Opportunity: A Theory of Delinquent Gangs* (Glencoe, IL: Free Press, 1960).

34. Michel Foucault, *Discipline and Punish: The Birth of the Prison*, trans. Alan Sheridan (New York: Vintage Books, 1995), 297.

35. Jean Comaroff and John Comaroff, "Criminal Obsessions after Foucault: Postcoloniality, Policing, and the Metaphysics of Disorder," *Critical Inquiry* 20, no. 4 (Summer 2004): 806 (emphasis added).

36. Ibid., 824.

37. Ibid. (original emphasis).

38. Dr. Dre, *The Chronic* (Death Row/Interscope/Priority, 1992).

39. "Chapter 5," WDR.

40. "Chapter 6," WDR.

41. Snoop Doggy Dogg, *Doggystyle* (Death Row/Interscope/Atlantic, 1993).

42. "Chapter 9," WDR.

43. Ibid.

44. "Chapter 12," WDR.

45. Ibid.

46. Ibid.

47. Ro, *Have Gun Will Travel*, 131.

48. "Chapter 12," WDR.

49. Ibid.

50. Ro, *Have Gun Will Travel*, 118.

51. "Chapter 13," WDR.

52. "East vs. West," *Beef*.

53. Ro, *Have Gun Will Travel*, 190.

54. Joel Bakan, *The Corporation: The Pathological Pursuit of Profit and Power* (New York: Free Press, 2004).

55. Joseph E. Stiglitz, *Globalization and Its Discontents* (New York: Norton, 2003), 3.

56. Kai Erikson, "Notes on Trauma and Community," in *Trauma: Explorations in Memory*, ed. Cathy Caruth, 183-99 (Baltimore: Johns Hopkins University Press, 1995).

57. Ibid., 192.

58. Ibid.

59. Ibid. (original emphasis).

60. Ibid., 192-93.

61. Rosemary J. Coombe, "Properties of Culture and the Politics of Possessing Identity: Native Claims in the Cultural Appropriation Controversy," *Canadian Journal of Law and Jurisprudence* 6, no. 2 (1993): 266.

62. Rosemary J. Coombe, *The Cultural Life of Intellectual Properties: Authorship, Appropriation, and the Law* (Durham, NC: Duke University Press, 1998), 62.

63. Ibid.

64. All quotations attributed to Ice-T in this passage can be found here: "East vs. West," *Beef*.

65. All quotations attributed to 50 Cent in this passage can be found here: 50 Cent, Interview, Bonus DVD, *Get Rich or Die Trying*.

66. "East vs. West," *Beef*.

67. Jay-Z, "Rap Game/Crack Game," *In My Lifetime, Vol. 1* (Roc-a-Fella, 1997).

CONCLUSION

1. All quotations from this article can be found here: Alexei Barrionuevo, "Cheap Cocaine Floods Argentina," *New York Times*, February 23, 2008, http://www.nytimes.com/2008/02/23/world/americas/23argentina.html (accessed August 15, 2010).

2. Clear, *Imprisoning Communities*, 20.

3. Cases can also be cleared by "exceptional means," which can include the death of the suspect or victim noncooperation.

4. For national clearance rates, see the Federal Bureau of Investigation's annual report, *Crime in the United States*. The numbers I have listed here are for 2008.

5. Barbara Boland, Paul Mahanna, and Ronald Stones, *The Prosecution of Felony Arrests, 1988* (Washington, DC: U.S. Department of Justice, Bureau of Justice Statistics, 1992), 2.

6. Nearly two-thirds of felony convictions are for property or drug offenses. Less than half of drug defendants are charged with trafficking. Seventy-two percent of those convicted of felonies are convicted of the original charge. See Thomas H. Cohen and Tracey Kyckelhahn, *Felony Defendants in Urban Counties, 2006* (Washington, DC: U.S. Department of Justice, Office of Justice Programs, Bureau of Justice Statistics, May 2010).

7. Sean Rosenmerkel, Matthew Durose, and Donald Farole, *Felony Sentences in State Courts, 2006: Statistical Tables* (Washington, DC: U.S. Department of Justice, Office of Justice Programs, Bureau of Justice Statistics, December 2009), section 4.

8. Ibid., section 1.

9. I have borrowed this descriptive phrase from an interview with historian Mike Davis in Cle "Bone" Sloan's documentary film, *Bastards of the Party*, about the development of black gangs in Los Angeles. I am indebted to Paul Kaplan for turning me on to this film, which is still one of the best yet made about gangs in general.

10. Quoting legal scholar Donna Coker, for example, political scientist Kristin Bumiller, in *In an Abusive State: How Neoliberalism Appropriated the Feminist Movement against Sexual Violence* (Durham, NC: Duke University Press, 2008), argues the following:

> "Mandatory arrest policies increase the risk of [punitive criminal intervention] . . . when women's (unrelated) criminal offending is exposed, when mandatory arrest practices threaten women's probation or parole status, when undocumented women are made more vulnerable to deportation, or when child welfare departments are prompted to investigate neglect or abuse claims based on a domestic violence incident report." The disappointing track record of mandatory policies has produced a cautionary tale for activists about the precariousness of relying on stepped-up police enforcement and attempting to control prosecutorial discretion. (*In an Abusive State*, 12; brackets and ellipses in Bumiller).

11. Meda Chesney-Lind, "Gender Matters: Trends in Girls' Criminality," in *Critical Issues in Crime and Justice: Thought, Policy, and Practice*, ed. Mary Maguire and Dan Okada (Los Angeles: Sage, 2011), 83.

12. Ibid.

13. Ibid., 84.

14. Currie, *Crime and Punishment*, 159.

15. Garland, *Culture of Control*, 152.

16. Clear, *Imprisoning Communities*, 186.

17. Michael Tonry, *Thinking about Crime: Sense and Sensibility in American Penal Culture* (Oxford: Oxford University Press, 2004), 200.

18. Tapio Lappi-Seppälä, "Penal Policy and Incarceration Rates in Finland," *Corrections Today*, February 2002, 32.

19. Matti Joutsen, "Finland," in *World Factbook of Criminal Justice Systems* (Washington, DC: U.S. Department of Justice, Bureau of Justice Statistics, 1993), http://bjs.ojp.usdoj.gov/content/pub/ascii/WFBCJFIN.TXT (accessed August 6, 2010).

20. Ibid.

21. Lappi-Seppälä, "Penal Policy," 31.

22. James Lynch, "Crime in International Perspective," in Wilson and Petersilia, *Crime*, 33.

23. Ibid.

24. Ibid.

25. Lappi-Seppälä, "Penal Policy," 30.

26. Heather C. West, *Prison Inmates at Midyear 2009: Statistical Tables* (Washington, DC: U.S. Department of Justice, Office of Justice Programs, Bureau of Justice Statistics, 2010), 2.

27. Joutsen, "Finland."

28. Webb, "Why We Must Reform." Webb's efforts are both commendable and sorely needed, but he, too, relies on unsupported fear mongering when, in striving to rationalize American criminal justice policy, he simultaneously claims that,

> While heavily focused on non-violent offenders, law enforcement has been distracted from pursuing the approximately one million gang members and drug cartels besieging our cities, often engaging in unprecedented levels of violence. Gangs in some areas commit 80% of the crimes and are heavily involved in drug distribution and other violent activities. This disturbing trend affects every community in the United States.

Webb offers no evidence of these supposedly "unprecedented levels of violence," which, of course, he could not offer, since all violent crime rates have been in steep decline for the past fifteen years. Sadly, it seems that every effort at criminal justice rationality must be anchored by irrational premises.

29. Pew Center on the States, *Prison Count 2010: State Population Declines for the First Time in 38 Years* (Washington, DC: Pew Charitable Trust, April 2010), 1.

30. Ibid., 2.

31. Ibid., 5. The federal prison population grew by 3.4 percent in 2009, or over two thousand people.

32. See the Sentencing Commission's annual *Sourcebook of Federal Sentencing Statistics* for every year since 1995.

33. Pew Hispanic Center, *A Rising Share: Hispanics and Federal Crime* (Washington, DC: Pew Charitable Trusts, February 2009).

34. See, for example, the *Los Angeles Times*' often sensationalized account of Mexico's drug war, called "Mexico under Siege," which, as of August 2010, can be found at http://projects.latimes.com/mexico-drug-war/#/its-a-war.

35. In its "systematic review of the available English language scientific literature" on "the impacts of drug law enforcement interventions on drug market violence," for example, the nonprofit International Centre for Science in Drug Policy found that 87 percent of the studies revealed the same stark reality discussed in chapter 2:

> [I]ncreasing the intensity of law enforcement interventions to disrupt drug markets is unlikely to reduce drug gang violence. Instead, the existing evidence suggests that drug related violence and high homicide rates are likely a natural consequence of drug prohibition and that increasingly sophisticated and well-resourced methods of disrupting drug distribution networks may unintentionally increase violence. From an evidence-based public policy perspective, gun violence and the enrichment of organized crime networks appear to be natural consequences of drug prohibition.

In a perverse form of reasoning, however, many drug war advocates have argued that Mexico's increased lethality is actually a sign of success. In the words of former "drug czar" John Walters, "'They're shooting each other, and the reason they're doing that is because they're getting weaker.'" Or, in the words of Michele Leonhart, acting DEA administrator in 2010: "'Our view is that the violence we have been seeing is a signpost of the success our very courageous Mexican counterparts are having. . . .The cartels are acting out like caged animals, because they are caged animals.'" In contrast to this line of argument, I cannot imagine a prison official claiming that, say, increased lethality among inmates—whom Leonhart, no doubt, would also call "caged animals"—signaled the success of an inmate safety initiative. This is irresponsible logic of the highest order. See International Centre for Science in Drug Policy, *Effect of Drug Law Enforcement on Drug-Related Violence: Evidence from a Scientific Review* (Vancouver, BC, Canada, 2010), 5-6. John Walters's quotations can be found in Martha Mendoza, "Study Links Drug Enforcement to More Violence," *San Diego Union-Tribune*, April 26, 2010, http://www.signonsandiego.com/ news/2010/apr/26/ study-links-drug-enforcement-to-more-violence/ (accessed August 6, 2010). Michele Leonhart's quotations can be found in Katherine McIntire Peters, "DEA: Mexican Drug Violence Is a Sign of Progress, Not Failure," *Government Executive*, April 15, 2009, http://www.govexec.com/dailyfed/0409/041509kp1.htm (accessed August 6, 2010).

36. Williams, *The English Novel*, 186.

37. Ibid.

38. Ibid., 26.

39. Ibid., 192.

40. Ibid.

41. Ibid., 13.

42. Ibid., 10.

43. Ibid., 25.

METHODOLOGICAL ESSAY

1. Grounded theory's origins are to be found in Barney G. Glaser and Anselm L. Strauss, *The Discovery of Grounded Theory: Strategies for Qualitative Research* (Chicago: Aldine, 1967). Since then, there have been numerous reformulations by many authors. The version that most resonates with my sensibilities is that of Kathy Charmaz. See, for example, Kathy Charmaz, *Constructing Grounded Theory: A Practical Guide through Qualitative Analysis* (Los Angeles: Sage, 2006).

2. Robert J. Cover, "Violence and the Word," in *Narrative, Violence, and the Law: The Essays of Robert Cover*, ed. Martha Minow, Michael Ryan, and Austin Sarat, 203-38 (Ann Arbor: University of Michigan Press, 1993), 203.

Bibliography

Albini, Steve. "The Problem with Music." http://www.negativland.com/albini.html (accessed August 16, 2010).

Alexander, Frank, with Heidi Siegmund Cuda. *Got Your Back: Protecting Tupac in the World of Gangsta Rap*. New York: St. Martin's Griffin, 2000.

Anderson, Elijah. *Code of the Street: Decency, Violence, and the Moral Life of the Inner City*. New York: Norton, 1999.

Andreas, Peter, and Ethan Nadelmann. *Policing the Globe: Criminalization and Crime Control in International Relations*. Oxford: Oxford University Press, 2006.

Anti-Drug Abuse Act of 1988, Pub. L. No. 100-690, 102 Stat. 4181 (1988).

Anti-Drug Abuse Act of 1986, Pub. L. No. 99-570, 100 Stat. 3207 (1986).

Apprendi v. New Jersey, 530 U.S. 466 (2000).

Archibold, Randal C. "California, in Financial Crisis, Opens Prison Doors." *New York Times*, March 23, 2010. http://www.nytimes.com/2010/03/24/us/24calprisons. html?hp (accessed August 16, 2010).

A Tribe Called Quest. *The Low End Theory*. Jive, 1991.

Austin, James, and John Irwin. *It's about Time: America's Imprisonment Binge*, 3rd ed. Belmont, CA: Wadsworth, 2001.

Avalon, Moses. *Secrets of Negotiating a Record Contract: The Musician's Guide to Understanding and Avoiding Sneaky Lawyer Tricks*. San Francisco: Backbeat Books, 2001.

Bakan, Joel. *The Corporation: The Pathological Pursuit of Profit and Power*. New York: Free Press, 2004.

Baker, Houston A., Jr. *Black Studies, Rap, and the Academy*. Chicago: University of Chicago Press, 1993.

Barber, Benjamin. *Jihad vs. McWorld: How Globalization and Tribalism Are Reshaping the World*. New York: Random House, 1996.

Barrionuevo, Alexei. "Cheap Cocaine Floods Argentina." *New York Times*, February 23, 2008. http://www.nytimes.com/2008/02/23/world/americas/23argentina.html (accessed August 15, 2010).

Baum, Geraldine. "Rapper's Upbeat Spirit Recalled." *Los Angeles Times*, November 6, 2002.

Becker, Howard S. *Outsiders: Studies in the Sociology of Deviance*. New York: Free Press, 1963.

Beckett, Katherine. *Making Crime Pay: Law and Order in Contemporary American Politics*. New York: Oxford University Press, 1997.

Beef. Image Entertainment, 2003.

Bennett, William J., John J. DiIulio Jr., and John P. Walters. *Body Count: Moral Poverty . . . and How to Win America's War against Crime and Drugs.* New York: Simon & Schuster, 1996.

Blakely v. Washington, 542 U.S. 296 (2004).

Bluestone, Barry, and Bennett Harrison. *The Deindustrialization of America: Plant Closings, Community Abandonment, and the Dismantling of Basic Industry.* New York: Basic Books, 1982.

Blumstein, Alfred, and Joel Wallman, eds. *The Crime Drop in America.* Cambridge: Cambridge University Press, 2000.

———. "The Recent Rise and Fall of American Violence." In Blumstein and Wallman, *Crime Drop*, 1-12.

Boatman, Robert H. *Living with Glocks: The Complete Guide to the New Standard in Combat Handguns.* Boulder, CO: Paladin, 2002.

Boland, Barbara, Paul Mahanna, and Ronald Stones. *The Prosecution of Felony Arrests, 1988.* Washington, DC: U.S. Department of Justice, Bureau of Justice Statistics, 1992.

Boot Camp Clik. *Chosen Few.* Duck Down, 2002.

Boucher, Geoff, and Paul Lieberman. "Fatal Shooting of Rap Pioneer in Studio Jolts Fans and Peers." *Los Angeles Times*, November 1, 2002.

Bourgois, Philippe. "In Search of Horatio Alger: Culture and Ideology in the Crack Economy." In Reinarman and Levine, *Crack in America*, 57-76.

———. *In Search of Respect: Selling Crack in El Barrio*, 2nd ed. Cambridge: Cambridge University Press, 2003.

Boyd, Todd. "Intergenerational Culture Wars: Civil Rights vs. Hip Hop (interview by Yusuf Nuruddin)." *Socialism and Democracy* 18, no. 2 (2004): 51-70.

———. *The New H.N.I.C.: The Death of Civil Rights and the Reign of Hip Hop.* New York: New York University Press, 2002.

Boyle, James. *Shamans, Software, and Spleens: Law and the Construction of the Information Society.* Cambridge, MA: Harvard University Press, 1997.

Brown, Ethan. *Queens Reigns Supreme: Fat Cat, 50 Cent, and the Rise of the Hip-Hop Hustler.* New York: Anchor Books, 2005.

Brown, Michelle. *The Culture of Punishment.* New York: New York University Press, 2009.

Bry, David. "New York State of Mind: The Resurgence of East Coast Hip Hop." In Light, *Vibe History*, 327-37.

Bumiller, Kristin. *In an Abusive State: How Neoliberalism Appropriated the Feminist Movement against Sexual Violence.* Durham, NC: Duke University Press, 2008.

Business Wire. "Russell Simmons Presents: Hip Hop Justice." July 22, 2004. http://www.allbusiness.com/crime-law-enforcement-corrections/law/5200009-1.html (accessed August 17, 2010).

California State Senate. *Personal Service Contracts: Seven-Year Rule; Exception for Recording Artists.* Hearing before the Select Committee on the Entertainment Industry, September 5, 2001.

———. *Record Label Accounting Practices.* Joint Hearing of the Committee on the Judiciary and Select Committee on the Entertainment Industry, July 23, 2002.

———. *Record Label Accounting Practices*. Joint Hearing of the Judiciary Committee and the Select Committee on the Entertainment Industry, September 24, 2002.

Caramanica, Jon, Jack Erwin, Saptosa Foster, Keith Murphy, and Vanessa Satten. "Victim." *XXL*, March 2005.

Castells, Manuel. *Rise of the Network Society*. Oxford: Oxford University Press, 1996.

Catalano, Shannan M. *Criminal Victimization, 2005*. Washington, DC: U.S Department of Justice, Office of Justice Programs, Bureau of Justice Statistics, September 2006.

Caulkins, Jonathan P., C. Peter Rydell, William L. Schwabe, and James Chiesa. *Mandatory Minimum Drug Sentencing: Throwing Away the Key or the Taxpayers' Money?* Santa Monica, CA: Rand, Drug Policy Research Center, 1997.

Chambliss, William J. "The Law of Vagrancy." *Social Problems* 12, no.1 (Summer 1964): 67-77.

Chang, Jeff. *Can't Stop Won't Stop: A History of the Hip-Hop Generation*. New York: Picador, 2005.

Charmaz, Kathy. *Constructing Grounded Theory: A Practical Guide through Qualitative Analysis*. Los Angeles: Sage, 2006.

Chesney-Lind, Meda. "Gender Matters: Trends in Girls' Criminality." In *Critical Issues in Crime and Justice: Thought, Policy, and Practice*, edited by Mary Maguire and Dan Okada. Los Angeles: Sage, 2011.

Christie, Nils. *Crime Control as Industry: Towards Gulags Western Style*, 3rd ed. London: Routledge, 2000.

Clear, Todd R. *Imprisoning Communities: How Mass Incarceration Makes Disadvantaged Neighborhoods Worse*. Oxford: Oxford University Press, 2007.

Clinard, Marshall B., and Peter Yeager. *Corporate Crime*. New York: Free Press, 1980.

Clipse. *Lord Willin'*. StarTrak, 2002.

Cloward, Richard A., and Lloyd C. Ohlin. *Delinquency and Opportunity: A Theory of Delinquent Gangs*. Glencoe, IL: Free Press, 1960.

Cohen, Albert K. *Delinquent Boys: The Culture of the Gang*. Glencoe, IL: Free Press, 1955.

Cohen, Thomas H., and Tracey Kyckelhahn. *Felony Defendants in Urban Counties, 2006*. Washington, DC: U.S. Department of Justice, Office of Justice Programs, Bureau of Justice Statistics, May 2010.

Coker, Cheo Hodari. "N.W.A." In Light, *Vibe History*, 251-63.

Comaroff, Jean, and John Comaroff. "Criminal Obsessions after Foucault: Postcoloniality, Policing, and the Metaphysics of Disorder." *Critical Inquiry* 20 (Summer 2004): 800-824.

———. "Millennial Capitalism: First Thoughts on a Second Coming." *Public Culture* 12, no. 2 (2000): 291-343.

Company Flow. *Funcrusher Plus*. Rawkus, 1997.

Coombe, Rosemary J. *The Cultural Life of Intellectual Properties: Authorship, Appropriation, and the Law*. Durham, NC: Duke University Press, 1998.

———. "Properties of Culture and the Politics of Possessing Identity: Native Claims in the Cultural Appropriation Controversy." *Canadian Journal of Law and Jurisprudence* 6, no. 2 (1993): 249-85.

Cover, Robert J. "Violence and the Word." In *Narrative, Violence, and the Law: The Essays of Robert Cover*, edited by Martha Minow, Michael Ryan, and Austin Sarat, 203-38. Ann Arbor: University of Michigan Press, 1993.

Cullen, Francis T. "Rehabilitation and Treatment Programs." In Wilson and Petersilia, *Crime*, 253-89.

Cunningham v. California, 549 U.S. 270 (2007).

Currie, Elliott. *Crime and Punishment in America: Why the Solutions to America's Most Stubborn Social Crisis Have Not Worked—and What Will*. New York: Henry Holt, 1998.

———. *Reckoning: Drugs, the Cities, and the American Future*. New York: Hill and Wang, 1993.

Dannen, Frederic. *Hit Men: Power Brokers and Fast Money inside the Music Industry*. New York: Vintage Books, 1991.

Davis, Mike. *City of Quartz: Excavating the Future in Los Angeles*. New York: Vintage Books, 1992.

Dead Prez. *Let's Get Free*. Loud, 2000.

Demers, Joanna. *Steal This Music: How Intellectual Property Law Affects Musical Creativity*. Athens: University of Georgia Press, 2006.

Dershowitz, Alan M. *The Abuse Excuse: And Other Cop-Outs, Sob Stories, and Evasions of Responsibility*. Boston: Back Bay Books, 1994.

DiIulio, John J., Jr. "The Coming of the Super-Predators." *Weekly Standard*, November 27, 1995.

Dimitriadis, Greg. *Performing Identity/Performing Culture: Hip Hop as Text, Pedagogy, and Lived Practice*. New York: Peter Lang, 2001.

Ditton, Paula M., and Doris James Wilson. *Truth in Sentencing in State Prisons*. Washington, DC: U.S. Department of Justice, Office of Justice Programs, Bureau of Justice Statistics, January 1999.

Dr. Dre. *The Chronic*. Death Row/Interscope/Priority, 1992.

Durkheim, Emile. "The Normal and the Pathological." In *The Rules of the Sociological Method*, translated by Sarah A. Solovay and John H. Mueller, edited by George E. G. Catlin. Glencoe, IL: Free Press, 1938, 1966.

Erikson, Kai. "Notes on Trauma and Community." In *Trauma: Explorations in Memory*, edited by Cathy Caruth, 183-99. Baltimore: Johns Hopkins University Press, 1995.

Fair Sentencing Act of 2010, Pub. L. No. 111-220 (2010).

Feld, Barry C. *Bad Kids: Race and the Transformation of the Juvenile Court*. Oxford: Oxford University Press, 1999.

Feldman, Allen. *Formations of Violence: The Narrative of the Body and Political Terror in Northern Ireland*. Chicago: University of Chicago Press, 1991.

Ferrell, Jeff. "Cultural Criminology." *Annual Review of Sociology* 25 (1999): 395-418.

Ferrell, Jeff, Dragan Milovanovic, and Stephen Lyng. "Edgework, Media Practices, and the Elongation of Meaning." *Theoretical Criminology* 5, no. 2 (2001): 177-202.

Feuer, Alan. "Rap World Baffled by Killing of Star with Peaceful Image." *New York Times*, November 1, 2002.

50 Cent with Kris Ex. *From Pieces to Weight: Once upon a Time in Southside Queens*. MTV Books, 2005.

————. *Get Rich or Die Trying*. Shady/Aftermath/Interscope, 2003.

Foucault, Michel. *Discipline and Punish: The Birth of the Prison*. Translated by Alan Sheridan. New York: Vintage Books, 1995.

Fox, James Alan, and Marianne W. Zawitz. *Homicide Trends in the United States*. Washington, DC: Department of Justice, Office of Justice Programs, Bureau of Justice Statistics, 2007.

Frank, Thomas. *One Market under God: Extreme Capitalism, Market Populism, and the End of Economic Democracy*. New York: Anchor Books, 2001.

Friedman, Lawrence M. *Crime and Punishment in American History*. New York: Basic Books, 1993.

Friedrichs, David O. *Trusted Criminals: White Collar Crime in Contemporary Society*. Belmont, CA: Wadsworth, 2006.

Galanter, Marc. "Why the 'Haves' Come Out Ahead: Speculations on the Limits of Legal Change." *Law and Society Review* 9, no. 1 (Autumn 1974): 95-160.

Garland, David. *The Culture of Control: Crime and Social Order in Contemporary Society*. Chicago: University of Chicago Press, 2002.

————. *Punishment and Modern Society: A Study in Social Theory*. Chicago: University of Chicago Press, 1993.

Garot, Robert. *Who You Claim: Performing Gang Identity in School and on the Streets*. New York: New York University Press, 2010.

Genius/GZA. *Liquid Swords*. Geffen/MCA, 1995

Ghostface Killah. *Fishscale*. Def Jam, 2006.

————. *The Pretty Toney Album*. Def Jam, 2004.

Gibson, James William. *Warrior Dreams: Paramilitary Culture in Post-Vietnam America*. New York: Hill and Wang, 1994.

Gilroy, Paul. "'After the Love Has Gone': Bio-Politics and Etho-Poetics in the Black Public Sphere." *Public Culture* 7, no. 1 (Fall 1994): 49-76.

————. *The Black Atlantic: Modernity and Double Consciousness*. Cambridge, MA: Harvard University Press, 1993.

————. "It's a Family Affair." In *That's the Joint! The Hip-Hop Studies Reader*, edited by Murray Forman and Mark Anthony Neal, chapter 9. New York: Routledge, 2004.

Glaser, Barney G., and Anselm L. Strauss. *The Discovery of Grounded Theory: Strategies for Qualitative Research*. Chicago: Aldine, 1967.

Glasser, Ira, and Loren Siegel. "When Constitutional Rights Seem Too Extravagant to Endure: The Crack Scare's Impact on Civil Rights and Liberties." In Reinarman and Levine, *Crack in America*, 229-48.

Goldstein, Paul. *International Copyright: Principles, Law, and Practice*. Oxford: Oxford University Press, 2001.

Goldstein, Paul J., Henry H. Brownstein, Patrick I. Ryan, and Patricia A. Bellucci. "Crack and Homicide in New York City: A Case Study in the Epidemiology of Violence." In Reinarman and Levine, *Crack in America*, 113-30.

Gottfredson, Michael R., and Travis Hirschi. *A General Theory of Crime*. Stanford, CA: Stanford University Press, 1990.

Grand Upright Music, Ltd v. Warner Bros. Records, Inc., 780 F. Supp. 182 (S.D.N.Y. 1991).

Green, Tony. "The Dirty South." In Light, *Vibe History*, 265-75.

Greene, Judith A. "Zero Tolerance: A Case Study of Police Policies and Practices in New York City." *Crime and Delinquency* 45, no. 2 (April 1999): 171-87.

Gundersen, Edna. "Rights Issues Rock the Music World." *USA Today*, September 16, 2002. http://www.usatoday.com/life/music/news/2002-09-15-artists-rights_x.htm (accessed August 11, 2010).

Hall, Stuart, Chas Critcher, Tony Jefferson, John Clarke, and Brian Roberts. *Policing the Crisis: Mugging, the State, and Law and Order*. New York: Palgrave Macmillan, 1978.

"Handbook of the Business Revolution—Manifesto." *Fast Company*, October 1995. http://www.fastcompany.com/magazine/01/edpage.html (accessed August 16, 2010).

Harcourt, Bernard E. *Illusion of Order: The False Promise of Broken Windows Policing*. Cambridge, MA: Harvard University Press, 2005.

———. *Language of the Gun: Youth, Crime, and Public Policy*. Chicago: University of Chicago Press, 2006.

Hart, Timothy C. *Reporting Crime to the Police, 1992-2000*. Washington, DC: Department of Justice, Office of Justice Programs, Bureau of Justice Statistics, March 2003.

Hebdige, Dick. *Cut 'n' Mix: Culture, Identity, and Caribbean Music*. London: Routledge, 1987.

Heller, Jerry, with Gil Reavill. *Ruthless: A Memoir*. New York: Simon Spotlight Entertainment, 2006.

International Centre for Science in Drug Policy. *Effect of Drug Law Enforcement on Drug-Related Violence: Evidence from a Scientific Review*. Vancouver, BC, Canada, 2010.

Jacobs, Bruce. *Dealing Crack: The Social World of Streetcorner Selling*. Boston: Northeastern University Press, 1999.

Jay-Z. *The Blueprint*. Rock-a-Fella, 2001.

———. *In My Lifetime*, vol. 1. Rock-a-Fella, 1997.

Jeru The Damaja. *Wrath of the Math*. Fontana London, 1996.

Johnson, Bruce, Andrew Golub, and Eloise Dunlap. "The Rise and Decline of Hard Drugs, Drug Markets, and Violence in Inner-City New York." In Blumstein and Wallman, *Crime Drop*, 164-206.

Johnson, Lynn d. "Hip-Hop's Holy Trinity." *Pop Matters*, August 8, 2003. http://www.popmatters.com/music/features/030808-50cent.shtml (accessed August 16, 2010).

Jones, Steve. "Hip-hop's Rap Shifts toward Social Activism." *USA Today*, January 12, 2002.

Joutsen, Matti. "Finland." In *World Factbook of Criminal Justice Systems*. Washington, DC: U.S. Department of Justice, Bureau of Justice Statistics, 1993. http://bjs.ojp.usdoj.gov/content/pub/ascii/WFBCJFIN.TXT (accessed August 6, 2010).

Juelz Santana. *What the Game's Been Missing!* Def Jam, 2005.

Junior M.A.F.I.A. *Conspiracy*. Big Beat, 1995.

Karmen, Andrew. *New York Murder Mystery*. New York: New York University Press, 2006.

Katz, Jack. *Seductions of Crime: Moral and Sensual Attractions in Doing Evil*. Basic Books, 1988.

Kelley, Robin D. G. "Kickin' Reality, Kickin' Ballistics: Gangsta Rap and Postindustrial Los Angeles." In Perkins, *Droppin' Science*, 117-58.

Kelling, George L., and William J. Bratton. "Declining Crime Rates: Insiders' Views of the New York City Story." *Journal of Criminal Law and Criminology* 88, no. 4 (Summer 1998): 1217-32.

Kelling, George L., Tony Pate, Duane Dieckman, and Charles E. Brown. *The Kansas City Preventive Patrol Experiment: A Technical Report*. Washington, DC: Police Foundation, 1974.

Kelling, George L., Antony Pate, Amy Ferrara, Mary Utne, and Charles E. Brown. *Newark Foot Patrol Experiment*. Washington, DC: Police Foundation, 1981.

Kelling, George L., and James Q. Wilson. "Broken Windows." *Atlantic Monthly*, March 1982. http://www.theatlantic.com/doc/198203/broken-windows (accessed August 16, 2010).

Kennedy, Randall. *Race, Crime, and the Law*. New York: Pantheon Books, 1997.

Kimbrough v. United States, 552 U.S. 85 (2007).

Klein, Malcolm, Cheryl L. Maxson, and Jody Miller, eds. *The Modern Gang Reader*. Los Angeles: Roxbury, 1995.

Krasilovsky, M. William, and Sidney Shemel. *This Business of Music: The Definitive Guide to the Business and Legal Issues of the Music Industry*, 10th ed. New York: Billboard Books, 2007.

KRS-One. "Sound of the Police." Vinyl single. Jive, 1993.

Lappi-Seppälä, Tapio. "Penal Policy and Incarceration Rates in Finland." *Corrections Today*, February 2002.

Laqueur, Walter. *No End to War: Terrorism in the Twenty-first Century*. New York: Continuum International Publishing Group, 2003.

Lessig, Lawrence. *The Future of Ideas: The Fate of the Commons in a Connected World*. New York: Vintage Books, 2002.

Light, Alan, ed. *The Vibe History of Hip Hop*. New York: Three Rivers, 1999.

Liptak, Adam. "Right and Left Join to Challenge U.S. on Criminal Justice." *New York Times*, November 24, 2009. http://www.nytimes.com/2009/11/24/us/24crime.html (accessed August 16, 2010).

Lynch, James. "Crime in International Perspective." In Wilson and Petersilia, *Crime*, 5-41.

MacLeod, Jay. *Ain't No Makin' It: Aspirations and Attainment in a Low-Income Neighborhood*. Boulder, CO: Westview, 1995.

Maher, Lisa. *Sexed Work: Gender, Race, and Resistance in a Brooklyn Drug Market*. Oxford: Oxford University Press, 1997.

Martin, Mark. "Maximum Insecurity: California's Prison System Produces Bizarre and Dangerous Results Harmful to Inmates and Public." *San Francisco Chronicle*, August 27, 2006. http://www.sfgate.com/cgi-bin/article.cgi?f=/c/a/2006/08/27/INGD3KNS441.DTL (accessed August 16, 2010).

Martinez, George. "The Politics of Hip Hop (interview by Ron Hayduk)." *Socialism and Democracy* 18, no. 2 (2004): 195-206.

Martinson, Robert. "What Works? Questions and Answers about Prison Reform." *Public Interest* 35 (Spring 1974): 22-54.

McPhee, Michele. "Bullets Riddle Busta Ride." *New York Daily News*, February 24, 2003.

Meares, Tracey L., and Dan M. Kahan. *Urgent Times: Policing and Rights in Inner-City Communities.* Boston: Beacon, 1999.

Mendoza, Martha. "Study Links Drug Enforcement to More Violence." *San Diego Union-Tribune,* April 26, 2010. http://www.signonsandiego.com/news/2010/apr/26/study-links-drug-enforcement-to-more-violence/ (accessed August 6, 2010).

Merton, Robert K. "Social Structure and Anomie." *Annual Review of Sociology* 3, no. 5 (October 1938): 672-82.

"Mexico under Siege." *Los Angeles Times.* http://projects.latimes.com/mexico-drug-war/#/its-a-war (accessed August 25, 2010).

Miller, Jody. *Getting Played: African American Girls, Urban Inequality, and Gendered Violence.* New York: New York University Press, 2008.

Miller, Walter B. "Lower-Class Culture as a Generating Milieu of Gang Delinquency." *Journal of Social Issues* 14, no. 3 (1958): 5-19.

Mitchell, Tony, ed. *Global Noise: Rap and Hip Hop outside the USA.* Middletown, CT: Wesleyan University Press, 2002.

Mobb Deep. *The Infamous.* Loud/RCA/BMG, 1995.

Morgan, Joan. *When Chickenheads Come Home to Roost: A Hip-Hop Feminist Breaks It Down.* New York: Touchstone, 1999.

Morgan, John P., and Lynn Zimmer. "The Social Pharmacology of Smokeable Cocaine: Not All It's Cracked Up to Be." In Reinarman and Levine, *Crack in America,* 131-70.

Morris, Norval. "The Contemporary Prison: 1965–Present." In Morris and Rothman, *Oxford History of the Prison,* 202-31.

Morris, Norval, and David J. Rothman, eds. *The Oxford History of the Prison: The Practice of Punishment in Western Society.* New York: Oxford University Press, 1998.

Musto, David F. *The American Disease: Origins of Narcotic Control,* 3rd ed. New York: Oxford University Press, 1999.

Naggar, David. *The Music Business (Explained in Plain English): What Every Artist and Songwriter Should Know to Avoid Getting Ripped Off!* 2nd ed. San Francisco: DaJe´ Publishing, 2000.

Nas. *God's Son.* Columbia, 2002.

———. *Illmatic.* Sony, 1994.

———. *It Was Written.* Columbia, 1996.

Newman, Andy, and Al Baker. "Was It a Bad Business Deal or a Music Industry Feud?" *New York Times,* November 1, 2002.

Newman, Katherine S. *No Shame in My Game: The Working Poor in the Inner City.* New York: Vintage Books, 2000.

Notorious B.I.G. *Life after Death.* Bad Boy, 1997.

———. *Ready to Die.* Bad Boy, 1994.

O.C. *Word . . . Life.* Wild Pitch, 1994.

Ogbar, Jeffrey. *Hip-Hop Revolution: The Culture and Politics of Rap.* Lawrence: University Press of Kansas, 2009.

Ogunnaike, Lola. "Sweeten the Image, Hold the Bling-Bling." *New York Times,* January 12, 2004.

Organized Konfusion. *Stress: The Extinction Agenda.* Hollywood BASIC/Elektra, 1994.

Packer, Herbert L. *The Limits of the Criminal Sanction*. Stanford, CA: Stanford University Press, 1968.

Padilla, Felix. *The Gang as an American Enterprise*. New Brunswick, NJ: Rutgers University Press, 1993.

Pareles, John. "Latest Violence Is Not Typical of Previous Gunplay." *New York Times*, November 1, 2002.

Parker, Derrick, and Matt Diehl. *Notorious C.O.P.: The Inside Story of the Tupac, Biggie, and Jam Master Jay Investigations from NYPD's First "Hip-Hop Cop."* New York: St. Martin's, 2006.

Parker, Laura. "Several Cities Snapping over Baggy Pants." *USA Today*, October 15, 2007. http://www.usatoday.com/news/nation/2007-10-14-Baggy_N.htm (accessed March 31, 2008).

Passman, Donald S. *All You Need to Know about the Music Business*. New York: Simon & Schuster, 2000.

Patterson, Lyman Ray. *Copyright in Historical Perspective*. Nashville, TN: Vanderbilt University Press, 1968.

Perkins, William Eric, ed. *Droppin' Science: Critical Essays on Rap Music and Hip Hop Culture*. Philadelphia: Temple University Press, 1996.

Perry, Imani. *Prophets of the Hood: Politics and Poetics in Hip Hop*. Durham, NC: Duke University Press, 2004.

Peters, Katherine McIntire. "DEA: Mexican Drug Violence Is a Sign of Progress, Not Failure." *Government Executive*, April 15, 2009. http://www.govexec.com/dailyfed/0409/041509kp1.htm (accessed August 6, 2010).

Petersilia, Joan. *When Prisoners Come Home: Parole and Prisoner Reentry*. New York: Oxford University Press, 2003.

Pew Center on the States. *One in 100: Behind Bars in America, 2008*. Washington, DC: Pew Charitable Trusts, February 2008.

———. *One in 31: The Long Reach of American Corrections*. Washington, DC: Pew Charitable Trusts, March 2009.

———. *Prison Count 2010: State Population Declines for the First Time in 38 Years*. Washington, DC: Pew Charitable Trusts, April 2010.

Pew Hispanic Center. *A Rising Share: Hispanics and Federal Crime*. Washington, DC: Pew Charitable Trusts, February 2009.

Philips, Chuck. "Musicians Urge N.Y. Rights Reform." *Los Angeles Times*, November 1, 2002.

———. "Rap Feud Prompts Universal to Cancel Party, Sources Say." *Los Angeles Times*, February 4, 2003.

———. "State Senate to Examine Music Firms." *Los Angeles Times*, August 26, 2002.

Pough, Gwendolyn. *Check It While I Wreck It: Black Womanhood, Hip-Hop Culture, and the Black Public Sphere*. Boston: Northeastern University Press, 2004.

Provine, Doris Marie. *Unequal under Law: Race in the War on Drugs*. Chicago: University of Chicago Press, 2007.

Quinn, Eithne. *Nuthin' but a "G" Thang: The Culture and Commerce of Gangsta Rap*. New York: Columbia University Press, 2005.

Quinney, Richard. *Class, State, and Crime*. New York: David McKay, 1977.

Raekwon. *Only Built 4 Cuban Linx*. Loud/RCA/BMG, 1995.

———. *Only Built 4 Cuban Linx . . . Pt. II*. Ice H2O/EMI, 2009.

Rafter, Nicole Hahn. "Criminal Anthropology in the United States." Reprinted in *The Criminology Theory Reader*, edited by Stuart Henry and Werner Einstadter, 78–91. New York: New York University Press, 1998.

"Rapper C-Murder Sentenced to Life in Prison." *USA Today*, August 14, 2009. http://www.usatoday.com/life/people/2009-08-14-cmurder-sentencing_N.htm (accessed August 11, 2010).

Rashbaum, William K. "Investigating Murder of a D.J., Police Use Detectives Specializing in the World of Hip-Hop." *New York Times*, January 25, 2003.

Redman. *Dare Iz a Darkside*. Def Jam, 1994.

Reiman, Jeffrey. *The Rich Get Richer and the Poor Get Prison: Ideology, Class, and Criminal Justice*, 6th ed. Boston: Allyn and Bacon, 2000.

Reinarman, Craig, and Harry G. Levine. *Crack in America: Demon Drugs and Social Justice*. Berkeley: University of California Press, 1997.

———. "Crack in Context." In Reinarman and Levine, *Crack in America*, 1–17.

Rita v. United States, 551 U.S. 338 (2007).

Ro, Ronin. *Have Gun Will Travel: The Spectacular Rise and Violent Fall of Death Row Records*. New York: Broadway Books, 1998.

Rose, Mark. *Authors and Owners: The Invention of Copyright*. Cambridge, MA: Harvard University Press, 1993.

Rose, Tricia. *Black Noise: Rap Music and Black Culture in Contemporary America*. Middletown, CT: Wesleyan University Press, 1994.

———. *The Hip Hop Wars: What We Talk about When We Talk about Hip Hop—and Why It Matters*. New York: Basic Civitas Books, 2008.

Rosenmerkel, Sean, Matthew Durose, and Donald Farole Jr. *Felony Sentences in State Courts, 2006: Statistical Tables*. Washington, DC: U.S. Department of Justice, Office of Justice Programs, Bureau of Justice Statistics, December 2009.

Rusche, George, and Otto Kirchheimer. *Punishment and Social Structure*. New York: Columbia University Press, 1939.

Sampson, Robert J., and John H. Laub. "A Life-Course View of the Development of Crime." *Annals of the American Academy of Political and Social Science* 602 (November 2005): 12–45.

Sampson, Robert J., Stephen Raudenbush, and Felton Earls. "Neighborhoods and Violent Crime: A Multilevel Study of Collective Efficacy." *Science* 277 (1997): 918–24.

Sanchez, Reymundo. *My Bloody Life: The Making of a Latin King*. Chicago: Chicago Review Press, 2000.

Sanders, William. *Gangbangs and Drive-Bys: Grounded Culture and Juvenile Gang Violence*. New York: Aldine de Gruyter, 1994.

Sanjek, Russel. *American Popular Music and Its Business: The First Four Hundred Years*. 3 vols. New York: Oxford University Press, 1988.

Scott, Peter Dale, and Jonathan Marshall. *Cocaine Politics: Drugs, Armies, and the CIA in Central America*, updated edition. Berkeley: University of California Press, 1991.

Segall, Laurie. "New York Politician Hopes to End Youths' Pants-Sagging Trend." CNN, March 29, 2010. http://www.cnn.com/2010/LIVING/03/29/new.york.baggy.pants/ index.html?iref=allsearch (accessed August 17, 2010).

Sentencing Reform Act of 1984, Pub. L. No. 104-38 (1984).

Shakur, Sanyika. *Monster: The Autobiography of an L.A. Gang Member.* New York: Grove, 1993.

Shapiro, Susan. "Collaring the Crime, Not the Criminal." *American Sociological Review* 55, no. 3 (June 1990): 346-65.

Sharpley-Whiting, T. Denean. *Pimps Up, Ho's Down: Hip Hop's Hold on Young Black Women.* New York: New York University Press, 2007.

Shaw, Clifford R., and Henry D. McKay. *Juvenile Delinquency in Urban Areas.* Chicago: University of Chicago Press, 1942.

Simon, Jonathan. *Governing through Crime: How the War on Crime Transformed American Democracy and Created a Culture of Fear.* Oxford: Oxford University Press, 2007.

Simpson, Colton, with Ann Pearlman. *Inside the Crips: Life inside L.A.'s Most Notorious Gang.* New York: St. Martin's, 2006.

Skolnick, Jerome. "Gangs and Crime as Old as Time: But Drugs Change Gang Culture." Reprinted in Klein, Maxson, and Miller, *Modern Gang Reader,* 222-27. Originally published as "Commentary" in *Crime and Delinquency in California, 1980-1989.* Sacramento: California Department of Justice, Office of the Attorney General, Bureau of Criminal Statistics and Special Services. 171-79.

Smith, Alexander, and Harriet Polack. "Curtailing the Sentencing Power of Trial Judges: The Unintended Consequences." *Court Review.* Williamsburg, VA: American Judges Association, Summer 1999.

Smith, Philip. *Punishment and Culture.* Chicago: University of Chicago Press, 2008.

Snoop Doggy Dogg. *Doggystyle.* Death Row/Interscope/Atlantic, 1993.

Stanton, Sam. "California Inmate Release Plan Begins." *Sacramento Bee,* January 25, 2010. http://www.sacbee.com/topstories/story/2486280.html?storylink=omni_popular (accessed August 16, 2010).

———. "Early Jail Releases in California Worry Former Violent Offender." *Sacramento Bee,* February 6, 2010. http://www.sacbee.com/2010/02/06/2517364/early-releases-worry-former-violent.html (accessed August 16, 2010).

Stephenson, Neal. *Snow Crash.* New York: Bantam Books, 1992.

Stiglitz, Joseph E. *Globalization and Its Discontents.* New York: Norton, 2003.

Street Terrorism Enforcement and Prevention Act, *California Penal Code* § 186.20-186.33 (West Supp. 1996).

Sullivan, Randall. *LAbyrinth: A Detective Investigates the Murders of Tupac Shakur and Notorious B.I.G., the Implications of Death Row Records' Suge Knight, and the Origins of the Los Angeles Police Scandal.* New York: Grove, 2002.

Sutherland, Edwin. *Principles of Criminology,* 4th ed. Philadelphia: Lippincott, 1947.

———. *White Collar Crime.* New York: Holt, Rinehart, and Winston, 1949.

———. "White-Collar Criminality." *Annual Review of Sociology* 5, no.1 (February 1940): 2-10. Excerpts reprinted in *Classics of Criminology,* 3rd ed., edited by Joseph E. Jacoby, 13-18. Long Grove, IL: Waveland, 2004.

Terror Squad. *True Story.* Umvd Labels, 2004.

Thomas, Bethany. "La. Proposes Crackdown on Belly-Baring Pants." *NBC News,* May 13, 2004. http://www.msnbc.msn.com/id/4963512/ (accessed March 31, 2008).

Thomas, Donald. *A Long Time Burning: The History of Literary Censorship in England.* New York: Praeger, 1969.

Tonry, Michael. *Malign Neglect: Race, Crime, and Punishment in America.* New York: Oxford University Press, 1995.

———. *Thinking about Crime: Sense and Sensibility in American Penal Culture.* Oxford: Oxford University Press, 2004.

Toop, David. *Rap Attack 3,* 3rd ed. London: Serpent's Tail, 2000.

United States Department of Justice. *Crime in the United States, 2008.* Washington, DC: Federal Bureau of Investigation, September 2009. Available at http://www.fbi.gov/ucr/cius2008/index.html (accessed August 15, 2010).

United States Sentencing Commission. *Guidelines Manual,* §3E1.1 (Nov. 2007).

———. *Report to the Congress: Cocaine and Federal Sentencing Policy.* Washington, DC: Sentencing Commission, May 2007. http://www.ussc.gov/r_congress/cocaine2007.pdf (accessed August 15, 2010).

———. *Report to the Congress: Cocaine and Federal Sentencing Policy.* Washington, DC: U.S. Sentencing Commission, May 2002. http://www.ussc.gov/r_congress/02crack/2002crackrpt.htm (accessed August 15, 2010).

———. *Sourcebook of Federal Sentencing Statistics, 1995-2009.* http://www.ussc.gov/annrpts.htm (accessed August 15, 2010).

———. *Special Report to the Congress: Cocaine and Federal Sentencing Policy.* Washington, DC: U.S. Sentencing Commission, February 1995. http://www.ussc.gov/crack/exec.htm (accessed August 15, 2010).

———. *Special Report to the Congress: Cocaine and Federal Sentencing Policy.* Washington, DC: U.S. Sentencing Commission, April 1997. http://www.ussc.gov/r_congress/NEWCRACK.PDF (accessed August 15, 2010).

United States v. Booker, 543 U.S. 220, 224 (2005).

Venkatesh, Sudhir. *Gang Leader for a Day: A Rogue Sociologist Takes to the Streets.* New York: Penguin, 2008.

———. *Off the Books: The Underground Economy of the Urban Poor.* Cambridge, MA: Harvard University Press, 2006.

Wacquant, Loïc. *Body and Soul: Notebooks of an Apprentice Boxer.* Oxford: Oxford University Press, 2004.

———. "Deadly Symbiosis: When Ghetto and Prison Meet and Mesh." *Punishment and Society* 3, no. 1 (January 2001): 95-134.

———. "Whores, Slaves, and Stallions: Languages of Exploitation and Accommodation among Boxers." *Body and Society* 7, no. 2-3 (2001): 181-94.

Walker, Samuel. *Taming the System: The Control of Discretion in Criminal Justice, 1950-1990.* New York: Oxford University Press, 1993.

Wallace, Voletta. *Voletta Wallace Remembers Her Son, Christopher Wallace, AKA Notorious B.I.G.* New York: Atria Books, 2005.

Webb, Senator Jim. "Why We Must Reform Our Criminal Justice System." *Huffington Post,* June 11, 2009. http://www.huffingtonpost.com/sen-jim-webb/why-we-must-reform-our-cr_b_214130.html (accessed August 16, 2010).

Welcome to Death Row. Xenon Pictures, 2001.

West, Heather C. *Prison Inmates at Midyear 2009: Statistical Tables.* Washington, DC: U.S. Department of Justice, Office of Justice Programs, Bureau of Justice Statistics, 2010.

Williams, Juan. "Banish the Bling: A Culture of Failure Taints Black America." *Washington Post*, August 21, 2006. http://www.washingtonpost.com/wp-dyn/content/article/2006/08/20/AR2006082000527.html (accessed August 16, 2010).

———. *Enough: The Phony Leaders, Dead-End Movements, and Culture of Failure That Are Undermining Black America—and What We Can Do About It.* New York: Three Rivers, 2007.

———. "What Bill O'Reilly Really Told Me." *Time*, September 28, 2007. http://www.time.com/time/nation/article/0,8599,1666573,00.html (accessed August 16, 2010).

Williams, Raymond. *The English Novel.* New York: Oxford University Press, 1970.

———. *Marxism and Literature.* Oxford: Oxford University Press, 1977.

Wilson, James Q., and Joan Petersilia, eds. *Crime: Public Policies for Crime Control.* Oakland, CA: Institute for Contemporary Studies, 2002.

Wilson, William Julius. *When Work Disappears: The World of the New Urban Poor.* New York: Vintage Books, 1996.

Woodiwiss, Michael. *Gangster Capitalism: The United States and the Globalization of Organized Crime.* New York: Carroll and Graf, 2005.

Wright, Kristine. "Rise Up Hip Hop Nation: From Deconstructing Racial Politics to Building Positive Solutions." *Socialism and Democracy* 18, no. 2 (2004): 9-20.

Wu-Tang Clan. *Enter the Wu-Tang (36 Chambers).* Loud/RCA, 1993.

Young, Jock. "Merton with Energy, Katz with Structure: The Sociology of Vindictiveness and the Criminology of Transgression." *Theoretical Criminology* 7, no. 3 (2003): 410-11.

Youth Communication. *Things Get Hectic: Teens Write about the Violence That Surrounds Them*, edited by Philip Kay, Andrea Estepa, and Al Desetta. New York: Touchstone, 1998.

Zimring, Franklin E., and Gordon Hawkins. *Crime Is Not the Problem: Lethal Violence in America.* Oxford: Oxford University Press, 1997.

Index

About the Author

DIMITRI A. BOGAZIANOS is Assistant Professor in the Division of Criminal Justice at California State University–Sacramento.